and the World

FREDERICK A. PRAEGER, *Publishers*

New York • Washington

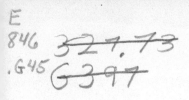
BOOKS THAT MATTER

Published in the United States of America in 1966
by Frederick A. Praeger, Inc., Publishers
111 Fourth Avenue, New York, N.Y. 10003

© 1966 by Frederick A. Praeger, Inc.

Library of Congress Catalog Card Number: 66-13684

Printed in the United States of America

Those who are prone by temperament and character to seek sharp and clear-cut solutions of difficult and obscure problems, who are ready to fight whenever some challenge comes from a foreign Power, have not always been right. On the other hand, those whose inclination is to bow their heads, to seek patiently and faithfully for peaceful compromise, are not always wrong. On the contrary, in the majority of instances they may be right, not only morally but from a practical standpoint. . . .

If the circumstances are such as to warrant it, force may be used. And if this be so, it should be used under the conditions which are most favourable. There is no merit in putting off a war for a year if, when it comes, it is a far worse war or one much harder to win. These are the tormenting dilemmas upon which mankind has throughout its history been so frequently impaled. Final judgment upon them can only be recorded by history in relation to the facts of the case as known to the parties at the time, and also as subsequently proved.

—WINSTON S. CHURCHILL
in *The Gathering Storm*

Preface

It has been said that the full scope of the thought and power and personality of Lyndon B. Johnson can never be known to any one man, and this book does not defy that notion. It is not its purpose to pass judgment or pose as history, for not enough time has passed for that. It is, rather, an interim report on that aspect of the work of the President which has stirred more curiosity and controversy than any other—how he approaches foreign affairs and the making of foreign policy. The aim is to illustrate and to illuminate, rather than to compile a complete chronicle of Lyndon Johnson's dealings with the world.

I am grateful to the many who contributed their experiences and accounts and time. But it is no more possible to identify them here than it is possible to identify those who appear in ghostly anonymity in the course of the book itself. In every case, those referred to—regrettably, and all too often, by the time-honored resort of the daily journalists—as "close aides" or "high officials" or "distinguished observers" are men living or working somewhere within Lyndon Johnson's ken. All of them wish to continue to do so, effectively, whether to the President's profit and the nation's, or in the case of those outside the Government, to their own profit—or in some cases, to the profit of all concerned. In any case, it is in the nature of things, above all in Lyndon Johnson's Washington, that anonymity is the price of a reasonable degree of candor about an incumbent President. The authenticity of those judgments rendered here without attribution must therefore be taken on faith.

What I know of the reporter's trade and the field of foreign affairs I have learned largely on assignment in Washington, Europe, Asia, and Latin America for the *Wall Street Journal,* to whose management I am indebted for many things, including its cooperation in making time available for me to complete this book. However, I alone am responsible for its contents, and any opinions expressed or implied in this book should in no way be taken as a reflection of the editorial views of the newspaper for which I work. For invaluable help along the way, my gratitude goes to Morton Puner and Manuela Ditz.

Finally, without the faith of my wife, Sherry, and the tender solicitude of my children for my privacy, the book could not have been finished.

—PHILIP GEYELIN

Washington, D.C.
March, 1966

Contents

In the Beginning

The world rushed in like a tidal wave at Lyndon Johnson in the first minutes of his Presidency, then receded respectfully for an eerie interval. All that the new President and the stunned men around him knew—and knew with awful certainty—was that John F. Kennedy lay dead. What they did not, could not, know was that his murder was an insane, isolated deed. Through the numbed mind of Lyndon B. Johnson raced the thought of an international conspiracy, not just against the person of the dead President, but against the United States Government. Strategic Air Command aircraft were ordered aloft; U.S. troops went on world-wide alert; Washington officials tensed for an inkling of a wider plot. Such a possibility was no more unthinkable than

Soviet missiles in Cuba a year earlier—or what had happened along the parade route that dismal Friday.

So the first reflex of the new President was to assure the nation's security against some faceless foreign enemy, his first move to gather up those around him and get them back to Washington, his first decision to order his own swearing-in ceremony aboard the aircraft to assure continuity of the office, come what might.

The cool and orderly execution of these measures gave early reassurance to a stunned nation; the anxiety implicit in them served to remind Lyndon Johnson that the nation whose destiny had suddenly been thrust into his hands was engaged in deadly conflict with an unruly world. Other reminders were not long in following; even in the first days of mourning—indeed, before the slain President had been buried—the world was beginning to make its relentless presence felt upon a grieving nation and a government in shock.

Appropriately, though nobody then could know how much so, almost the first serious post-Kennedy foreign-policy session had Vietnam as its topic. Ambassador Henry Cabot Lodge had flown back from his post in Saigon for Sunday lunch at the Kennedy weekend retreat, Glen Ora. Instead, he had a somber conference with President Johnson in the Vice Presidential suite in the Executive Office Building across the street from the White House. The familiar Diem regime was gone, the successor military junta a question mark. There were grim portents, unrecognizable at that point, in the battlefield reports: Vietcong "incidents" were running at a monthly rate of 700 that November, roughly double the average up to then in 1963, and the raids were getting still bigger.

Mechanically, Johnson assured Lodge, "You're my man out there," told him to "do the best you can," and sent him back to work.

Anastas Mikoyan, craftiest of the Kremlin's leading figures, was Nikita Khrushchev's representative at the funeral; his visit to the President's office was a ceremonial obligation, but he would have been remiss not to take some measure of America's new man. Lyndon Johnson had to weigh his words, carefully balancing continued firmness of American resolve with just the right expression of willingness to press for peace. It was imperative to convey no hint of anything but continuity of American policy.

Pakistan's brash, young, Yankee-baiting Foreign Minister Bhutto had attended President Kennedy's funeral as the personal representative of Lyndon Johnson's old friend President Ayub Khan. Afterwards he called at the White House to deliver a message of condolence from his government, but he apparently couldn't resist a passing word or two about U.S. policy. As Bhutto rose to depart, Mr. Johnson ordered him to sit down and delivered an impromptu discourse on Pakistan's increasing antipathy to Western causes and growing preference for those of Peking—with pointed reference to the possible impermanence of U.S. aid to Pakistan. For once, the vocal, volatile Mr. Bhutto was nearly speechless; even U.S. officials present were taken aback. But Lyndon Johnson has a feel for foreign aid in his fingertips, and strong views about recipients whose conduct runs counter to U.S. interests. "Bhutto was asking for it," said one American official later; others who "asked for it," including Mr. Bhutto's boss, were to encounter the same hair-trigger Johnson response.

Also on hand for the funeral was Charles de Gaulle, now more than ever the senior man in the Western alliance, a towering relic of another era of allied relationships, and a symbol of new and serious alliance strains. He cruised majestically through the sea of foreign dignitaries at an official reception, leaving in his wake the judgment that by contrast with the raw, untested Texas rancher now at the head of the U.S. Government, *Moi, De Gaulle!* had become the man to reckon with in the councils of the free world.

For the new President of the United States, this was an irresistible challenge. At a meeting with De Gaulle, he wasted little time making his approach. Some say that the translation was faulty, and some that De Gaulle was simply being his old grandiloquent, inscrutable self. At any rate, Johnson thought he had a promise from the General that he would return to Washington early in the coming year, and he savored a sense of satisfaction that his faith in his favorite refrain from the Prophet Isaiah ("Come now, and let us reason together") was sounder than the defeatist advance briefings he had received from the State Department. Heading directly from his talk with De Gaulle to address a gathering of state governors, and arriving late, Johnson apologized; his conversation with President de Gaulle had lasted longer than he expected and "even then, we did not finish, so we have another meeting set up for early in the year when he comes back to this country." De Gaulle had previously told aides of his concern to remain noncommittal on the touchy question of a future meeting with Johnson, and suspected a misunderstanding. At the airport before departure, he told Hervé Alphand, his American Ambassador, to make sure there had been no confusion on the question; but by the time the Ambassador got back to town, Johnson had made his announcement to the governors, and new instructions on how to proceed were needed from Paris.

They came swiftly; three days later, Secretary Rusk was obliged to advise Johnson that Alphand had called on Assistant Secretary William Tyler with a clarification: De Gaulle had not intended to suggest that he would come to Washington to see Johnson. The new American President was welcome, of course, to come to Paris to see De Gaulle—as was only proper, of course, for a new junior member of the allied partnership.

Slowly at first, then swiftly, the world was resuming its rhythms, its sudden tempests, its ceaseless batterings. There would be riots in Panama, massacres in Cyprus, a U.S. aircraft gunned down over Berlin, comic-opera *brouhaha* over the Cuban waterworks supplying the U.S. base at Guantanamo Bay—all within the first few weeks. Briefly, the sudden brutality of the American change of government had rocked the world, for few were in doubt about where the power lay, and least of all Fidel Castro.

"Everything is changed," he blurted out, according to French journalist Jean Daniel who was with Castro when the news reached him. "The United States occupies such a position in world affairs that the death of its President affects millions of people in every country of the globe," Castro said. "The cold war, relations with Russia, Latin America, Cuba, the Negro question —all will have to be rethought. I'll tell you one thing; at least Kennedy was an enemy to whom we had become accustomed."

But if U.S. power was recognized, it was also resented. The temptation to flout it was strong. The tendency to criticize and criticize was stronger still, and under less restraint, and it was quick to show itself. The senselessness of the assassination could not be accepted on its face; in a world beset by political plotters and intriguers, there must have been a plot. It was to allay foreign suspicions, as much as to reassure Americans, that President Johnson moved quickly to establish the Warren Commission, headed by the Chief Justice and composed of the nation's most respected figures, to investigate every aspect of the Dallas tragedy. The Communists were calling it a rightist conspiracy and tying it to the Ku Klux Klan and the John Birch Society. The Arabs saw it as a Zionist plot, and Africans and Asians as a racist affair. Nigeria's President hurried off a message to President Johnson, saying that the killing of Kennedy "shows clearly that among some Americans there is a deep-seated hatred of the black man as a human being." A newspaper in Lebanon could not believe that "the craziest of crazy fools destroyed Kennedy with the ease of one swatting a fly."

Even less credible and more disturbing to foreigners was the immediate aftermath of the assassination—the murder of the murderer—which not only conveyed the image of abject lawlessness but heightened the suspicion that there had to be more to it than the bare, scarcely believable facts. *Le Monde,* a pillar of responsibility of the French press, was sure the police were in cahoots with the murderer. A leading Indian politician figured that Jack Ruby had shot Lee Harvey Oswald to cover up conspiracy and saw "big money behind the plot." In West Germany, an official government spokesman found it all "incredible" and asked: "How can you announce you're going to transfer a man and have the cameras there waiting? Do the TV networks run the United States today?"

From the United Nations, Adlai Stevenson reported to Washington that the Jack Ruby shooting had done more to tarnish the American image than the assassination itself—"We have been made the laughingstock of the whole cockeyed world," Stevenson declared at the time. And Dean Rusk, agreeing, said, "I will have to say that the double tragedy in Dallas was a great shock to people and has damaged us right around the world."

It was no help to Lyndon Johnson that a great many foreigners focused their criticism on Texas, or as *Time* put it, "on their vision of [Texas] as a lawless, uncontrollable little world of its own." "Texas was always a joke," said Britain's Denis W. Brogan, according to *Time,* and added: "Now Texas is a bad joke." For a new, untested, relatively unknown President—from Texas—this was a bad enough way to begin in the eyes of the world, but foreign opinion often went further, to the conclusion that the violence in Dallas was a serious symptom of social instability in the United States, quite out of keeping with the impression Americans had been seeking to project, an impression of a government of law seeking a rule of law for the world.

The ill effects were a long time receding, even in the face of the extraordinary evidence furnished by President Johnson and those around him that the United States could make an orderly, dignified, efficient, and entirely legal transfer of governmental authority out of an act of utter lawlessness. For Lyndon Johnson, the transition was a triumph. But it could not dispel the underlying antipathy to the United States, the quick reflexes toward harsh and hasty judgments, which were to confound his relations with the world from Santo Domingo to Saigon. Still less could the triumph of transition dispel the sharp, shocking contrast between John F. Kennedy and him. Comparisons were inevitable, often emotional, usually colored by personal prejudice, and by and large irrelevant. What was profoundly relevant, however, was that one was known, and one was not; one was proven and one untested; one had electrified a whole generation while the other was a dim figure out of a region of America fabled for oil, and high-heeled boots, and big hats, and a distinctive drawl. Only after his death did Americans discover the real reach of the Kennedy charisma. Young Cubans, encountered in the quiet of a Havana restaurant fully a year later, could not bring themselves to blame Kennedy for the fiasco at the Bay of Pigs, nor could they find any redeeming grace in his successor. Fully two years later, a Yugoslav diplomat in Washington was to say, "I am a Communist and I cannot talk about Kennedy now without emotion. He was against everything I believe in. He hated Marxism. But we had been through so much and lost so much, and he made us want to fight for something again. It didn't matter that what he wanted to fight for and what we wanted to fight for were completely different. He was a great man, like Lenin, the kind that comes along only once in a thousand years."

From all over the world, the emotions were the same. It wasn't just the tributes of public figures. It was the pictures of John F. Kennedy side by side with those of the Virgin Mary in peasant huts in remote Latin American villages—pictures still there two years after his death. It was the little tributes and the lasting ones encountered by any American traveler almost anywhere. Kennedy's great reservoir of respect and affection was a national asset in his conduct of this country's foreign policy. But the reverence was not transferable.

What had been a national asset became, for Lyndon Johnson, a liability. It was his fate to be almost the antithesis of John F. Kennedy. Though some would argue that this was a blessing in disguise—that total antithesis was better than a bad copy—in the world at large, where understanding of America is always imperfect, Lyndon Johnson's initial image was a debit against his account. He was the cowboy who had rent the Taj Mahal with a rebel yell. He was the wheeler-dealer master parliamentarian, a caricature out of an American Western, with an uncultivated accent and an often unintelligible turn of phrase. He was ungraceful and uninspiring. He was also Western rather than Eastern, and the world had long since grown accustomed to dealing in the international arena with Americans who were either Easterners or acted like them—with Harrimans and Roosevelts and Stevensons and Kennedys.

Lyndon Johnson was like none of these. He was a political pro, a throwback to the age of the Roosevelt whose name he was so quick to invoke. The torch that had been passed to young men all over the world had been snatched away; an older generation was in charge again, in the person of a man few foreigners knew and a good many tended, from what they did know, to distrust. A distinguished American authority on foreign affairs touring Europe shortly after Lyndon Johnson became President met a wide assortment of old and trusted figures on the European political scene and found that close friends who had long responded to his reasoning could not be persuaded that Johnson was anything but a "mountebank." A Soviet diplomat who had no particular reason to look fondly upon President Kennedy and no basis for judging Lyndon Johnson was convinced that the former was a great leader with whom the Soviet Union could do at least a limited amount of business, while the latter was somehow suspect. These judgments were widespread, difficult to dispel, and yet another inescapable burden upon the new President in his initial dealings with the world. There were other burdens, some of them self-imposed. For it was not in Johnson's nature to accept graciously what was inescapable. He was torn by doubt and inner conflict. He was also torn between a prudent awareness of the perils of an unfamiliar world and a fierce determination to prove his competence as President, between a sensible realization of the need for continuity and a powerful urge to put his own brand on everything that moved. He was preoccupied with the problems of transition; with the preparation of a legislative program; with projecting himself as a national, rather than a regional, figure, who could unify the land. He was making appeals to bankers and businessmen, trade-union men and consumers, Southerners and Northerners, Republicans and Democrats. He was championing civil rights and tax cuts, defending an embattled foreign-aid program, wrestling with a bulky federal budget, addressing Congress, the United Nations, and the Latin American diplomatic corps, en bloc. He was struggling to hold together a shaken administration, to console the inconsolable Kennedy men—and to establish his command.

He wanted nothing more of the world than for it to go his way, or to go away. Predictably, it went its own way, propelled by what Under Secretary of State George Ball described in the early weeks as "cataclysmic forces at work, giving new shape and new form to the world."

Lyndon B. Johnson

"Better to try and drain the Atlantic Ocean into a bathtub than to try and take one sentence to describe this President."—Bill D. Moyers, White House Press Secretary, in a television interview, October 24, 1965.

Lyndon B. Johnson could be called the personification of the American political system. He represents its logical extreme and he possesses all the system's strengths and liabilities. If one sentence is incapable of encompassing even the dimensions of the man, one incident, in October, 1960, toward the end of that year's Presidential campaign, may at least offer a way into the subject, and a measure of its complexity. Vice Presidential candidate Johnson had been barnstorming the North and Northeast, "preaching socialism" in the eyes of a good many of his fellow Texans. When he came home, he ran smack into a hornets' nest in the ill-fated city of Dallas. As he started diagonally across an intersection toward the Hotel Adolphus, an angry mob formed, organized by ultra-conservatives laboring in the Nixon-Lodge cause, egged on by a dashing, ultra-conservative Republican Congressman from Dallas. The mood was as mean as one of the placards ("Let's Beat Judas!") and it could not be made prettier by the Junior League matrons especially recruited for the occasion. Lady Bird was shouted at and spat upon; the intensity of the display frightened her as the two made their way into the teeming hotel lobby.

But somewhere in the long, craggy head of Lyndon Johnson, the political computers were spinning and humming furiously, and the data they disgorged added up to a warning as well as a vision of votes. The warning was that it wouldn't do at all to come home under police escort. So, chin high, a look of disdain on his face, and an anxious Lady Bird being hauled along at his side, Lyndon Johnson waded into the throng, and when a hapless pair of motorcycle policemen attempted to clear a path, he bellowed at them: "Get out of the way! This isn't Nazi Germany!" Slowly, he forced his way through to a staircase and on up to a second-floor ballroom where the Democratic faithful awaited him, unaware of the indignities being heaped upon their hero down below. Johnson's first reference to the incident, when he finally rose to speak, was gentle; his antagonists were more to be pitied.

But if he was magnanimous, he was also defiant, and with his voice rising and his face darkening as he warmed to the recounting, he leaned into the microphone and shouted: "I told the police to stand aside! When a man and his lady can't walk through the lobby of a hotel in Dallas, Texas, I want to know about it." At this punch line, his listeners rose from their seats, applauding thunderously.

It was plainly a triumph, perhaps a turning point, and a reporter set off in search of reaction. The policemen were bitter, one of them unreconcilably so. "I don't like to be called a storm trooper," he said sourly, as he mounted his motorcycle. "Johnson will never get my vote."

Later, a group of more moderate, responsible Republican leaders assembled and they, too, were bitter. The most conservative estimate among them was that the Adolphus affair would cost the Republican ticket at least 50,000 votes in Texas and some said the losses might go twice as high. Even the lower estimate would have been enough to transfer Texas into the Democratic column, and as the national election turned out, to tilt the outcome to John F. Kennedy. Nobody will ever know, of course, whether at this precise moment Lyndon Johnson's Presidency was preordained, and, anyway, that is not the point.

The point is that Lyndon Johnson is a hard man to measure—and this incident is a measure of the difficulty. More than most men, his performance must be looked at in the main. Judgment must await ultimate results, for initial appearances can grossly deceive. Rate him on his rude highhandedness with the police, and he is arrogant, inconsiderate, petty in the use of his power, reckless in his concern for the safety of others, and not even very smart about how to win friends. Place the matter in a larger frame, however, and Lyndon Johnson becomes a hero under fire, a political maestro, and a man whose every thought and every instinct is strictly attuned to his larger purpose, his fundamental aim.

One more observation, and the moral of the Adolphus affair is made: the incident obviously would never have occurred, and thus redounded to the benefit of Lyndon Johnson, had it not been for the unwitting cooperation of his enemies. Lyndon Johnson was not beyond innovation or initiation, but his penchant is for the judo principle in politics; it is his special genius to turn the initiatives of others—of allies as well as antagonists—to his ends. That's how it worked in Dallas in 1960 and that was the way it was to work more than once in his conduct of international policy as President.

It was a bloody Vietcong assault on an American base in Pleiku in February, 1965, that furnished the crucial element in his careful preparation of U.S. and world opinion for systematic U.S. air strikes against North Vietnam. It was a Communist torpedo-boat attack on U.S. warships that offered grounds for an earlier one-shot air strike in the North. It was the power hunger of an erratic, ruthless Dominican opportunist, Antonio Imbert, that enabled the United States to construct a counterweight to the leftist, rebel forces in Santo Domingo. A British proposal took the United States off the hook with its multilateral nuclear force; peace appeals from Pope Paul gave the United States a basis for beginning a bombing pause in Vietnam at the end of 1965, and another Papal appeal offered an opportunity for Lyndon Johnson to reverse course and refer the Vietnamese conflict to the United Nations, when a way was wanted to soften the impact of ending the "pause."

The technique is less haphazard than it sounds. Pleiku, or something like it, was quite predictable at the time. Antonio Imbert got some not-very-subtle U.S. encouragement. It is hardly likely that the Pope's peace pleas took the White House by surprise. Critics were to call such methods "finagling" and their practitioner a "courthouse Machiavelli," and to cry for straightforward U.S. leadership. Defenders saw it as American politics in its finest flowering. Both were right, for Lyndon Johnson brought a Byzantine talent for the intricacies of exercising political power to the White House. He also brought a masterful sense of timing, an intuition and a certain instinctiveness which he referred to as "that feeling in his gut."

What he could not bring, however, were a couple of ingredients essential to his prowess as a Senate straw boss. One was the luxury of doing nothing if his sense of timing told him the moment was not propitious. "Old Lyndon," he often said, liked to "get all his ducks in a row" before declaring himself, but if the Senate very nearly did work to Lyndon Johnson's bidding, the world would not. More important, he did not bring to world affairs anything like the expertise that had enabled him to hold sway over the Senate—the intimate insights, the detailed knowledge of men and their motivations and their source of power. He could acquire it, but slowly and secondhand, and it would never be any better than the quality of the counsel he got and his own capacity to make sound judgments about his counselors. This is the imprisoning effect of the Presidency and the problem for Lyndon Johnson was to be aggravated by the fact that he not only did not have the firsthand knowledge (few new Presidents do, after all) but he did not speak the language of those who did. It wasn't that he didn't know the technical jargon or the bureaucratese: he had sat through too many Senate Committee hearings not to be aware of the difference between polycentrism and polyethylene, between infrastructure and infrared. He had heard the fashionable concepts, be they containment or disengagement or neutralism or parallelism. But he didn't speak that language because he did not think in it; he thought in analogies to the New Deal or Munich, to "another Korea" or "another Cuba"; the Mekong Basin was to be "another TVA." He was in large measure, then, a self-taught statesman; he couldn't read the music, but he had come a long way on his ability to play by ear.

The Man

"A President has to be President in his own way," a close but reasonably dispassionate associate of Lyndon Johnson once said in a last exasperated effort to explain a specific aspect of President Johnson's performance in the wake of the upheaval in the Dominican Republic in the spring of 1965. He added:

"This President wants the world to work to his clock."

Neither commentary quite answered the questions that had been raised, but, taken together, they are not a bad way to begin a study of a man who has been variously described as titanic and petty, courtly and crude, compassionate and cruel, an authentic political genius and a cornball—and of his approach over more than two years to what is loosely described as foreign policy. To begin with, foreign *politics* is perhaps the better way to put it, for not since Franklin Roosevelt has the Presidency been in the hands of someone so completely a political animal.

And it seems also fair to say that not since Roosevelt, or perhaps ever, have foreign politics been integrated so inextricably into the processes of domestic politics. It was the essence of Lyndon Johnson's way, from the outset, that foreign affairs should be part and parcel of all that he was doing at home, that neither should interfere with the other; that both, in fact, should reinforce each other insofar as he could make them do so. Judgments would be handed down on how he handled the world at large, and they would vary violently, for this was to be the area of his greatest controversy. But the broad purpose was plain from the start: whatever he might do in one or another aspect of world affairs, foreign politics was not to be the primary preserve of any exclusive "establishment" of elders or professionals; it was not to be treated as a privileged, separate entity or a richly specialized art. It was to be a part of the total political process because Lyndon Johnson, more than most, *had* to be President his own way, and because that was the only way he knew to practice politics.

Every man arrives at the office of the Presidency more or less an amateur, and the more so in international affairs, given the criteria and the priorities and the preoccupations imposed by the American process of choosing Presidents. Each brings his own set of assets and liabilities, strengths and weaknesses. Time was when governors—Grover Cleveland, Theodore Roosevelt, Woodrow Wilson, and Franklin Roosevelt—were thought to be the best equipped. They brought executive experience and often a management team tried and tested in the state house. Harry Truman brought cool courage and a healthy humility; he was an up-from-the-ranks political pro. Secure in his reliance on his advisers most of the time, ready to go against their counsel some of the time, he was tough-minded enough to make hard decisions, stick to them, and not brood about them afterwards. Eisenhower had known large, fateful, heart-wrenching command and had worked intimately with foreign governments in great undertakings; he knew the Establishment crowd in this country and abroad; he had made his way through the Pentagon's political jungle; a lifetime with the Army staff system left him content to allow the governmental mechanism to do the bulk of his decision-making.

By 1960, political fashion had altered. The Senate had become the Presidential incubator; there were Nixon, and, briefly, Goldwater for the Republicans; Kennedy, Humphrey, Symington, and Johnson for the Democrats. According to the new vogue, the Presidency had come to require a national view and such first-hand familiarity with world problems as the Senate might offer.

John F. Kennedy brought a scholar's command of history to the

White House; he could place contemporary events in large perspective. He could speak the language and command the allegiance of the intellectuals. In his painstaking, relentless rush towards the Presidency, he recruited a brilliant brain trust on both foreign and domestic matters. While he later complained on occasion that he did not know nearly enough people to staff the modern bureaucracy, he had faith enough in those elder statesmen he did know (Robert Lovett, Dean Acheson, John J. McCloy, Eugene R. Black) and confidence enough in his own judgment to choose as his principal lieutenants three men whom he had never met before he interviewed them for their jobs—Secretary of State Dean Rusk, Secretary of Defense Robert McNamara, and Budget Director David Bell. Today's government holds no more important posts below the Presidency. For the crucial position of Special Adviser on National Security Affairs, he picked a brilliant young Harvard dean, McGeorge Bundy, who had been an almost lifelong Republican and whom he knew only casually.

Lyndon Johnson fitted none of these Presidential molds. He was unique in almost all respects. By political background, by temperament, by personal preference, he was the riverboat man. He was brawny and rough and skilled beyond measure in the full use of tricky tides and currents, in his knowledge of the hidden shoals. He was a swashbuckling master of the political midstream, —but only in the crowded, well-traveled familiar inland waterways of domestic politics. He had no taste and scant preparation for the deep waters of foreign policy, for the sudden storms and unpredictable winds that can becalm or batter or blow off course the ocean-going man.

He was king of the river and a stranger to the open sea.

The trouble with foreigners, the President once said, "is that they're not like folks you were reared with." Lyndon Johnson was reared with hill-country Texans, and his school was Congress and the New Deal. His interest and expertise were not in policies and still less in ideas. His interest was in instrumentalities, and his supreme talent was in making them work to his timetable and to his ends. He had also had, of course, an abiding concern with the political advancement of Lyndon Johnson, but he had seen it for most of his life in terms of domestic politics—or in the broad, black-or-white, war-or-peace aspects of foreign affairs. He was accustomed to talking about the world, when he talked about it at all, in terms of appeasement vs. military preparedness. There was something alien and inscrutable about foreign political leaders; he called them "potentates." He bridled when others suggested that foreign policy was not his forte. "I suppose sitting in on all those meetings with Eisenhower and passing on foreign aid and every major foreign-policy bill in the last twenty years isn't good experience," he would exclaim irritably to visitors. He even enjoyed tossing out a reminder that he had wangled a seat on the Senate Foreign Relations Committee for John F. Kennedy, adding in sarcastic tones that Kennedy had "even attended a few meetings, just a few."

But when he thought the circumstances called for it, he was equally capable of abject confession to inexperience with the finer points of foreign policy. On one occasion, after more than a year in office and a succession of bruising international encounters, he was to complain about the quality of the counsel he was receiving from his senior advisers—complain, because as he told the men around him, he was "new here" in terms of his knowledgeability about foreign policy and would be for another year or so until he had time to become an expert himself.

He was, he said, "in the position of a jack rabbit in a hailstorm, hunkered up and taking it."

If this was the case after a year on the job—after Panama and Cyprus, and the Congo and the Gulf of Tonkin—it had been all the more so on July 12, 1960, the second day of the Democratic nominating convention, when columnist Walter Lippmann dismissed the Presidential candidacy of Lyndon Johnson in two short sentences. In a column deploring the lost hopes of Adlai Stevenson and accepting the inevitability of John F. Kennedy's nomination, Lippmann said: "Johnson, for all his shrewdness and skill as a legislative manager, is not a genuine alternative to Kennedy. For Johnson knows little of the outer world."

That was pretty much the prevailing opinion among those who professed to know something about world affairs at the time. Three years later, when Lyndon Johnson inherited the Presidency, the prevailing estimate of his knowledgeability in world affairs was not much more generous. As Senate Majority Leader, Johnson had held power second only to that of the President, and he himself might put it a bit higher than that. He had been history's busiest Vice President. He had spent almost three decades at the seat of government. And while it is true that the really crucial questions of foreign policy do not come to Congress for decision, and while it is also true that the Vice Presidency, for all the recent efforts to enrich that office, is hardly a center of policymaking, the fact remains that an interested Congressman could become an authority on the world at large. Still more so could an interested Vice President, seated in the high councils of government and privileged to voyage in the President's name to all corners of the globe.

The point is that Lyndon Johnson never was really interested, except as a practical need to be interested arose.

So it was that in those first few weeks of Lyndon Johnson's Presidency, men with much at stake sought in vain to plumb Johnson's foreign policy. His own top lieutenants, career men of American diplomacy, foreign statesmen, and academicians all rushed to the record, parsing every public Johnson utterance, probing every private clue. What they came up with, however, was not a chronicle of statecraft and still less a preview of policy, but, rather, a catalogue of case histories of practical politics. Some of the cases were misleading or contradictory. Others would prove profoundly pertinent and prophetic in the months to come. But as one Johnson researcher counseled another at the time: "You will search without success for any evidence of deep commitment or firm philosophy."

More than two years later, the record was no longer barren. But the keys to it all were still very much with the man. And a search for answers that had been so baffling at the beginning of the Johnson Presidency was confounded by the fact that it was ever part of his purpose to keep those he dealt with always uncertain about where he stood—as well as where they stood with him. "I've known him for fifteen years and I don't think I could predict what he will do in any given circumstance," one of the White House men from Texas once said.

Few who have worked with him over the years would disagree.

At best, after more than two years in the hot glare of public and private scrutiny, it still is necessary to approach Lyndon Johnson as one approaches an artichoke—layer by layer, with each leaf yielding no more than a hint of what lies at the heart.

One of the President's closest advisers, and a warm admirer, once observed in a private conversation that the difference between John F. Kennedy and Lyndon Johnson was the difference between a John Stuart Mill and a combination of John C. Calhoun and Baron Munchausen. He was talking about style, articulation, and outward appearances. Kennedy made a fetish of precision; he could, of course, be devious when he felt circumstances demanded it, but, by and large, he struggled to be better understood.

Johnson, on the other hand, has always talked unceasingly, above all about himself. It did not seem to trouble him that what he said was trite or hopelessly generalized or outlandish or tasteless or patently self-serving or inconsistent with what he had said just a month or a day earlier. "The President," one of the Kennedy holdovers observed after a long association, "is a painter, not a historian."

There is, for example, the Johnson of the sweepingly simple pronouncements for peace, or for improving the lot of man the world over, or for standing up to the Communists, or for upholding the honor of the flag—the Johnson who recites a passage he learned as a schoolboy to the effect that the finest sight an American voyager can hope to see is the American flag in a foreign land. He has defined U.S. foreign policy in terms of one word (peace), or in terms of something more than 100 policies (one for each country), or in terms of his domestic program. (He once congratulated a delegation of Congressmen at the White House, after a busy session devoted almost wholly to the Great Society, for "legislating my foreign policy.") But his finest effort came on August 24, 1965, after signing a bill extending the authority for the Peace Corps for another year; the President invited a group of volunteers into his office afterward and read to them from the Scriptures. "They therefore that were scattered abroad went about preaching the word," the President intoned. "And Philip went down to the city of Samaria and proclaimed unto them that Christ . . . and many that were palsied, and that were lame, were healed . . . and besides this, giving all diligence, and unto your faith virtue; and to your virtue knowledge; and to your knowledge temperance; and to your temperance patience; and to your patience godliness; and to godliness brotherly kindness; and to brotherly kindness love." Striding back and forth behind the desk as he continued, the President said: "That's what the Peace Corps is to me. That is what my religion is—that is what the Great Society is . . . and that is the foreign policy of the United States."

His Calhoun-like statesmanship is shown by the fact that no one ever made the Senate run better. But there is the Munchausen in the man. His public and extemporaneous description of the carnage in Santo Domingo, during the April, 1965, uprising, went so far beyond the demonstrable facts that U.S. officials on the spot could only throw up their hands when badgered by newsmen for some supporting evidence. Friends dismissed it as Texas hyperbole, but to the war correspondents in Santo Domingo, Presidential hyperbole could only serve to widen an already widening credibility gap about Administration moves and motivations in the Dominican affair.

They might have believed him better, however, had the same correspondents accompanied Johnson on his 1960 campaign tour, and heard his pitch for his Presidential running-mate. The Johnson account of the celebrated adventures of PT-109 went something like this: "That little Massachusetts boy," he would shout from one stump to the next, "took his little ole torpedo boat and *rammed* it into the side of a Japanese cruiser." In fact, Kennedy's heroism began after his torpedo boat was sliced in two by a Japanese destroyer. But his heroic rescue of his crew was not enough for Johnson's oratorical purposes.

Nor, it seems, was the astonishing performance of the U.S. Congress in the record-setting session of 1965. Shortly after it ended, in one of those background sessions in which Presidential thinking is relayed for attribution to "informed sources," Lyndon Johnson let it be known that he thought the performance a mite disappointing; he also allowed as how his foreign-policy record was probably better than his performance on the domestic side;

this last, it seems to safe to say, was the view of a small minority.

The backstage Johnson, begging or badgering a foreign leader or Congressman or pundit to see things his way, is somewhat subtler, but not necessarily any more real. This Johnson was quite capable of telling one of the Senate's more serious students of foreign affairs that if "we don't stop the Reds in South Vietnam, tomorrow they will be in Hawaii, and next week they will be in San Francisco." Johnson was similarly capable of reassuring Alaska's Senator Gruening, a consistent critic of Johnson's Vietnam policy, the U.S. troops would be beginning to come home from Vietnam by the early part of 1966; this, the President argued, was one reason why he hoped the Senator would not press an amendment which would inhibit the President's right to send draftees to Vietnam. At that time, mid-1965, no responsible American official thought American troops could be withdrawing from Vietnam anything like that soon; the President didn't think so; and it is even doubtful if Senator Gruening really thought so. But the Johnson art of persuasion and influence is a nearly magical one; it works even when it isn't convincing. It operates on the theory that almost any argument that isn't demonstrably false is justified in a good cause; if contradictions develop, they can be ironed out and retribution made at a later date.

Finally, there is the off-the-record Johnson, brooding or ebullient, considerate or sarcastic or scathingly unkind, pious or posturing or unprintably uncouth. Further probing may well be beside the point—which is that after two years in the White House, Lyndon Johnson remained, to a considerable extent, a mass of contradictions and an enigma even to those closest to him. Incapable of solitary reflection, he was given to thinking aloud in the company of a captive audience; on occasions, he would even dragoon a Cabinet member into midnight talk-fests that dragged on aimlessly into the early hours of the morning, without any specific question to be answered or decision to be made. The time of his aides and advisers was his time; none of those who counted were beyond his call; those found not to be on the job were taken to task, sometimes savagely; he was always, as one subordinate put it, a "bully-ragger," and often not from rage at his immediate target, but from wrath over something his immediate target could do little or nothing about. Yet he would shower the faithful with mementos, and money, or other gestures of consideration in times of trouble.

A stark realist in assessing legislative prospects, he was not beyond self-deception, many who worked with him believed. Constant reiteration of his own accomplishments or of his reasons for a particular course sometimes seemed to transform his version into absolute truth, even when all the evidence contradicted him. Public challenge only seemed to harden his conviction that he had done whatever he had done for the reasons that he said he had done it. Thus, as Vice President, he would insist quite convincingly in private that he had seen to it that John F. Kennedy be placed on the Senate Foreign Relations Committee—and on the road to the Presidency—because "I knew he was Presidential timber from the first day he walked into the House of Representatives." Johnson's assessment of Kennedy's Presidential qualifications, however, were privately presented in considerably less glowing terms when he confronted him in competition for the nomination in 1960.

Possessed of an extraordinary feel for power, he had devoted a lifetime to its political application. But he always seemed uncomfortable in its military use. His first inclination was to avoid it, the second to overdo it, not because he relished the dispatch of Marines, or automatically inclined toward that course, but in part because he wanted to give those troops he did dispatch the best possible odds in their favor. Indeed, the President had a profound, even exaggerated distaste for war, an aversion beyond that of the ordinary man. Yet even this was counterbalanced by a simplistic approach to the evils of appeasement.

He had an astonishing record of political achievement and legislative accomplishment, but he felt compelled to devote time and energy in endless pursuit of public attention and affection and acclaim and still more recognition of his success.

The first instinct is to take refuge in contradiction, in the endless complexity of the man. These were the aspects that first struck most of the investigators from the beginning of the Johnson Presidency, and few were to record their sense of bafflement more graphically than Deputy Editor Michael Davie of the Lon-

don *Observer,* who plunged into the jungle of Johnson studies in
mid-1965 and emerged with this report [abridged by the author]:

> This President comes into a room slowly and wearily, as if he means
> to smell out the allegiance of everyone in it. There is a faint air of a
> mobster. His manner is restrained, his voice, usually, is almost a
> whisper. Afterwards you chiefly remember the eyes, steady and un-
> relenting under half-lowered lids.
>
> He is one of the most fascinating human beings ever to become
> President of the United States. He is more interesting because he is
> infinitely more alien and complex than was President Kennedy. To
> meet him is to be awed and excited. He is purely and aggressively
> American—the first uninhibited product of the American frontier
> to take over since Andrew Jackson. Washington is obsessed by him.
> No one is sure what kind of animal he is dealing with but under the
> anxieties the feeling is beginning to grow that he may be a great
> President.
>
> Inside the White House the atmosphere at first seems more normal
> than it does outside. Before long, however, the peculiarities of the
> man in the center begin to ripple outwards. First, there is the man's
> uncouthness in manners and language. He can, when discussing the
> highest matters of state, employ sexual imagery of a startling and
> unreportable directness.
>
> Then there are the stories of how he treats his subordinates. It is
> typical of Mr. Johnson that no one is quite sure whether the rages
> are uncontrolled or not. Some people claim to have seen him become
> enraged, break off to have a calm telephone discussion, and then
> resume the bawling-out.
>
> Certainly, as no one denies, the President gets frustrated. One of
> his closest associates puts all his frustrations and "erraticisms" down
> to his uneasiness in Washington, connected with his feelings of in-
> feriority in the inbred society of Washington where it is his uncon-
> cealed desire to be loved. He wants everybody to vote for him all the
> time and he is abnormally sensitive to criticism. His pride is as open
> as a wound. Whether any of these traits are important to the serious
> business of the Presidency, no one can yet be absolutely sure.
>
> It does seem true that he combines exceptional energy with excep-
> tional wariness. He is no idealist; yet he is a man of undoubted com-
> passion. He distrusts bankers, yet he uses them. He is suspicious of
> East Coast intellectuals, yet McGeorge Bundy of Harvard is one of his
> right-hand men. He was elected by a record majority, yet he feels

insecure. Asked how a journalist might rationalize these complexities, an old crony of the President advised: "Go West. The further West you go, the nearer you get to Lyndon Johnson."

A Son of Texas

The Texas image comes in handy stereotypes—big, blustering, conservative, insular, Southern, self-centered, combative, restless, rich and growing richer—and Lyndon Johnson fits some of these. But he doesn't fit them all. And, neither for that matter, does Texas. It may seem a far piece from the Pedernales to Peking, say, or to Punta del Este or Pankow. But it is no great leap for the Texas mind to the power center of Communist China, for mainland China once sold hog bristles to Americans in exchange for as much as 60 per cent of the Texas cotton crop; the capture of China by Communism was thus a heavy blow. Leaving aside what this may have done to Texas thinking on the China question, the fact is that a certain kind of internationalism comes more easily to most Texans than nationalism, because Texas, like many another Southern state, has almost always been crucially dependent on international trade.

Nor is it so far a piece from Texas to the Uruguayan seaside resort where the Alliance for Progress was born—or to the capital of Communist East Germany. Texas, after all, was once part of neighboring Mexico, and Mexican-Americans in large numbers are now very much a part of Texas politics. So are German-Americans, to an astonishing degree; just 15 miles from the LBJ Ranch along the Pedernales is the town of Fredericksburg, one of a large cluster of Texan-German settlements created by a mammoth mid-nineteenth-century influx of German immigrants who encountered such oppression and antipathy that they remain in essentially German enclaves to this day.

How the Mexicans or the Germans may have conditioned Texas thinking about Latin America or Germany is, again, beside the point. What is relevant is how they conditioned the thinking of a man who, as a youth, once agreed to take an eight-hour night shift while working as an elevator operator, in exchange for two hours off during the day to get a glimpse of a real live candidate for the U.S. Vice Presidency (Dawes), a man who had known poverty and hungered for wealth and power and had achieved both in large part because he applied himself early, with endless energy, to the art of politics. Lyndon Johnson may not have been reared with foreigners, strictly speaking, but he was reared with two categories of foreign-Americans and it became very much his business to know what made them tick. The effect of this on Lyndon Johnson cannot be established beyond a doubt. But a compelling case can be made that the effects were to influence significantly his actions and reflexes in his conduct of European and Latin American policy. Johnson was ever a man to draw, reflexively, on his own past experiences.

The cynical called him "Landslide Lyndon" when he reached the U.S. Senate in 1948 with a victory margin of 87 votes out of nearly 900,000 cast. Texas politics being a rough-and-tumble business, some suspicious people even thought he had not really won at all. But there he was, and this crucial step in his climb up the political ladder hung on the massive majorities, in the range of 100 to 1, that he piled up in South Texas among the Mexican-American *vaqueros*. "What rescued Johnson in the end was his old friendship for the Mexican ranch hands," according to William S. White, a dedicated student of the political history of LBJ. That friendship, in turn, rested heavily on Lyndon Johnson's early embrace of the New Deal, with all that it meant in terms of rural electrification and other improvements in the social and economic welfare of the workingman. It was a straightforward arrangement: Johnson brought the beneficence of Washington to the primitive back country of Texas, and the grateful *vaqueros* gave him the votes to send him back to Washington for more. As Mr. White put it, "Johnson, the *muy hombre,* was *simpatico* to them, always had been, and always would be."

It began, some Lyndonologists believe, when the young man was a schoolteacher for a year in the town of Cotulla, close to the Mexican frontier and composed, in the ratio of eight to one, of Mexican-Americans. He enjoyed it, became deeply interested in the experience, and even brought one laggard student back to Johnson City for the summer for special tutoring by his mother, who was a schoolteacher too. In 1960, the same student headed a local Johnson-for-President club. As a Senator, a more dramatic gesture earned him wider gratitude and lasting fame among the Mexicans on both sides of the frontier; when a Korean War casualty was refused burial in the little town of Dos Rios, where discrimination against the Mexican-Americans was strong, Johnson arranged for a military funeral, with full honors, at Arlington. Months later, a long-time associate recalls standing in a crowd in a Mexican village, 1,000 miles south of the border, while Johnson was delivering a speech, and hearing whispered through the crowd the words "Dos Rios."

Sensitive to all sources of political support, Johnson did not overlook the landholders, as indeed, he did not overlook the Texas business community, which is deeply engaged in commercial relations with Mexico. Because of all this, it was logical for Lyndon Johnson to have a special sense of identity with Mexican-Americans and with neighboring Mexico as well. As Senator and later as Majority Leader, he was on close terms with Mexican leaders, and particularly President López Mateos. He had visited him in Mexico City and counted him a friend. So, it was perhaps natural for Lyndon Johnson to see himself as something of an authority on everything south of the Rio Grande, all the way to Argentina, however unfamiliar he might find other regions of the world.

In a long series of talkathons with newsmen, in smoke-filled motel suites, and in the cramped confines of his chartered campaign aircraft, the "Swoose II," in 1960, he staked out the areas in which he thought he might be most useful as Kennedy's Vice President. The Pentagon and the space program were two—his Congressional dealings in both areas had been extensive. But a third was Latin America; there could be no doubt that Lyndon Johnson envisaged an active and influential role as principal adviser to President Kennedy in dealings with this Hemisphere—and little doubt about how he thought the dealing ought to be done. Mexico—which had suffered through a bloody revolution and achieved a reasonably stable, one-party political system with corruption a way of life and with almost all the political weight on the left—was his frame of reference. True, Mexico was a model of no particular pertinence to the political problems besetting most of the rest of the Hemisphere, where revolution simmered, or burned, and rightist military autocracies inflamed arch-leftist agitation and unrest. Still, Mexico worked, and Johnson was inclined to accept whatever worked. He also thought it important, old-time associates explain, to approach Latins always with a banker's hardheadedness; to make them aware that the United States would protect its own interests because that, supposedly, was something Latins could appreciate. He saw U.S. interests, more often than not, in commercial terms, because those were the dealings with Latin America he knew most about. Mutual self-interest, rather than ideology, thus struck him as the proper basis for relations with Latin Americans—or, as far as that goes, with anybody else. Plus, of course, good neighborliness, for he was ever an admirer of FDR, and aware of how successfully Roosevelt had maintained amiable relations in this Hemisphere by showering it with kind words, and continuing professions of interest, and an occasional Export-Import Bank loan.

Kennedy, of course, came to the White House firmly committed to changing all that; a brand-new "alliance for progress" was to become a major Kennedy theme. He spoke it first in a resounding campaign speech and wrote the phrase into the philosophy of his Administration in his Inaugural Address. The essence of the Kennedy approach was revolutionary and idealistic, rich in philosophic content, espousing financial support, as well as good neighborliness; its appeal was to the young and the progressive and the liberal, to those who cherished democratic process, and to those throughout the hemisphere, however, small in numbers, who were dedicated to the need for social and economic reform. It attempted, at any rate, to be the total antithesis of the pragmatism then in vogue—a pragmatism which argued, with Cuba as Exhibit A, that Latin American revolutionary movements were unreliable and that a stable, strong military regime, however indifferent to the needs of the masses, was the best bulwark against Communist intrusion in the hemisphere. It would be unfair to say that Lyndon Johnson, when he achieved the Presidency, was still anchored to this attitude or ever had been wholly tied to it. He certainly was not attuned to the initial Kennedy fixation with the "non-Communist left" as the one great hope for progress in the Hemisphere. He did not appear to accept the "pendulum theory" of Latin politics—that encouragement of military dictatorships of the right only invited upheaval and subsequent hard swings to the left. Even if the role of Vice President lent itself to delegation of authority in such a fashion, Lyndon Johnson could not have been John F. Kennedy's man for Latin America.

So Lyndon Johnson was somewhat of a frustrated Latin expert on arrival at the Presidency; this propelled him boldly and vigorously into Latin American policy from the start.

By contrast with the Mexican-Americans, the German-Americans were not on Johnson's side of the political fence. They were a proud and sturdy people—Johnson's maternal grandmother was one of them—and the discrimination and hostility they met in Texas made them move out into the bare hills. They called themselves *Die Landsleute,* (or,, roughly, "compatriots") and together worked the soil. Old friends say that they were part of Johnson's first brush with discrimination, and it offended him; his father had made a bold defense of *Die Landsleute* on the floor of the Texas legislature. But Lyndon Johnson could never win that German vote, and as a consequence he could never carry his home county. The Germans were not just Republicans; ultimately they became the leaders of the Texas Republican right wing; the chiefs of the Texas Taft delegation in the 1952 convention fight with the Eisenhower forces, and a voting bloc which, in the words of an old Johnson associate, "Lyndon could never crack." It might be too much to translate this lesson too literally to international affairs. But there is no doubt Johnson was impressed by the existence of a solid Republican vote, which, in the view of the same close associate, "had no basis except hatred and oppression." Lyndon Johnson, in brief, saw and was impressed by the inequity and folly of discrimination in general, and by the discrimination that makes second-class citizens of Germans, in particular. Years later, those who discussed this with him found him acutely sensitive to the subject as it applied to the thorny issue of whether to give West Germany a larger voice and greater participation in NATO nuclear defenses. "He was completely, instinctively, in tune with the whole thrust of our postwar policy to restore West Germany to a respectable place in the Western community," one of his most distinguished advisers was to report. Johnson himself was to express his concern in emphatic terms, in private meetings, that the Germans "will break out again like Kaiser Bill and get us into World War III" unless granted a reasonable, respectable role in the common defense. He did not doubt, he said at that time, that the Germans had the skill and the resources to fashion their own nuclear deterrent; the question was whether they would develop the will.

The Lawmaker

Inconsistencies, contradictions, a tendency to straddle fences—these are no black marks against a Congressman or a Senator. For Lyndon Johnson, they might even have been a positive plus, when, at the start of the Congressional session in 1951, the Senate Democratic elders were casting around for someone to take the number two job of Democratic Party Whip. They needed a hardworking, middle-of-the-road, not-too-controversial figure, a Southerner with some acceptibility to the liberal North—and, above all, an organization man. Lyndon Johnson was only three years into his first Senate term, but already he stood out as a man of exceptional energy and political talent, tough of mind, boundless of ambition—and quite incapable of being placed easily in any single category. His own self-analysis, made some years later, is a minor triumph in being all things to all men:

"I am a free man, an American, a United States Senator, and a Democrat, in that order," he said in 1958, in the *Texas Quarterly*. "I am also a liberal, a conservative, a Texan, a taxpayer, a rancher, a businessman, a consumer, a parent, a voter. . . ."

By way of hammering home the point, he added: "At the heart of my own beliefs is a rebellion against this very process of classifying, labeling, and filing Americans under headings." What better philosophy from a man who must make a maximum virtue of compromise? That was Lyndon Johnson's consummate skill, and he performed his Senate prodigies first as Whip, and then as Democratic Leader from 1953 to 1960, in large part by the extraordinary exercise of good timing, patience, and tactical restraint. While he may have voted with the minority on occasion, it is an interesting parlor game to ask old colleagues when they can remember Lyndon Johnson losing when his name or prestige or power was at stake. "Let's see," they are likely to say, furrowing their brows. "Of course, he lost the election for the Senate in 1941—but he was 'counted' out of that one. I think he lost a Senate vote in 1951 on Universal Military Training. He got beaten once on Hell's Canyon, but he always figured that was Wayne Morse's bill, so it doesn't really count. And that's about it."

Such a record, of course, does not derive from taking unpopular positions or backing losing causes, and Lyndon Johnson never could see much point in doing either one. "The key word was to win," is the way one man puts it, a man who was with him throughout much of his Congressional career. "He will change any time he thinks he has to in order to win." This is what makes close perusal of his Congressional voting record a wasted exercise, if one is searching for philosophy. In the early House days, Johnson was largely preoccupied with making his way in Washington, which meant building a political base in Texas. He dealt with problems whose solutions were neatly interlocked with early espousal of New Deal programs to bring water and roads and electricity to the dirt-poor hills of central Texas. Even so, Johnson later disclaimed the New Deal label. While favoring elements of the Roosevelt revolution, he had always insisted that fundamentally he was a free-enterprise man.

He did not fit the familiar mold of a Texas politician beholden to the oil-and-gas lobby. He did, however, fit the Southwestern image of a rurally oriented Populist, with an abiding interest in the elementals—electricity, water, flood control, education and health. He also showed suitable antipathy to Wall Street and bankers—to high interest rates, high tariffs, or to anything else that placed the poor in bondage to the rich or collided with the region's agricultural interests. This was enough to impel him toward the New Deal, and against isolationism. It also placed him in favor of free trade and, more recently, as his Presidential responsibilities brought him to grips with problems of the U.S. dollar, in favor of international collaboration rather than domestic austerity, as the best means of keeping the currency strong. He deplored resorting to higher interest rates.

As a Congressman, he made his mark mostly as a member of the Naval Affairs Committee (hardly the best training ground in foreign policy), and his performance on that Committee is perhaps best remembered by his ability to browbeat witnesses and bring naval installations to Texas. In the Senate, his preoccupations were with military preparedness and appropriations (which are not commonly considered the best avenue to an education in world affairs, either). As chairman of a Senate Appropriations Subcommittee on the State Department, he developed a keen appreciation that foreign policy costs money—and usually, the tone and content of his questioning implied, too much money.

"How much did you spend last year?" was almost his first question of a witness, a scanning of the hearings shows; there is little evidence, from the questioning, of interest in programs or practices for their own sake. Indeed, as President, he was to recall one aspect of his Congressional approach to foreign aid by chiding a delegation of Congressmen, in the presence of senior Administration officials: "One of the troubles with the aid program is that you fellows place all the incompetent people you know in aid jobs." He added, "I know, because I used to do it myself."

Johnson was not against foreign aid, as such; he was merely against handing it out without a clear-cut return, either in terms of demonstrable economic improvement, or in political favors, or both. That he later moved, as President, to cut back foreign-aid spending, tighten eligibility, and crack down on those who refused to engage in their own self-help efforts or who caused trouble should come as no surprise. While in Congress, he had voted to halt aid to Egypt's Gamal Abdel Nasser unless Israeli shipping was permitted to pass through the Suez Canal; supported aid to Britain in his first (and losing) Senate campaign in 1941; and supported the Marshall Plan during his close shave in 1948. However, by 1954, he had begun to talk about shutting the whole thing off, "unless some nations can offer us deeds instead of promises." Then he was up for re-election, and the memory of that 87-vote 1948 victory margin was still vivid in his mind; he decried "foreign give-aways" and denigrated Africa and

Asia as "suburbs" in terms that stirred suspicion that his concern lay largely with the "big-city" world—the U.S. and industrialized Europe.

Indeed, Lyndon Johnson did have a split vision of the world, a tendency to divide it neatly between the poor and downtrodden, who should be helped if they would help themselves, and the well-to-do, the European allies, who should also be helped in bad times, but should be counted on to do their share—and in some cases, more of it than they seemed to be doing. In the case of the Indochina war, for example, while no clear line is detectable, he thought the British as well as the French were not being tough enough. In an obvious reference to British efforts—ultimately successful—to promote the partition of Indochina, he deplored a "doctrine which smacks strongly of the appeasement of Munich." He assailed the French, also by implication, for failure "to take necessary steps in time or in quantity" to check the Communist gains in Vietnam. "The American people," he concluded, in a speech on July 2, 1954, "have become very uneasy over the objectives and intentions of our allies."

Yet Johnson was plainly leery of U.S. involvement in the war, and especially of the proposal by Admiral Radford that American forces rush to the rescue of the French at Dienbienphu. He argued, according to some accounts, that it would be risky to plunge in without knowing "who was going to put up the troops." He was to answer this question for himself, more than a decade later, when he discovered just who was left to put up troops, if the nations of Southeast Asia were to be defended against the threat of Communist encroachment. As a Senator in the mid-1950's, however, he overestimated the will or ability of others to do the job.

Yet, in Korea, Johnson saw a direct challenge to the United States—and saw it in broader, bolder terms than even the Truman Administration did. Early in the conflict, he wanted full mobilization and "an over-all global plan of strategy," and he warned of war for "ten or twenty years or more." When U.S. prestige was on the line, Lyndon Johnson was always fast on the draw.

Johnson's approach to the military, however, was mixed. He

tended to see world events in military terms, because that was his greatest field of expertise; his experience on the Preparedness Subcommittee in the Senate had brought him far more insights into the workings of the Pentagon than his review of State Department budgets (with their emphasis on ambassadors' expense accounts and the proper management of language schools) had brought him to the workings of foreign policy. He was knowledgeable on military matters, on hardware, and on the workings of the military mind—and he was hardheaded. Shortly after reaching the White House, he was to boast that he had called in the Joint Chiefs and told them: "You've done a good job of protecting my two girls for seventeen years, but you're the biggest wasters and spenders in the country."

The rest is a potpourri, but some of it prophetic. If he was steadfast in his emphasis on military preparedness and more than necessarily martial at some moments, he was also strongly in favor of opening up cultural contacts with the Russians—a portent of later Presidential emphasis on the promoting of East-West trade and other contacts with the Russians. His dim view of the timing and purpose of Eisenhower's invitation to Khrushchev in 1959 was to find an echo in his instinctive reluctance, as President, to enter into talks with Khrushchev or his successors without plain promise of something to be gained. He was always interested in outer space and even engaged in a rare exchange of strong language with the Eisenhower Administration on that issue; when Sherman Adams dismissed the first Sputnik as an "outer-space basketball," and Ike proclaimed matter-of-factly that while Johnson had his head in the sky, he, Eisenhower, had his feet on the ground, Johnson correctly read the public disquiet over Soviet space achievements as an issue he could safely seize without violating his prudent policy of statesmanlike bipartisanship.

Bipartisanship, indeed, was an article of faith with him, though some of his colleagues saw in it nothing more than clever partisanship; taking on a war-hero father figure, whose popularity was enormous and unassailable, Johnson recognized, was simply bad politics. One of his closest Senate colleagues recalls imploring Johnson to fight Ike on the Eisenhower Doctrine, to no avail. "He didn't support Eisenhower out of any profound conviction," this high-ranking Democratic figure now insists. "He did it out of some larger political purpose." In any event, having played the bipartisan game, Johnson came to believe that bipartisanship was any President's due—and was able to argue with shining consistency, and to some effect, that it was his due when he became President.

If the voting record is an unrewarding source of insights into a firm Johnson philosophy, there are perhaps more meaningful portents in his methods.

He was, to begin with, a middleman, which meant, in practice, that before moving into the middle he had to find out where it was; the outer limits had to be defined, the contenders had to declare their positions.

That was the signal for Lyndon Johnson to move in, not as initiator or creator or prime mover or driving force, but as the pilot or navigator with the special knacks to harness all the other forces at work in the interests of compromise. This background ill-equips a man to play the role of adversary, to be party to a dispute. Yet, with the world he inherited, that was to be Lyndon Johnson's lot. It is the United States which is in conflict with international Communism in Latin America, in Asia, in Europe. If this conflict is to be compromised, other men must play the Lyndon Johnson role. But in Lyndon Johnson's world, there never has been much room for more than one Lyndon Johnson. This, in the view of many students of the man, accounted for his often uncertain touch, especially in the earlier part of his administration, as he moved to deal with the great cold war confrontations; it accounted, in part, for his initial inability to accept with grace, let alone encourage, the honest brokerage offered by Canada's Lester Pearson or the United Nations' U Thant.

As the Senate maestro, Johnson traded heavily on his intimate knowledge of all the important personalities that mattered—the Eastlands, the Byrds, the Dirksens, the Fulbrights. In the world at large, he began with no such intimate knowledge of men's strengths and weaknesses, of the little levers that can move them, of the special favors or fetishes that can be turned to a particular purpose. Never much for arguing the merits of a case at great length, his talent lay in the forceful application of just such influence, whether by skillful horsetrading or irresistible appeals. Without the same touch for international leverage, he was all the more on uncertain ground abroad. The result was an initial insecurity and awkwardness, a disinclination to do business, a fit of temper, or a rude disdain, which, in turn, only served to make matters worse.

Mastery of the Senate, moreover, is a special art. It calls not for creation, but for improvisation, exploitation, implementation. This is not to say that legislative battles cannot be rugged and intricate and demanding of special skills. But eventually they end. Ultimately there is a vote, and then, in the nature of things, rough treatment, harsh words, or indiscretions in the heat of the battle are usually forgotten in the fraternity of the Senate lobby. But very few foreign-policy questions are ever voted up or down; they linger on.

He was never a reader. By his own account, he cannot remember having read "six books all the way through" since college, but this too might be exaggerated. He once observed that he could learn more from a lunch with a knowledgeable newspaper columnist than from any books. This is not to say he is not a quick student, or that he does not read anything. He wades through stacks of magazines and newspapers and reports and briefing documents when he is interested. He reads inexhaustibly about himself.

But his scholarship in history or philosophy or any of the arts and sciences is negligible; his learning lies largely in what he had managed to absorb in a lifetime of public service, as a Congressional inquisitor, and as a Vice President, and finally as President.

Because as a Senator he had to vote on an endless number of subjects, and because as Majority Leader he had to know a great deal of detail about every major piece of legislation, he developed an impressive capacity to absorb all the necessary background and fact. His logical line of thought and quick eye for essentials was the marvel of a number of men who worked with him and could boast much gaudier academic and intellectual credentials. But he tended to learn what he needed to know only for as long as he needed to know it and then to move on to the next item on the docket. The inevitable result was to leave him with a "smattering of everything and a knowledge of nothing" in Dickens' phrase. This can, of course, be more perilous than starting out with no smattering at all. Indeed, it can have the effect of inhibiting the embrace of new ideas or even a change of mind, as was daily evidenced in Lyndon Johnson's recourse to comparisons between contemporary events and almost anything that was even faintly relevant in his experience, even before the New Deal days. "The most striking discovery one makes in examining the Johnson history," wrote Selig S. Harrison, in the *New Republic* in June, 1960, "is how little he has changed. . . . Johnson seems to have been from the beginning more or less what he is today."

The Stand-in

If Texas and the U.S. Congress offer their own peculiar views of the world, surely the modern office of Vice President ought to be more broadening. But for Lyndon Johnson, it was largely three years of frustration—all the more acute for a man of his temperament. He voyaged abroad, and on one occasion—his quick trip to West Berlin as the Wall was going up—to especially good effect. Berliners, sensitive to any inkling that the West is indifferent to their plight, were visibly fortified in their faith in the United States by the Johnson treatment—big, boisterous, brimming with reassurance for them and defiance against the Communists. Somewhat the same thing can be said for his 1961 Southeast Asian tour, coming as it did on the heels of the chilling Kennedy-Khrushchev encounter in Vienna, and at a time when Asians needed visible tokens of U.S. resolve. But his celebrated, Texas-sized accolade to South Vietnam's Ngo Dinh Diem—the "Winston Churchill of Asia"—did not make the already authoritarian, independent-minded Diem easier to deal with. "The trouble was that Diem believed it," said an old Asia hand later, putting his finger on a problem that was to dog Lyndon Johnson throughout the first two years of his Presidency: the world did not readily understand Texas hyperbole.

The world that was visited by Vice President Johnson didn't always take to him, either. One official who traveled with him later remarked: "Like some wines, Lyndon Johnson does not travel well." Prior to assuming the Vice Presidency, he had one short wartime tour in the South Pacific, two trips to Europe, a four-day visit to Mexico City, and little else in the way of a first-hand view. Touring as Vice President, with all the trappings of office, he was often as much concerned with the splendor of the welcoming ceremony and the comfort of his accommodations as with the content of the discussion he was to have with a foreign head of state. One man who knew him well considered his Vice Presidential odysseys not only "countereducational" but "counterproductive." Not the least of the reasons he offered was the picture Lyndon Johnson painted of himself as he leapt out of automobiles to kiss babies and distribute fountain pens, and to "howdy and shake" with everybody within reach. On his Southeast Asian tour, he offended the Thais, who eschew handshaking as a matter of custom, by persisting in this American gesture despite the entreaties of local diplomats. In Bangkok, he stopped his motorcade, jumped into a bus stalled in a traffic jam, and handshook his way up and down the aisle; then he dashed exuberantly into a crowded Chinese shop, believing it to be run by Thais, and apparently assuming those present spoke English, delivered a speech that few of the local people could comprehend.

If the Johnson travels were not always broadening, many would argue that, on balance, they were better than no traveling at all —that, for example, when the Cyprus situation flared into a dangerous confrontation between Turks and Greeks, Johnson almost certainly was the better for having at least seen that tormented island and talked to its leaders.

Probably more important than all this was the fact that as Vice President, Johnson was meticulously briefed right up to the moment. Technically, he arrived at the top job better prepared than any of his predecessors. He had sat in the high councils— through the Cuban missile crisis, among others—and of necessity would have soaked up not only a feel for high-level policy-making but a considerable range of knowledge. He was not always attentive; but when he did his homework, those who saw him in action all agree he had done it well.

On one occasion, when he was on his mettle, the results were dazzling. Kennedy, it seems, had taken to chiding Johnson in good spirit when they differed, with the remark, "You do not have to make the decisions that I do." By way of proving the point, Kennedy once abruptly asked Johnson for an independent reading on the controversial issue of U.S. Government support for construction of a supersonic airplane, and gave him forty-eight hours to submit his conclusions. Then Kennedy suddenly called a high-level meeting for the following afternoon. It was the sort of challenge Lyndon Johnson dotes on, and after the usual meticulous presentation of Defense Department thinking by Secretary MacNamara, Johnson ostentatiously pushed aside the documents piled in front of him and proceeded, in the words of one official who was present, "to shoot the Defense Department position full of holes. He zeroed in on five instances where the Pentagon was wrong on the facts. It was like a tennis match. There was some consternation in the room. But Kennedy thought it was great—not just the Johnson arguments but the Johnson one-upmanship."

Defense, of course, was one of the areas of Johnson's greatest interest. The number of prominent people in Washington who claim never to have chatted seriously with him about foreign affairs before he became President include one highly talented ambassador of a major ally, and one prestigious elder statesman and good friend with a rich background in foreign affairs. Johnson did talk foreign policy with a select circle of top Kennedy Administration men, including, of course, President Kennedy himself. That he did not range wider was partly—it is only fair to say—out of awareness that it was not his business to take foreign policy leads: his every word would be weighed. But even his inclusion in the most portentous policy-making assemblages was in a sense, a secondhand experience. There is reason to believe that Kennedy prized most highly Johnson's assessment of the domestic political implications in a given foreign-policy course, not his view on the substance of the matter at hand.

The fact, little recognized at the time, was that Lyndon Johnson was often out of step with his chief—on foreign aid, on Latin America, on the whole Kennedy approach to the emerging world. Johnson had his own heroes—Chiang, Diem, Tshombe, Ayub. But by the time Johnson reached the White House, Chiang Kai-shek was more than ever an anachronism, Diem was gone, and Moise Tshombe had fled into exile after the Katangan secession effort (which Johnson silently admired) had been crushed by the United Nations. Later, Johnson was to welcome Tshombe's return to leadership of the central government in Léopoldville and comment acidly to his advisers on the "circular" nature of America's Congo policy. But all three, whether still in power or out, were relics of an earlier day, symbols of an earlier U.S. policy with which Lyndon Johnson felt more comfortable, however much they may have represented the wave of the past in the eyes of Kennedy men.

Johnson had taken a strong liking to Ayub on his Asian tour, but he was rapidly falling from U.S. grace when Johnson reached the White House, joining the wave of the future as he worked his way into the territory of neutralism and beyond, into seeming sympathy with the interests of Peking.

If Johnson had scant sympathy for Kennedy's wooing of the Third World, he was not without his own, fixed notion about how to deal with it. One of his notions was eventually to bring about a revolution in the U.S. approach to foreign aid. He envisioned a massive, world-wide approach to uplifting the less developed nations, broken down in regional mutual self-help plans for Asia and Africa as well as Latin America; for such schemes, properly managed and soundly conceived, he would have the United States give generously, in the company of other industrialized countries. It was a concept that sprang from his Texas background and his New Deal experience, and his firsthand familiarity with the plight of the poor and the uneducated. For this concept, he also had his own evangelist and his favorite creed. The former was British economist Barbara Ward; the latter, her book *The Rich Nations and the Poor Nations.*

A passage, taken at random, could serve as preamble for the foreign-aid approach Lyndon Johnson, as President, was to adopt —as indeed, it could serve as the guiding principle for his Great

Society at home. "When we talk so confidently of liberty," Miss Ward wrote, "we are unaware of the awful servitudes that are created by the ancient enemies of mankind; the servitude of poverty when means are so small that there is literally no choice at all; the servitude of ignorance when there are no perspectives to which the mind can open because there is no education on which the mind can begin to work; the servitude of ill-health which means that the expectation of life is almost too short to allow for any experience of freedom, and the years that *are* lived are dragged out without the health and strength which are themselves a liberation."

International health and international education were to be the subject of special Presidential messages to Congress in early 1966; the phrase "ancient enemies of mankind" was to appear and reappear in Presidential speeches, and *The Rich Nations and the Poor Nations* was to become required reading for members of the President's staff.

Johnson, however, was insistent on grafting hardheaded political and financial terms to high principle, even before he became President. His belief, as described by a man who served with him for more than a decade, was profoundly held: that the distribution of foreign aid for the sake of sheer charity or benevolence was an invitation to be taken for a ride; respect from others, he had long felt, derived from a sensible concern with one's own self-interest and an awareness by others that such a thing exists. Lyndon Johnson was for doing favors to those who showed themselves to be appreciative—in what they did for themselves to make the favors count and what they did, or did not do, that might run counter to the larger interests of the benefactor. With Lyndon Johnson this was basic, and he was to move within two years to serve notice to foreign-aid recipients that actions detrimental to U.S. interests—and detrimental to Lyndon Johnson's political interests at home as well as abroad—would not be countenanced. As one official put it, after Johnson was in the White House, "If mobs sack our libraries in some foreign country, and nothing much is made of it, that's one thing; but if it stirs a row in Congress, and gets the President into hot water, or the foreign-aid program into hotter water, then watch out."

Vice President Johnson had other foreign-aid tutors as well as Barbara Ward. One was Arthur Goldsmith—a Fredericksburg, Texas, native—who worked for the United Nations in economic development and was an authority on the Mekong Basin. He had much to do with Johnson's flaming enthusiasm for Mekong development, as evidenced by Johnson's public embrace of the idea on his 1961 Southeast Asian tour, and again, more meaningfully, in 1965, when as President he threw the weight of the United States for the first time behind the Mekong development scheme.

"Any help—economic as well as military—we give less developed nations [in Southeast Asia] . . . must be part of a mutual effort," Johnson reported to President Kennedy on his return from the Southeast Asian tour. In his confidential memorandum to the President, he argued that "these nations cannot be saved by United States help alone. To the extent the Southeast Asian nations are prepared to take the necessary measures to make our aid effective, we can be—and must be—unstinting in our assistance. It would be useful to enunciate more clearly than we have —for the guidance of these young and unsophisticated nations— what we expect or require from them.

"In large measure, the greatest danger Southeast Asia offers to nations like the United States is not the momentary threat of Communism itself; rather that danger stems from hunger, ignorance, poverty and disease. We must—whatever strategies we evolve—keep these enemies the point of our attack, and make imaginative use of our scientific and technological capability in such enterprises."

Here, with astonishing fidelity, were the guidelines of what was to be Johnson's foreign-aid policy five years later, when as President he gave Congress the outline of "basic changes" he wished to make in American assistance efforts overseas.

That same report included some interesting insights on Johnson's thinking on the broader question of his country's proper role in Asia. By 1961, he had abandoned the notion that the European allies could handle the responsibility. "Asian Communism is compromised and contained by the maintenance of free nations on the subcontinent," he declared, adding: "there is no alternative to United States leadership in Southeast Asia." Apparently he had also soured on the old pacts and treaties—but not on the concept of having pacts that worked. "We should consider an alliance of all the free nations of the Pacific and Asia" with a "clear-cut command authority" and a readiness to devote due attention to "measures and programs of social justice, housing and land reform," he urged.

Johnson advised Kennedy that Asian leaders "do not want American troops involved in Southeast Asia other than on training missions," and avowed that "American combat troop involvement is not only not required, it is not desirable." Five years later, he was to feel compelled to reverse this judgment—at least as to the necessity—but in 1961 he felt strongly that "possibly Americans fail to appreciate fully the subtlety that recently colonial peoples would not look with favor upon governments which invited or accepted the return this soon of Western troops." Indeed, he argued that "to the extent that fear of ground troop involvement dominates our political responses to Asia in Congress or elsewhere, it seems most desirable to me to allay those paralyzing fears in confidence, on the strength of the individual statements made by leaders consulted on this trip."

But he added this prophetic afterthought: "This does not minimize or disregard the probability that open attack would bring calls for U.S. combat troops."

Finally, he posed the need for a "fundamental decision . . . whether we are to attempt to meet the challenge of Communist expansion now in Southeast Asia by a major effort . . . or throw in the towel. This decision must be made in full realization of the very heavy and continuing costs involved in terms of money, of effort and U.S. prestige. It must be made with the knowledge that at some point we may be faced with the further decision of whether we commit major United States forces to the area or cut our losses and withdraw should our efforts fail. We must remain master in this decision."

"Throwing in the towel," the then Vice President had explained at another point in his report, would mean pulling back our defenses to San Francisco and a "Fortress America" concept. "More important, we would say to the world in this case that we don't live up to our treaties and don't stand by our friends," he declared, and concluded flatly: "This is not my concept."

In short, there, with minor variations, was the script, as followed by President Lyndon Johnson four years later, in 1965, when he took the view that North Vietnam had indeed "attacked" South Vietnam, when South Vietnam did indeed call for U.S. troops, and when he decided on a massive expansion of the U.S. effort there. The difference was that he was the man to make the decision he sketched with such eerie clairvoyance for John F. Kennedy.

Whatever Lyndon Johnson saw and touched, and whatever touched him, he thought he knew, and conclusions thus reached were not lightly discarded. He thought he knew Southeast Asia, and he also thought he knew Berlin; he was remembered as a hard-liner on the latter issue long before he became President. "He was more stalwart than some of the Administration," said a French diplomat who had occasion to discuss the matter with Vice President Johnson. "I talked to him at length and he knew all about it and was very sound. He said we should give nothing, and the Russians would back down, and we agreed, of course, and we both were right, as we saw later."

About Europe, he had other fixed and firmly held views. One was that U.S.–British relations, or more specifically, those between Kennedy and his longtime friend the able diplomat Sir David Ormsby-Gore were uncomfortably close; the British, he felt, were getting the best of the bargain in the so-called special relationship. He balanced this off with the realization, politically rooted, that it didn't do to be seen pushing the British around. "You don't kick England in the teeth and get away with it," he once told a visitor, "particularly in the press or on the Hill."

By contrast, Johnson thought relations with De Gaulle were needlessly icy. He came to the Presidency determined, as one confidant described it, to "put an end to low-level State Department attacks and provocations against the French. Johnson believes that if you can create a different atmosphere, you can make progress; you can find a little something to make De Gaulle happy."

Yet the same Johnson, as Vice President, had been taking a line on Europe that could hardly be expected to make De Gaulle happy. He had a habit then of hounding the State Department for new ideas for Johnson speeches, even something that could be called a Johnson Doctrine, as long as it did not put him at odds with the President (he was ever faithful on that score), and, perhaps unwittingly, he threw in with that activist element in the State Department which was busily making De Gaulle angry on a daily basis. In November, 1963, he delivered a speech in Brussels which placed him in the forefront of those adventurous spirits that wanted to remake Europe, if need be, without De Gaulle. In that address, he not only endorsed the controversial multilateral force concept, but went further in stating that "evolution toward European control [of nuclear weapons] as Europe marches toward unity is by no mean excluded." This was Europeanism with a capital E, carried to its grandest extreme, and while both McGeorge Bundy and George Ball had hinted at an independent collective European deterrent in earlier speeches, it was by that time no more than a faint and flickering gleam in the eye of President Kennedy.

On the issue of Latin America, Lyndon Johnson carried to the White House one conviction that turned out to be somewhat more meaningful; he accepted the unacceptability of "another Cuba" as a commandment beyond serious dispute. "He and Kennedy had talked about it many times," one of the President's old Texas friends explained in the wake of the Dominican affair in the spring of 1965, "and they both agreed that any President who permitted a second Communist state to spring up in this Hemisphere would be impeached." Johnson would have argued this case on a number of grounds, beginning with the interests of U.S. security and including the impact in Congress on the Alliance for Progress, on all foreign aid, and indeed on the total power position of any President.

Something else Kennedy and Johnson had apparently discussed was the whole question of the East-West *détente,* and again, their discussions had gone beyond the intrinsic appeal of easing East-West tensions to the domestic political appeal. Kennedy had been concerned about Congressional resistance to the partial nuclear test ban and, consequently, gratified by the public response he had encountered on the "peace" issue in a swing through the Northwest in the fall of 1963. He had discovered that crowd reaction to the tired old hydroelectric-power issue was as nothing in comparison with crowd reaction to his peace theme. Johnson, according to his advisers, had heard Kennedy talk of it and·was never to forget it.

Beyond all this, Johnson brought to the Presidency a personal and amorphous concept of foreign policy based on the simple thesis that the best offense abroad was a good defense at home: a sound domestic program, an impression of a nation dealing forcefully and effectively with its own problems, a nation plainly in sound social and economic health. This, like so much else about Lyndon Johnson, originated, in part, with Roosevelt. He was not unaware how far FDR had gone in becoming a respected world figure with a bare minimum of foreign initiatives. Johnson, in short, arrived at the Presidency with little respect for foreign policy as such. While President, he once told senior advisers that he didn't think the United States had accomplished much of anything in foreign affairs since Truman's day and made clear he was not excluding in this indictment the three years of Kennedy.

Finally, old friends reported·at the time, Johnson came to the White House with one overriding concern. He had a theory that the United States was made to be misunderstood, that the U.S. system was essentially strange and hardly understandable to foreigners, and that most of the ills that had befallen the United States in the world—World Wars I and II and Korea, for example—stemmed from miscalculation of American intentions and American will. The answer, he reckoned, lay not in what was said but what was done—in demonstrable, unmistakable, larger-than-life action to make clear that the United States, in his own, oft-repeated phrase, won't be taken as "fat and fifty, like the country-club set."

Many months after Lyndon Johnson assumed the Presidency, an old and close associate who had spent long hours with him discussing the basic nature of U.S. relations with the world, tried to sum up the pre-Presidential Johnson credo:

"Johnson doesn't believe that relations between nations turn on minor understandings, on cultural differences, or on what you say in speeches or formal diplomatic exchanges. He thinks relations turn on fundamentals, on what you do, and more important, what your motives are thought to be, whether people think you have a tough-minded view of your own self-interest. People have seen us move to another continent to protect our interests, and yet they never seem to believe we will do it again—the readings of American leaders have always been wrong. This is an obsession with Johnson. It stems from all he saw in the 1920's and 1930's; all he saw in his closeness to Roosevelt, who so obviously wanted to prepare the nation for war. Yet the Axis believed Roosevelt's critics; they should have known, and they didn't. Johnson has always believed that this makes it necessary for the United States, unlike any other country, to communicate its purpose and make plain its awareness of its own self-interest loud and clear and over and over, and by deeds rather than words."

THREE

–And the World

John F. Kennedy used to express the frustrations of three Presidents by citing a favorite remark of Franklin D. Roosevelt: "Lincoln was a sad man because he couldn't get it all at once. And nobody can."

But certainly it was Lyndon Johnson's initial temptation to try. In his second month in office, confronted with anti-American rioting in Panama, he startled his advisers by grabbing for the phone and calling the Panamanian President direct. He mobilized considerable segments of top officialdom in a crash effort to get a compromise solution in the Dominican Republic. He yearned for an easy way out of Vietnam, an opportunity to do business profitably with De Gaulle, and above all, a breakthrough towards *rapprochement* with the Russians that might offer some lasting prospect of peace.

He reached none of these goals, for this was not the way of the world early in his Presidency. There had been a time when it was possible for American power and policy to find expression in pro-Western and anti-Communist pacts and alliances, when departures and new directions came in the form of doctrines, when it was all rather tidy and neat. There was even a moment in October, 1962, when it seemed clear-cut; then Kennedy could stare down Khrushchev and win a stunning victory over the course of twelve tense and terrible days. But this exception only reinforced an illusion that international conflict could be quick and conclusive. The world had long since ceased to be tidy and neat.

Long before Lyndon Johnson assumed the office, the cold war—East vs. West for the allegiance of all the rest—had begun to break up into a profusion of conflicts. "East" was increasingly in conflict with "East" within the high councils of the world Communist movement and everywhere that Communism was seeking to extend its sway. The struggle was waged in Communist parties in dozens of countries, by propaganda, by intrigue, by maneuvering for influence down to the smallest party cell in Asia and Africa and Latin America. The Communist monolith was no longer a monolith.

The great confrontation in Europe between the West and Soviet Russia was easing off; Russian Communism collided with U.S. and Western interests almost everywhere, but new rules had been written, perhaps indelibly, in the deadly test of wills over Nikita Khrushchev's Cuban missile bases. In the last days of the Kennedy era, the bare beginnings of "parallelism"—the concept that envisioned a Russia working at least tacitly in concert with the West to contain the expansion of Communist Chinese power —were visible in Soviet withdrawal from the Communist effort to subvert Laos, in the 1963 nuclear-test ban, in Moscow's quickening interest in shoring up the great Asian subcontinent against Chinese encroachment.

Increasingly for the United States, the cold war was coming to mean the contest between the United States and Communist

China, and while this clash of interests centered in Asia, it was a global conflict too. Meantime, the nations of the West were more and more at odds among themselves over the shape of the Atlantic Alliance and the weight a resurgent Western Europe should have in it, and over the conduct and content of "Western" policy around the world. Finally, there was a North-South struggle overlaid upon all the other struggles, pitting the rich or the relatively rich against the poor; the advanced, industrialized half of the world against the impoverished rural half, lying largely in the southern latitudes and comprised in the main of the so-called emerging nations or pseudo-nations that have sprouted like weeds—or wildflowers—in the abandoned formal gardens of the old empires.

In these struggles, the cockpits were no longer Berlin or Austria or Greece; they were Zanzibar and Laos and Yemen. The terrain was unfamiliar—and remote. Only in rare instances were the circumstances clear, the choices easy, the execution quick. Of course, they had never been entirely so. But the Truman Doctrine, the Marshall Plan, the North Atlantic Treaty Organization, the Bretton Woods monetary accords—all the great postwar initiatives—had powerful impulses and motivations behind them. They profited from the legacy of Allied collaboration in the war against Hitler and from a sense of common interest and danger against a common foe, a legacy that remained strong enough to sustain common initiatives in a cold war against the new threat of international Communism.

President Eisenhower, however, could summon up only one "doctrine" to bear his name; the emptiness of his effort to rally the Middle East against Soviet encroachment suggests how limited was the capacity of the U.S. Government, even by the late 1950's, to find practical ways to apply the package approach to foreign policy. By Kennedy's time, international events were fast developing immunity to sweeping shifts in policy (as witness the fate of the Kennedy "Grand Design" for Europe). Ultimately, President Kennedy was to recast U.S. ambitions in the world by settling on an effort to make it "safe for diversity." Ultimately, Lyndon Johnson was to settle for this objective, too.

Less and less was it possible to shape the world from Washington. More and more it had become necessary to lead from behind the scenes, to exploit existing forces (including some that seemed on their face to be alien to proper U.S. objectives), or even to stand aside. U.S. hopes for Europe rested on Europe's ability to build a common market, which was something the United States could scarcely talk about aloud without being accused of "interference." U.S. hopes for Latin America and for much of the rest of the so-called Third World hinged on the self-help efforts that the emerging nations were prepared to make. The United States alone could not stop Indians and Pakistanis from shooting each other, however much the shooting might undercut the American objectives of bolstering the subcontinent of Asia; they could be stopped only under U.N. auspices. A triumph of U.S. policy could be seen in the mere fact that the United States did not quite sever all relations with Indonesia, and thereby stood to profit when the Communist Chinese badly bungled an effort to overthrow the Sukarno Government. Vietnam could not be pacified by U.S. force alone; somehow it would have to be accomplished through the creation of a stable, cooperative government in Saigon.

The Asian Time Bomb

"We have a very simple policy in Vietnam," said President Kennedy in a news conference on September 12, 1963. "We want the war to be won, the Communists to be contained, and the Americans to go home. That is our policy."

By contrast with what it was to become, the war in Vietnam did look relatively simple in September, 1963, and only moderately more complicated by the time Lyndon Johnson took over responsibility for U.S. policy there. The familiar, seemingly stable, authoritarian, and distinctly unpromising regime of President Ngo Dinh Diem had been brutally demolished only three weeks before Kennedy was killed. But the military junta that seized power, under Lieutenant General Duong Van Minh, better known as Big Minh, was pursuing the fight against the Vietcong with admirable vigor.

The monsoon rains were ending and U.S. officials saw no reason to depart from the timetable confidently laid down by

Defense Secretary McNamara for the progressive withdrawal of the U.S. military adviser contingents by the end of 1965. There were about 25,000 American troops on duty in South Vietnam and if anybody then believed that the number would in fact be expanded more than tenfold by the end of 1965, and that this number would include six combat divisions actively engaged in a full-dress war on the Asian mainland, nobody was saying so. Indeed, though the fighting was to become still fiercer, and the Minh junta was to give way quickly to yet another military government under General Khanh within a few months, dogged optimism was still the rule. Nor was it reasonable to expect the U.S. war planners in Washington or Saigon to foretell Hanoi's intent to intensify its efforts, or the degree of political disintegration that would follow the removal of the Diem Government's ironhanded rule. So it is important, in assessing Lyndon Johnson's inheritance in Asia, to distinguish between what was known to be happening and what was later revealed to have been happening.

What was actually happening was that the Communist Government was getting ready to administer to South Vietnam what it expected would be the *coup de grâce*. The rate of infiltration of agents, military cadres, and trained troops into South Vietnam was already rising—though intelligence reports lagged well behind the fact. It is also clear that the Communist hierarchy in Hanoi had concluded that the United States would not make the necessary effort to salvage South Vietnam.

What may have been developing, simultaneously, was an increased willingness on the part of Hanoi—if not Peking—to explore a negotiated settlement, secure in the belief that it would be bargaining from strength. The terms are a matter for conjecture, and also, as a practical matter, irrelevant. The conviction in Washington, widely shared among the counselors inherited by Lyndon Johnson, was that there was no hope of doing profitable business with what Dean Rusk referred to collectively as "the other side," that Hanoi and Peking were hell-bent on total victory, and that the only sensible U.S. response under those circumstances had to be total resistance.

Lyndon Johnson's most dangerous Vietnam legacy, in short, was not so much a state of war as a state of mind, or rather several states of mind. The guessing was that the war in Vietnam was being conducted, according to the assessment of one high-ranking authority who served President Kennedy and would serve President Johnson, by a "North Vietnamese holding company in which the Chinese have at least sixty per cent of the shares." This was the assumption upon which U.S. policy was based. But nobody knew nearly enough about "the other side" to be able to do more than guess about the intentions of the "holding company," about its real make-up, about who was really running the war. That became more and more the crux of the controversy over Vietnam policy. The point that mattered at the outset was that it was not being debated much within the small group of men upon whom Lyndon Johnson was relying for counsel. For the new President, the state of mind that really mattered most was the prevailing view among his advisers of the mind of Hanoi and, in the last analysis, Peking.

Of all the new forces at work in the world, the most menacing to U.S. interests was mainland China. Even by the end of 1963, China remained, for most Americans, a great unknown, a time bomb whose fuse stretched to Vietnam. There were no official contacts, save for a dreary round of empty conversations between U.S. and Chinese diplomats in Warsaw; there was no trade, no cultural exchange, indeed, no tangible Chinese presence in the American consciousness, except for that of Chiang Kai-shek. The world's most populous nation was simply something to be denounced regularly, resisted rigidly, and otherwise ignored. Before Lyndon Johnson's first Presidential year was up, however, Peking was to join the nuclear club (at least technically), widen its ideological warfare with the Soviet Union, receive the diplomatic blessings of De Gaulle, egg on Communist escalation in South Vietnam—and, in all these ways, bring closer a major realignment of the fundamental power relationships of the world.

By their efforts to outdo each other in the conflict against the West, the two great Communist powers had managed simultaneously to advance as well as retard their common interest in stirring up troubles for the United States. One effect was to intensify Sino-Soviet competition for the favors of the international Communist movement, which meant more Communist subversion, propaganda, and infiltration to undermine governments friendly to the West. But a contrary effect of this intramural tugging and hauling was, of course, to split and weaken Communist movements in a number of countries. The result was ferment and conflict amid a tangle of crosspurposes. If there was much in all this for the United States to exploit, few ways had been found to do so profitably. The confusion was contagious; nations of the neutralist Third World, from Algeria to India and Cambodia to Zanzibar were wondering how best to make the most of the dissensions in the Communist bloc, as well as the larger conflict between Communism and the West.

Partial paralysis afflicted the Russians as well. They were pulled two ways—toward competition with Peking on something resembling Peking's terms (which would have meant a more vigorous and risky Soviet cold war campaign), and toward competition of a different sort, which would have meant a real effort to reach *rapprochement* with the West—an easing of the Soviet line in the cold war and greater Soviet internal concentration on consumer goods instead of missiles. For lack of a clear course, the Russians were trying both, and making it that much harder to achieve East-West *rapprochement*. Later, the vast expansion of the Vietnam fighting would make *rapprochement* even more remote. But even without the Vietnamese escalation, Peking, by the end of 1963, had achieved a considerable capacity to play the spoiler's role. And the U.S. Government had yet to come up with anything that could properly be called a policy for Peking.

Publicly and officially, the United States was positioned solidly against recognition of the Communist government, against its admission to the United Nations on any basis (barring a fundamental change in its character), against its acceptance in world society. The grounds were legal and moral; Communist China was held to be in violation of the U.N. resolution condemning her aggression in the Korean War; the argument was that technically the United States was still at war with Communist China. Hardly anybody, including most Western or pro-Western U.N. members, accepted this view. General de Gaulle was to abandon it as French policy during Johnson's first few Presidential months. Even the top men of government who faithfully upheld the American position in public agreed in private that the position was difficult to defend on anything but moralistic grounds—or in terms of practical domestic policies. Although there was no way of telling, beyond the samplings of the pollsters, the assumption was that the American public stood stoutly with Nationalist China as the rightful government of China and against recognition in any form of the Communist government.

Whatever the case, the United States was stuck with its line, and Lyndon Johnson could hardly have been expected to change it, even if he had been so inclined. Obviously, some event or series of events would be required to knock the Chinese problem off dead center. A Vietnamese solution could yield a breakthrough, but the view of a good many China experts at the time was that a new generation of Chinese leaders would probably be required as a forerunner to a new Chinese policy which might pave the way for a change in the U.S. attitude.

In the meantime, almost all the thinking was along familiar lines. In December, 1963, long before Johnson had gotten into the China question, Assistant Secretary of State for Far Eastern Affairs Roger Hilsman had dared to discuss the China problem publicly and proclaim the "open door" approach favored by President Kennedy. The most careful reading of his address could not uncover any evidence that U.S. policy had really shifted; the point of Mr. Hilsman's discourse was simply to attempt to fix the blame more squarely upon the Communist Chinese for U.S.–Chinese antagonisms. But the incident served to underscore how touchy a topic Communist China was at that time, for there was a quick outcry of protest, and the State Department offered public reassurance that there was nothing new in U.S. thinking on China.

On the contrary, what Lyndon Johnson inherited, in the person of Dean Rusk as Secretary of State, was a rigidly doctrinaire approach to Peking with which the most fanatic China lobbyist could hardly quarrel. Not just in public, but in private, and in regular conversations with the President himself, Mr. Rusk hammered the point that Communist China was actively promoting aggression in Vietnam, that aggression in Vietnam was no different than aggression in Europe by Hitler, and that appeasement in

Vietnam could have the same consequences as appeasement in Munich. By appeasement, Mr. Rusk meant any solution of the war in Vietnam which would reward the use of force. Though the U.S. position on negotiations over Vietnam was to soften steadily in the first two Johnson years, the fundamental demand, as set forth by Dean Rusk, remained unchanged—the North Vietnamese and their Communist Chinese sponsors must "leave their neighbors alone."

If Rusk took a puritanical view and offended some critics by what they considered to be moralistic preaching, there was heavy pressure for a much more radical course—a calculated escalation of the war effort in Vietnam, leading logically to the crowning achievement of a nuclear strike at Chinese atomic-weapons plants. The Pentagon had detailed contingency plans for this purpose. Though the segment of military thought that favored it was by no means predominant, the idea of denuclearizing the Chinese before they had really gotten started was preached with considerable force by high-ranking and responsible officials while Kennedy was still alive. Their argument was that there was no time like the present to eliminate China as a nuclear power; why wait a decade to be subjected to Communist Chinese nuclear blackmail?

But the Chinese, for all their bluster, were giving little direct help to the Vietcong movement in South Vietnam—Peking's war against American "imperialism" was to be fought, as far as possible, down to the last North Vietnamese. So there was no provocation for the sort of direct retaliation against China that appealed to the planners in the Air Force and the Strategic Air Command. There was pressure for expansion of the U.S. war effort in the South and for extending it to the North, but Kennedy had it firmly in check. All there really was in the way of a Vietnam policy, then, was a determination to go on supporting the government in the South. Even that had been hedged significantly by Kennedy in the last months of his Administration, in declarations suggesting strongly the practical limits of U.S. assistance to any government which would not do more than the Diem Government was held to be doing to promote social justice, economic reform, and constitutional process.

And all there really was in the way of a U.S.–China policy was unstinting hostility to Peking and a determination to contain the expansion of Chinese Communism, somehow. For this purpose, there was no single U.S. strategy and still less a cohesive Western effort, but rather a mishmash of efforts concocted to cope with a mishmash of situations.

Though there was no formal pact, the United States and Britain had a mutual understanding to help India if the Chinese repeated their 1962 attack on a major scale. The Chinese intrusion in India had been carefully restrained, but it lasted long enough and struck deep enough to elicit from the United States an expanded program of arms aid to New Delhi, a program which further alienated the Ayub Government in Pakistan and drove him into closer connection with Communist China. The United States was committed in two ways to defend Pakistan from either the Russians or the Chinese; under the Central Treaty Organization (CENTO), (which was formerly the Baghdad Pact until Iraq pulled out, forcing a change of name), and under the Southeast Asian Treaty Organization (SEATO), which still had some status, though it had proved so unreassuring in Southeast Asia that Thailand felt it necessary to take out additional insurance through a mutual-defense arrangement with the United States.

The weaknesses of both CENTO and SEATO were the same; in theory they could be invoked against aggression of any sort, and all members would cheerfully pitch in. In practice, the European members, especially the French, had long since lost interest in Asia's defense; lacking the power to do anything effectively, De Gaulle had fallen back on the rationalization that nothing effective could be done; to a large degree, the over-extended British were of the same mind, except where vital British interests (Hong Kong, for example, or Kuwait) were concerned. A second weakness was that neither of these mutual-security arrangements was designed or equipped to cope with the form of warfare that any Communist "aggression" was most likely to take—subversion and infiltration, outside incitement of internal dissidents, hit-and-run guerrilla tactics, terrorism. For this new and virulent strain of aggression, the old pacts of the Dulles days, as a practical matter, offered little more than mustard plasters where the critical need was for wonder drugs. They could be invoked, as SEATO was to be in Vietnam, for legal and moral and psychological purposes, to give a collective, and, more important, Asian cast to a U.S. effort. But they could not compel collaboration by America's Atlantic allies; still less could they compel moral support or even sympathy. Such political backing as Britain was willing to give the U.S. effort in Vietnam, for example, derived largely from a simple horse trade; the U.S. end of the deal was support for Britain's Malaysian defense effort.

For all practical purposes, the United States stood alone in fighting Communism on the far side of the globe. If the British Government did not quarrel openly with U.S. policy in Asia, its private thinking was closer to the French than to the Washington view; and the thinking of both Britain and France had less to do with the merits of the matter than it had to do with their practical inability to do much about it.

In any event, the argument of both these allies, and a good many American critics, was that the United States was expecting too much, that it was trying to promote a greater degree of independence from and defiance of Communist China by the far smaller countries on the Chinese rim than could reasonably be expected. It was De Gaulle's claim, advanced in a series of talks with American diplomats, that the Chinese were inner-directed, preoccupied with economic problems, and both unlikely and unready to try to swallow up the Southeast Asians or to move into the populous and impoverished subcontinent. Short of that, however, Chinese influence was bound to be strong, and China's neighbors could not prudently ignore the towering weight of the colossus to their north. As a practical matter, a good many countries were moving toward middle ground and beyond, in an effort to reach an accommodation with Peking. A wobbly sort of neutralism prevailed in Burma and Cambodia. Pakistan was perhaps a special case, due to her preoccupation with India. Indonesia was another special case with the canny Sukarno in charge and a powerful Communist Party forcing his hand. India was being driven in the other direction by Chinese militancy.

Thailand, the Philippines, Malaysia, South Korea, and Nationalist China—these remained the beaux ideal of America's

Asian policy. But Laos, or rather that half of it not under total Communist control, had lapsed into uneasy neutralism with U.S. encouragement under the Kennedy Administration, joining Burma in a halfway house between pro-Westernism and open alignment with Peking. Cambodia was at odds with all her neighbors, but with Prince Sihanouk, anti-Americanism was a favorite sport.

Even in the case of Vietnam, the U.S. predilection for Western-oriented governments was wearing thin. The Kennedy Administration still talked about "winning" the war and leaving behind a stable, anti-Communist government. It is doubtful if President Kennedy really believed such an objective feasible; men close to him are confident that he would have been willing to settle in time for something far less than staunch and sterling anti-Communism in Saigon. In Asia, as elsewhere, events were encouraging the United States to apply the doctrine of diversity. And not the least of the reasons was that the Western allies were less and less willing to offer even token backing of the U.S. stand in Asia on any other terms. Nowhere were they less prepared to follow an American lead.

The State of the Atlantic Union

The European Alliance inherited by Lyndon Johnson was not exactly rudderless. Rather, it was "lost in the horse latitudes" —a treacherous reach of the Atlantic Ocean which runs, geographically, in the region of 30° N and is characterized by high pressure, calms, and light baffling winds. As legend has it, when ancient sailing vessels became becalmed too long in this dead air, the horses which were so often a part of their cargo became first restive, then demented; as fresh water supplies ran low, they would kick crazily at the sides of the ship, sometimes causing it to sink.

In late 1963 and early 1964, the North Atlantic Treaty Alliance was far from sunk. Indeed, as an effective deterrent against Soviet ambitions in Europe, it was a stunning success militarily, even though it fell far short of the sort of integrated defense instrument instantly responsive to the collective will of its membership that many devoted Alliance strategists would have preferred. But the bare beginnings of a *détente* with the Soviet Union had robbed it of the adrenalin of demonstrable danger, and its most important members, the United States included, were beginning to kick. Increasingly, Washington had come to believe that the Europeans were not pulling their weight in the manning of NATO defenses, and that, beyond this, they were insensitive to the further need of presenting a solid front wherever Western interests were threatened around the globe. Generalizing, the Europeans felt with varying intensity that the United States had far too large a voice in the affairs of a resurgent Europe, and that for all its talk about "consultation" on Western policy it did not really want collective decision-making as much as it wanted loyal, unquestioning backing of U.S. efforts to counter Communism from Cuba to the Congo to South Vietnam.

There was much to be said for both sides of this broad debate. At a time when a flourishing Europe was flaunting its growing economic strength, and basing its claim for a larger voice in world affairs on its remarkable recovery from postwar prostration, its share of the total Western defense burden remained disproportionately small. In West Germany alone, only half as many men per hundred population were bearing arms as in the United States. For all of Europe, defense spending averaged $53 per capita, only a fraction of the figure of $277 in the United States. Even then, long before the Vietnam build-up, the United States had about as many men under arms as all the European NATO countries combined, despite Europe's considerable population edge. The American nuclear deterrent, constructed at a cost roughly estimated at $150 billion by 1963, accounted alone for more than twice the total defense expenditure of all the European NATO allies together; it accounted for more than 10 times the money all of the European allies together spend annually on all defense costs. Indeed, the total annual defense budgets of all European NATO members was a mere one-third of annual U.S. defense outlays, and scarcely one country among them was not complaining of having to spend too much. The British, claiming Commonwealth commitments around the globe, shied away from military conscription, while the United States was drafting men for service in the armed forces.

Such statistics were bound to impress a man like Lyndon Johnson, with his strict adherence to the principle of reciprocity. Yet the Europeans could argue, with some justice, that the statistics misled, that it was not easy to distinguish between that part of the American defense effort which would have been essential, in any event, for the maintenance of its world-power position and that part which was devoted to the defense of Europe. Nor could it be denied that the nub of the Alliance deterrent was U.S. nuclear power, and that the control of this power was almost exclusively in the hands of the United States. Kennedy had talked of "interdependence" in his memorable Fourth of July address in Philadelphia in 1962, but he was careful to offer "equality" only to a Europe united as one sovereign entity. The United States was in the habit of talking grandly about close collaboration, and a growing role for Europe in the total defense effort. But balance-of-payment pressures impelled the United States to insist that the Germans buy much of their military hardware in the United States to offset the cost of maintaining U.S. troops along the Western front in Europe. On the matters that counted, U.S. "consultation," as in the striking instance of the Cuban missile crisis, had come to mean notification. Nationalism, or at least a strong sense of the sanctity of its own sovereign status, afflicted the United States as well as its allies.

So it wasn't all De Gaulle, even though his more virulent expressions of French nationalism constituted the most acute threat to Alliance collaboration. On January 14, 1963, he slammed the door on British membership in the Common Market. In mid-1963, he stepped up his war of nerves against NATO as an organization even while reiterating his undying devotion to the spirit of the Alliance. He sounded more loudly than ever his call to the Continental Europeans to resist the influence and encroachments of the "Anglo-Saxons" (by which he meant primarily the dominance of the United States in Europe's defense). "France has provided herself with an atom bomb," he said, and the result is that "for the French Government, important changes must be made in the conditions of its means of participating in the Alliance, for this organization was built on the basis of integration, which no longer is of any value for us." Skillfully, the French President played on gnawing West German fears that the United States would somehow sell out Bonn's interests in a big deal with the Soviet Union; just as skillfully, he played on wider European anxiety that in the last analysis, the United States would not risk its cities in a nuclear exchange with the Russians to save Europe.

Meantime, the General was groping for a global role, for anything that would enhance French prestige at a time when France had, for all practical purposes, withdrawn within her national boundaries and was no longer a world power of consequence, even with the pinch of nuclear capability implicit in the embryonic French *"force de frappe."* He was undercutting the U.S. effort in Vietnam by promoting a "neutralist" solution at a time when the mere suggestion was enough to shake the government in Saigon. In the interests of French agriculture, he was making trouble in the Common Market and threatening to scuttle the Geneva trade negotiations before they even began. He was withdrawing his officers from the NATO high command, refusing to commit French forces where they were needed on the German front. He was contemptuous of the Kennedy peace offensive and its one positive product, the partial nuclear-test-ban treaty negotiated in the middle of 1963; this did not fit France's purpose, which was to build its own nuclear strike force. He was on the Soviet side of the argument in the United Nations on the obligation of members to pay for special peace-keeping operations in the Middle East, the Congo, and elsewhere. As Lyndon Johnson came to power, Charles de Gaulle was eyeing Latin America as a fresh field for intensified French diplomacy. With the same fine disregard for what the United States took to be its urgent interests, France bestowed diplomatic recognition upon Communist China, just a few weeks after Lyndon Johnson took office.

In all of this, French action or influence was not of much significance, except in a negative sense. Still, mere mulishness was enough to thwart U.S. objectives on a number of fronts, and as practiced by a master like De Gaulle, it was sufficient to immobilize the Western Alliance, even if there had been no other immobilizing forces at work.

But the British, for their part, were not much more cooperative. The Profumo affair had shattered Tory rule, though it was not until October, 1964, that the changeover to a Labour Government came. In the interim, however, the British were incapable of strong initiatives in any direction. They were caught up in internal political upheaval, increasingly menaced by the chronic threat to the ever vulnerable pound sterling, and all the more in need of asserting their place in the world as Commonwealth leader, as a power to be reckoned with, and as somebody the United States must not be allowed to take for granted or push around. Trade with Communist Cuba, violently opposed by the United States, had been elevated to an inalienable British right; in a time of political turbulence, the sanctity of free trade for a nation so dependent on trade was not something to trifle with. *Rapprochement* with the Germans was likewise something to be resisted; fear of German nationalist revival is almost universal in the British Isles. *Rapprochement* with the Communists, on the other hand, was something to be fervently pushed, because in Britain this is everybody's dream. Even while accepting the latter, and understanding the former, the United States found its job of concerting Alliance thinking complicated because of the intensity of British feeling on both counts.

The Germans, as Lyndon Johnson came to power, were in political transition, too. The Adenauer age was actually over, but the Erhard era would not be officially ushered in until German elections in 1965. Meantime, the ruling Christian Democratic Union Party, lacking a fresh mandate from the public, was more than ever sensitive to the conflicting tugs and hauls of European politics. De Gaulle was beckoning Bonn into closer bilateral alliance, but the United States was still West Germany's only real protector. The cdu was deeply split and anxious not to be asked to choose between the Atlanticism preached from Washington and De Gaulle's blandishments, which would have tied West Germany tightly into a Continental combine of European nations over which France, with its claim to nuclear-power status, would naturally wish to preside.

The rest of Europe was divided, confused, and for the most part noncommittal. It also reveled in unprecedented prosperity, thanks to the success of the Common Market; the Belgians, Dutch, and Italians, as well as Luxembourg, wanted nothing more than for The Six to get on with their work of economic integration. Increasingly, this process was hung up in the agricultural quarrel between West Germany and France. Most Europeans, including many Frenchmen, also yearned for a closer political community, a bigger collective voice for Europe, and strong trans-Atlantic ties in a wider Western Alliance. But they had heard and harkened to President Kennedy in the summer of 1963 without seeing many specific indications that the "Grand Design" discussed so eloquently in the early stages of the Kennedy Administration was anything more than a design—anything more than a blueprint for which there seemed to be no builders and not much common interest in getting on with the job.

On both sides of the Atlantic, there were, at the beginning of the Johnson Presidency, at least two established schools of thought about how to proceed. Lyndon Johnson was to enroll in first one and then the other and ultimately to become a dropout from both.

One school, embedded in the State Department's Policy Planning Council and led by Under Secretary of State George Ball, was all for action. It argued that the Alliance ought not to be allowed to flounder for lack of French cooperation; the thing to do was to work around De Gaulle, in hopes of someday bringing him around. "It is not possible to persuade, bribe, or coerce General de Gaulle from following a course upon which he is set," said Dean Acheson, professor emeritus of the activist school. "But he can and does in time recognize the inevitable and adjust his conduct to it, as he did in Algeria. It has been wisely said that 'the mode by which the inevitable comes to pass is effort.' The power of the United States to shape the inevitable for General de Gaulle is immense."

That was the credo, and the proposal dearest to the hearts of those who believed it was the multilateral nuclear force (MLF). Its principal, practical purpose for almost all of its five years of active life as a proposal was nothing more than to give Atlantic-minded, integration-minded Europeans something they could sink their teeth into in company with the United States. This point was often discounted by traditionalists, who persisted in taking the idea of a small nuclear navy for NATO quite literally, in judging it on its military merits and finding it, naturally enough, deficient, in feasibility or effectiveness. It wasn't all that wanting, however, on any count, and it had the supreme virtue of being useful even if nothing came of it. It was, indeed, an almost essential diplomatic doorstop, holding open the option of a communal, Atlantic solution to the difficult nuclear-defense issue against the relentless pressures of nationalism and narrow European Continentalism generated by De Gaulle.

The activists also backed monetary reform as something the allies could possibly act like allies about, even when they couldn't act like allies about nuclear affairs. They pressed a rich variety of proposals designed to promote concerted Western action and policy around the world. They favored a rough-tough U.S. attitude toward those team members found working against U.S. interests. Off on the edge of the horizon, they saw glimmering the vision of a truly united Europe, with West Germany inextricably tied up in it, a Europe in boldface, an entity which would constitute a second great power on the Western side of the scale. And they saw no need not to work toward this ambition just because De Gaulle was against it; for the other allies, there was more than enough leverage, if the United States was ready to risk strong-arm techniques.

The opposing school was less easy to place. It had adherents in the Pentagon, a group traditionally against any measures which might dilute U.S. authority and ability to make its own military decisions. It had others in the State Department among those officials who had to deal daily with the repercussions of Gaullist wrath, whether vented on the Common Market, or the West Germans, or NATO, or the United Nations and still others among the arms controllers who saw MLF as a red flag to Russia and an insuperable obstacle to disarmament.

This school had powerful support on the continent of Europe, from the U.S. diplomatic corps, from France's smaller neighbors, from all those most directly influenced by the style and implacable will and grand majesty of the solitary, unyielding figure in the Elysée Palace. For them, De Gaulle was a natural force, and life in his midst was like life on the slope of a live volcano. Like aborigines, they worried over every wisp of smoke, wrung their hands over every rumble, and paid daily homage to a force they feared and could not fathom. From this came two conclusions: that De Gaulle was supreme and all wise, and the corollary that any U.S. policy designed to confound this force was the muddle-headed work of mere mortals.

If it sounds illogical, it was no more so than, for example, sun worship; when enough people believe in it, it becomes a force to be reckoned with. By the time Lyndon Johnson became President, France was odd man out, one day threatening the future of the Common Market, another day of NATO, the next of the United Nations. The head man seemed lost in visions of a world 20 or 30 or 50 years away—either way—and the content and quality of French diplomacy on the big European questions was often measured most eloquently by the presence of an empty chair. As a power in the world, France was probably overrated; the towering presence of an undoubted great man of unflinching will and purpose has a capacity to mesmerize. But in an Alliance operating by unanimity, progress can be quite effectively foreclosed, not just by saying "no," but by De Gaulle's more maddening technique of saying "not now" or "maybe" and icily declining to elaborate.

The Latin Legacy

In the last months of 1963, things were going awry in the southern half of the Western Hemisphere. Communist Cuba had been cleansed of Soviet missiles, but the U.S. Government had only Nikita Khrushchev's word to Dean Rusk that it had also been cleansed of Russian combat troops. Castro was up to his familiar tricks and was soon to be caught red-handed fomenting revolution in Venezuela. A pro-Communist candidate was the winter-book favorite to win the next presidential election in Chile, then a year away. The Goulart Government in Brazil was sliding out of control, carrying the nation toward economic catastrophe and deep political penetration by the extreme left. A constitutional government in the Dominican Republic, warmly embraced by the United States when it was installed in February, had been pulled down in September by a right-wing military coup; the United States had declined to recognize the new government and closed down aid operations, but a decision could not be delayed for long. In open defiance of the high hopes and noble principles of the Alliance for Progress, rampant militarism was more and more becoming a threat to progressive economic and social development.

And the fabled *Alianza* itself was increasingly gripped by the growing pains that afflict great international undertakings in their early years. Kennedy was beginning to move toward a major overhaul just before his death. Part of the problem was management, but a lot of it lay in the very enormity of the task that had been laid out at Punta del Este in 1961 and in the lamentable absence of any real social, political, or ethnic homogeneity in the Hemisphere.

Not in December, 1963—and, for that matter, not at any time —did Latin America lend itself to one grand master plan. The temptation remained to talk glibly about Latin America in terms suggesting that there was something common between a giant military autocracy such as Brazil; a minuscule democracy such as Costa Rica; a polyglot, European-oriented Argentina; a voodoo-istic, African-oriented Haiti; a Communist Cuba; a totalitarian Paraguay; a Mexico living always under the shadow of the presence to the north; and a remote, free-wheeling, social-reforming Christian Democracy such as Chile. Venezuela, which had suffered firsthand from Castro-Cuban subversion, could have one view of the Communist threat to this Hemisphere, and share it with some of its Caribbean neighbors. To others to the south, Cuba looks like a tiny island nation several thousand miles away. Brazil, spread over half of the Latin American land mass, is Portuguese-speaking. Travel and communications facilities between most Latin countries are inadequate, and despite recent efforts to promote free trade and common markets, intra-Hemisphere commerce has never amounted to much, if only because most Latin nations produce raw materials for export to other parts of the world and import consumer goods and industrial items which none of their neighbors produce in large amounts. Economic sophistication, social development, and political structure vary widely; so, historically, has U.S. policy and approach varied widely toward individual nations. However, most Latin countries share poverty and social injustice; it had been the great hope of John F. Kennedy to find in this common denominator the basis for a pan-Hemispheric approach.

In varying degree, he had succeeded. There were progressive, young, reform-minded Latin Americans almost everywhere; some were in power, some were in powerful opposition, some were almost in hiding; but they were there and he spoke to them and they heard. His was a household name, and in death he became a martyr as only Latins can make a martyr of a man. And because John F. Kennedy could have done no wrong in Latin eyes, the tendency was strong across the Hemisphere to believe that his successor could do no right, even when, as was sometimes the case, he was pursuing, in his way, policies little different from those of Kennedy. Indeed, all the liabilities that Lyndon Johnson inherited by the mere fact of not being John F. Kennedy were magnified many times over in Latin America. Johnson was not a patrician, or an intellectual, or an obviously charismatic figure— and Latin Americans of all stripes had long grown accustomed to finding some measure of these qualities in the men who led them, as well as in the U.S. leaders they most admired.

Lyndon Johnson's Latin American inheritance, therefore, was an especially harsh burden. One president of a Latin nation told a visitor from the United States: "If there is one person we find it hard to trust, it is a Texas American who speaks a little Spanish —we have not forgotten the Mexican War." Though Lyndon Johnson was to speak movingly and act constructively on numerous occasions dealing with the area of Latin America's vital needs, there was nothing he could do about appearances. And with Latin Americans, appearances matter; worse, even if they did not matter, it suited the purpose of a good many Latin leaders to act as if the appearance of things mattered tremendously. One high U.S. official who toured the Hemisphere in 1965 encountered a stock response as self-serving as it was sentimental: the Alliance for Progress, the line was, had died with John F. Kennedy; Lyndon Johnson didn't really care; therefore, there was no incentive for the Latins themselves to do the hard things that were absolutely vital if the Alliance for Progress were to make *any* progress. Even without this handicap, the fact is that Lyndon Johnson inherited a soggy *Alianza*. It had been launched by Kennedy with tremendous force as a "vast cooperative effort, unparalleled in magnitude and nobility of purpose, to satisfy the basic needs of the American people for homes, work, and land, health and schools." Money—in large, round numbers—had been promised; the Punta del Este conference had pledged the Hemisphere to unending mutual good works. But enthusiasm, as is so often the case, had outstripped performance; projects were slow in developing, funds trickled down rather than arriving soon in the hoped-for torrents. The mystique was wearing thin, along with the patience of *Alianza* beneficiaries, and so was the zest for self-help that had been so splendidly in evidence at the founding conference.

And as the mystique wore thin and momentum slowed, the natural forces from the right and from the left—and from nothing more than sheer nationalism—were beginning to reassert themselves. This was measurable in the rash of military coups; Honduras and Guatemala were recent victims. As the right reached for more power, so did the left, with the first faint traces of Communist-encouraged guerrilla movements becoming a source of anxiety in Guatemala, Ecuador, Peru, and the tormented, star-crossed Dominican Republic, which was to bulk so large in Lyndon Johnson's second year. Concurrently, the apostles of pragmatism in the State Department's centers of Latin American policy-making were making themselves felt. They had an instinctive preference for the *status quo,* were against revolutionary change with all its uncertainties, and had a general, prudent disposition to play the Hemisphere by ear. Lyndon Johnson was later to be charged with robbing the *Alianza* of its ideology. But principle was already giving ground to practicality at the management level before Lyndon Johnson took over. President Kennedy's Assistant Secretary of State for Inter-American Affairs, Edwin Martin, whose liberal outlook toward the Latin Americans was not in question, stated the case for those in the middle ground of official U.S. thinking in October, 1963. With militarism seemingly renascent in the Hemisphere and the U.S. attitude about it seemingly equivocal, he prepared a policy statement for publication in the *New York Herald Tribune.*

"We all have respect for motherhood and abhor sin," he began. "We may observe, however, that while motherhood has prospered, so has sin." It was Mr. Martin's point that the Latin military was a fact of life and, further, that it need not necessarily always be equated with sin. He listed the Latin dictators, Perón in Argentina, Jiménez in Venezuela, and Rojas Pinilla in Colombia, who had eventually been dislodged from absolute power by their own military. He pointed out that the military men who had recently grabbed power in Peru and Ecuador had supplanted corrupt and ineffective constitutional regimes and, under careful U.S. pressure, had been encouraged to turn both nations back towards constitutionalism after cleaning house. Martin insisted he was making no apology for coups. "They are to be fought with all the means we have available." What he was saying, however, and what a lot of Latin American experts in the U.S. Government accepted with a good deal more cynicism than Martin, was that "democracy is a living thing which must have time, and soil and sunlight in which to grow. We must do all we can to create these favorable conditions and we can do and have done much. But we cannot simply create the plant and give it to them; it must spring from seeds planted in indigenous soil."

As for the state of the "soil" in the mid-1960's, Mr. Martin noted that "genuine concern with an overturn of the established order; fear of left-wing extremism; frustration with incompetence in an era of great and rising expectations; and a sheer desire for power are all formidable obstacles to stable constitutional government—especially in countries where the traditional method of transferring political power has been by revolution or *coup d'état.* In most of Latin America, there is so little experience with the benefits of political legitimacy that there is an insufficient body of opinion, civil or military, which has any reason to know its value and hence defend it."

Martin's declaration reportedly was not well received in at least some White House circles, but it comes close to defining the mean between the thinking of the Kennedy idealists (without whose idealism, it must be noted, the *Alianza* would not have gotten off the ground), and the native instincts of average Latin American hands in the bureaucracy, most of whom were quite aware that fortune had not smiled upon the hapless colleague who happened to be holding down the Cuban desk when Fidel Castro delivered himself up to Communism. The system encourages the belief among civil servants that their safety and security is most often assured by clinging to the status quo, and, as noted by more than one observer, the civil servants stay on while Presidents come and go; Arthur M. Schlesinger, Jr., labored both points on behalf of President Kennedy in his history of the Kennedy era, *A Thousand Days.* Another Kennedy aide and speechwriter, Richard Goodwin, who had much to do with breathing the ideological fire into the Alliance for Progress in the first place, learned the lesson the hard way. Abandoning his White House sanctuary to become Martin's deputy and the White House's principal liberal apostle in residence in the State Department on behalf of Latin America, Goodwin plunged joyously into the bureaucratic breakers and barely made it back to shore. He was in line, at the time of Kennedy's death, for a new post as White House cultural adviser.

There were, then, native forces at work eroding the *esprit* and beginning to alter the character of the Alliance for Progress before Johnson assumed the Presidency. To them must be added a particular and powerful element now built into the reflexes of any prudent professional. This was the "Cuban syndrome," which, in reality, was very close to qualifying as a piece of U.S. policy for the Hemisphere. Briefly stated, it was that one Cuba was one thing, but that two would be intolerable, not just in strict terms of U.S. security but as a domestic political proposition as well. Indeed, the principle had been handed down by John F. Kennedy in more guarded terms on two occasions, the first right after the Bay of Pigs debacle in his first year and the second in a major address in Florida just before his death.

The essence of the Kennedy policy was that for all the devotion the United States might have to the principle of nonintervention in the internal affairs of Hemisphere states, if the Latin Americans would not move collectively to head off a Communist takeover threat, the United States would feel compelled to move unilaterally. Kennedy's first exposition of this principle could have been read as the over-the-shoulder shout of defiance of a defeated fighter, but the second was a measured declaration of policy which no American official on the spot or in a Washington office could safely ignore. And safety, in the eyes of almost any responsible U.S. official, could be found only in throwing the weight of the U.S. against not only "another Cuba," but against another anything that looked as if it might be a Communist-inspired movement that could evolve into another Cuba.

It can be argued that this was not a healthy state of mind. It is plain, however, that these natural forces within the bureaucracy were a critical element in the Johnson legacy in Latin America. It is an element that must be cast into the balance in weighing his performance in that part of the world.

Indeed, the total international inheritance of Lyndon Johnson cannot be measured by any arbitrary judgment on the state of the world as he found it. It must be measured also by what people, politicians, and policy-makers actually thought was going on in the world and what they thought the proper role of the United States should be.

Myths and Realities

"We can't expect these countries to do everything the way we want them to do it," President Kennedy declared just a short time before his assassination. "They have their own interest, their own personality, their own tradition. We can't make everyone in our image, and there are a good many people who don't want to go in our image."

Yet, as Secretary Rusk was to say just a few days after Kennedy's death in summing up the U.S. position in the world as Lyndon Johnson found it: "We made a national decision to involve ourselves in the fate of the world (after World War II) because, among other things, our own fate was deeply involved in what happens elsewhere."

That was the quandary confronting Lyndon Johnson, as it had confronted Kennedy and Eisenhower before him. On the one hand, there were growing limitations on the U.S. capacity to

exert positive influence on the forces at work in the world; and
on the other, there were firm commitments as well as compelling
reasons to try—though some would find the reasons more compelling than others.

"The problem of our foreign policy today," said Walter Lippmann fully a year after Lyndon Johnson moved into the White
House, at a time when the war in Vietnam was beginning to expand alarmingly, "will not be fully understood until historians
explain how our intervention in the Second World War to defeat
the Nazis and the Japanese became inflated into the so-called
Truman Doctrine of the late 1940's, in which the United States
said it was committing itself to a global ideological struggle
against revolutionary Communism. For it is this global commitment which is at the root of our difficulty in appraising coolly
the extent and the importance of our engagement in Vietnam."
Lippmann thought there had to be a "stopping point between
globalism and isolationism" and that the "test of statesmanship"
was to find it.

It was not an easy test for a new U.S. President in the last days
of 1963. Vietnam was one case in point, and Lyndon Johnson was
to move quickly to tie himself to the commitment Dwight Eisenhower had made to the Diem Government, in another day, under
vastly different circumstances, to help the South Vietnamese
stand off Communist subversion. Anywhere he turned, there
were obligations that were hard to duck, crises in the making that
would engage U.S. interests and invite U.S. intervention. The
United Nations was getting ready to withdraw from the Belgian
Congo after three bloody years of peace-keeping, and the U.S.
Government was seeking a delay, knowing full well who would
be called on to fill that vacuum if trouble started up all over
again. The State Department's George Ball, only a few months
earlier, had tried to bring U.S. influence to bear on the Kashmir
quarrel between India and Pakistan in the interests of shoring
up the Asian subcontinent against the Communist Chinese. The
coup in the Dominican Republic spelled trouble for the United
States, though nobody could then foretell the form it would take.

That the United States was deeply involved in a complicated
world, that it could quickly become entangled in tiny conflicts,

that these could rapidly blow up into major international confrontations, and that these conflicts had robbed the word "war" of much of its meaning—all this Lyndon Johnson had every reason to know before he reached the White House. From 1945 until 1963, there had been three dozen "wars," if the term is broadened to take in all the uprisings and incipient or active guerrilla insurrections from Venezuela to Cyprus and Algeria to Kuwait, and to include the bloodless but deadly nuclear showdown over Cuban missiles. There were few in which the United States had not become engaged in one way or another; Cyprus was about to demonstrate that what had been for a thousand years only a Mediterranean trouble spot, reserved for Mediterraneans (and Great Britain), could suddenly erupt into a matter of crucial concern to the United States, requiring urgent U.S. action.

But if Lyndon Johnson accepted the dimension of American involvement in the world, what he may not have accepted—what any new President would find difficult to accept immediately— was the hard reality implicit in all this strife and conflict: the comparative impotency of the world's greatest power in the face of the tiniest of pinpricks from the puniest of nations.

The two great Gullivers of the globe could obliterate each other, but possession of the mightiest arsenals of destructive weapons in the history of mankind did not endow them with special magic or absolute authority in dealing with the Lilliputians. Indeed, the awesome arsenals of the Russians and the Americans had cancelled themselves—and each other—in a way that put more, not less, premium on diplomacy and a rich mix of conventional weaponry. Eisenhower had found this out first at Suez and later in Lebanon, but little was done then to adjust Pentagon planning or procurement accordingly.

Kennedy learned the lesson first in West Berlin, then in Laos and in the Congo, and more conclusively in the Cuban episodes, both One and Two. Not the least of his legacies to Lyndon Johnson was a far more flexible, versatile military force than he himself had inherited. In the space of just three years, Kennedy and his able, energetic Defense Secretary, Robert McNamara, had added nearly $10 billion a year to the defense budget and applied a large part of this increase to the expansion of American capacity to meet the burgeoning demands of "limited war." McNamara added five combat divisions to the army, greatly increased combat readiness, and, with the help of the ultimate weapon—the helicopter—greatly increased mobility. Where Dwight D. Eisenhower and John Foster Dulles had placed their reliance on massive retaliation, the Kennedy men moved rapidly to expand U.S. ability to bring pressure to bear in little ways.

"A minimum of force obtained a maximum gain," wrote Kennedy aide Theodore C. Sorensen, in the chapter of his book *Kennedy* summing up the Cuban missile confrontation. In the last analysis, Sorensen pointed out, it was the U.S. ability to clamp an effective naval blockade around Cuba and pose a credible invasion threat that won the day. Kennedy had no illusions that the U.S. had crowned itself cock of the walk, by standing up to Nikita Khrushchev on that occasion, Sorensen relates in his account of the Kennedy years. When aides McGeorge Bundy and Carl Kaysen suggested to the President just after the Cuban missiles had been removed that he now must look "ten feet tall" to such bystanders as India and Pakistan, Mr. Kennedy is said to have answered: "That will wear off in about a week, and everyone will be back thinking only of his own interests."

For India and Pakistan, that prophecy proved all too accurate three years later when fighting broke out over the Kashmir question. For the wider world, Kennedy's judgment proved all too valid, also. The world situation inherited by Lyndon Johnson was roiled by national, regional, religious, ideological, and personal political self-interest as it had been rarely before in history. It did not lend itself to sweeping solutions or brilliant diplomatic master strokes any more than it was ready to bend to American military power. Not since the Eisenhower era had responsible American policy-makers talked in terms of a grand and global crusade against a monolithic Communist menace. There was also less tendency, at least among the high officials of the Government, to talk of "winning" the struggle against international Communism in any finite sense. In his Inaugural Address, Kennedy had summoned the nation to a "long twilight struggle," and his administration marked the beginning of a concerted effort to win public acceptance of the complexity and timelessness of the task confronting American diplomacy around the world.

The Kennedy men did not claim to have all the answers by any means, nor time enough to test the answers they did have. But they had blocked out the right concerns—the control of the spread of nuclear weapons; the promotion of peaceful revolution against outmoded autocracies in Latin America and elsewhere; the future shape of a Western Alliance strained as much by Europe's growing sense of self-sufficiency as by De Gaulle's nationalism; the containment of an increasingly separatist Chinese Communist threat in Asia; the opportunities for exploiting community of interest between the West and an increasingly separatist Russian Communist movement; the urgent need for a new and different and much expanded effort to narrow the widening disparity between the wealth of the Northern Hemisphere and the poverty of the Southern Hemisphere; the merits of at least limited trade with Eastern Europe as a way of opening a window on the West; the need, ultimately and perhaps even urgently, for a modicum of flexibility in U.S. thinking about Communist China, if only to the extent of beginning to *think* of Mainland China as China rather than as a region ruled by a temporary usurper.

These were some of the "unthinkables" that Senator Fulbright was to put forth early in the Johnson first year, in a catalogue of "old myths and new realities," which touched off more controversy than thought.

"The character of the cold war," Fulbright declared, "has, for the present, at least, been profoundly altered: by the drawing back of the Soviet Union from extremely aggressive policies; by the implicit repudiation by both sides of a policy of 'total victory'; and by the establishment of an American strategic superiority which the Soviet Union appears to have tacitly accepted because it has been accompanied by assurances that it will be exercised by the United States with responsibility and restraint. These enormously important changes may come to be regarded by historians as the foremost achievements of the Kennedy Administration in the field of foreign policy. Their effect has been to commit us to a foreign policy which can accurately—though perhaps not prudently—be defined as one of 'peaceful coexistence.'"

The turning point, historians may also come to believe, was not the Cuban missile confrontation itself as much as one speech, delivered at American University by John F. Kennedy on June 10, 1963. This most memorable of the Kennedy state papers led almost directly to the partial nuclear-test-ban accord with the Soviet Union the following month. More important, perhaps, it called on a skeptical American public and a hidebound Congress to accept a degree of common interest and common purpose with the Soviets which was very nearly revolutionary in scope. He decried the notion that peace is only possible when the Soviet Union adopts "a more enlightened" attitude. "I hope they do," Kennedy said. Pointedly he added: "I believe we can help them do it but I also believe that we must re-examine our own attitude—as individuals and as a nation—for our attitude is as essential as theirs."

There was the rub. For in mid-1963, and indeed, long after Lyndon Johnson became President, the American "attitude," as reflected in the Congressional power centers and in large segments of public opinion as well, was still strapped to the familiar cold war order of things, to the old pacts and alliances and alignments, still inhibited by refusal to accept the decline in the power and influence of the monoliths, in both East and West; or the nation explosion which had given birth to 50 new and often unruly sovereign entities since World War II; and to the true nature of the neutralism, or more properly, nationalism, in the Third World of these new nations. China was still something to be debated in terms of who lost it, rather than how to live with it. The test of U.S. policy still was whether Peking could be kept out of the United Nations, not how the West might work together to keep Peking out of the rest of Asia. Congress still approached foreign aid or East-West trade not in terms of how to improve the former and promote the latter, but how to make it harder for the Executive Branch to exercise its own day-to-day judgment on what should be proffered and what should be withheld and from whom. Annually, while the spotlight focused on the foreign-aid money totals, the legislators were busily adding barnacles to the bill—amendments to bar aid or trade, in many cases, with specific

countries. As Fulbright had put it, in seeking to explain the disquieting impact of the cold war's new course on both public and
official opinion in the U.S.: "We are a people used to looking
at the world, and indeed at ourselves, in moralistic rather than
empirical terms. We are predisposed to regard any conflict as a
clash between good and evil rather than as simply a clash between
conflicting interests."

The total effect, then, was deceptive. The Kennedy Administration was moving—and in time would have probably moved the
country as well—toward new approaches and away from the old
shibboleths and anachronisms. But official action, not to mention
public attitudes, had not moved very far; Kennedy was finding
the remaking of U.S. foreign policy uphill work.

It would, therefore, have been less than reasonable to expect
stunning new breakthroughs from whoever followed him. Any
judgment of Lyndon Johnson's performance, over the relatively
short span of less than three years, must accordingly take into
account the discrepancy between what Kennedy was trying to do
and what the American public and the U.S. Congress were ready
to do; between the new thinking of policy-makers and the old
thinking of lawmakers; between the world as it was and the world
as it still appeared to be to many Americans.

All this must be taken into account for the very elemental
reason that all this is what Lyndon Johnson, the man of Congress
and the master practitioner of practical politics, would instinctively, reflexively, compulsively, take into account.

FOUR

First Flings

This was the way it was supposed to be, if only everybody would cooperate: Orderly transition, with no unsettling policy departures. Lyndon Johnson, humble but hardheaded, ever the peace-seeker, never the appeaser—and always the can-do man.

But not everybody would cooperate. The new President was soon to be caught up in a campaign to outdo Nikita Khrushchev in protestations of peaceful intent, while simultaneously struggling to stamp out big and little brushfires around the globe.

As Lyndon Johnson was later to reconstruct it, the breathing spell at home lasted about a month. It was broken by a Republican challenge on the issue of using U.S. Government credit to finance the sale of surplus American wheat to Russia. That was the first time "we had to take a position and stand up," the President recalled afterward, and while it wasn't earth-shaking as a test, the topic was singularly appropriate. For Johnson's quick readiness to fight for the right to finance wheat sales to Russia reflected a burning preoccupation that was to dominate his approach to world affairs in the early days and remain unflagging even in the face of seeming futility as the United States worked its way ever deeper into the Vietnam war. Stated simply—and even Lyndon Johnson's warmest admirers would concede a certain simplistic quality to his approach to foreign affairs—it was a preoccupation with finding peace, with *rapprochement* with the Russians, with bridge-building to the Communist countries of Europe, with anything that might serve to diminish hostility and ease the awful menace of nuclear war.

Many would question the way the President went about it. Some would find his quest fatally flawed by concern over the appearance of "appeasement," and others would argue that at times he wasn't tough enough. But none would question his fervor or his intent, certainly not the working-level operatives of the State Department once they had recovered from their initial bemusement over the marching orders they received before the new man in the White House had barely settled in.

The command, as it was handed down in the first few days, was in essentially these words: "Give me your programs for peace."

Meantime, riots erupting in Panama were propelling the President into his first foreign crisis, one with powerful domestic impact. As the weeks wore on, there was a Communist grab for Zanzibar; unrest in East Africa; and massacres in Cyprus with ugly implications for war between Greece and Turkey and the collapse of NATO's southern flank. There was a revolution in Brazil carrying with it a brief threat, as Johnson saw it, of not just "another Cuba" but "another China" in this Hemisphere. Chile looked as if it might become the first country to vote in a Communist government in a free election. Castro was quiescent by comparison with the trouble he caused Kennedy, but the water shutdown at Guantánamo rubbed raw nerves in the United States, and Fidel was to bring Johnson into abrasive conflict with old allies in Europe whose trade with Cuba was fast undercutting the U.S. effort to strangle Castroism with an economic squeeze. Pathet Lao forces were on the move again in Laos; Tshombe slipped back into power in the Congo, and the Congo was slipping toward chaos, with help from a half-dozen of Africa's "nonaligned" recipients of U.S. aid. The generals were at one another's throats in Saigon, and by the middle of the year there was to be that quixotic Communist torpedo-boat foray against U.S. warships in the Gulf of Tonkin.

In those transition days, Johnson was under heavy strain, initially in a state near shock. He was torn between his unfamiliarity with an unpredictable world and a fierce yearning to prove his capacity to conduct the nation's foreign affairs. The celebrated Johnson ego, which not even his closest associates would deny was king-sized, was working, as it always was to work, two ways. If it impelled him toward crowd-pleasing heroics, it also warned him away from anything that might cause him to fall on his face. The result was what William S. White has called "this odd metronomic effect . . . [of] violent sortie followed by prudent reticence," as the new President sought to pick and choose between what was desirable and what was achievable, what would be scintillating and what would be safe. And in those early weeks and months, this made it all the harder to distinguish between what was real and of enduring significance and what was unreal and intended largely for appearances. What was unreal was some of the frenzy, some of the flailing about in search for approval, some of the early floundering; some of the intensity with which all things were set against the vital test of "continuity" and against the backdrop of the approaching November vote; some of the ease of the embrace of familiar formulas, tried, tested, and in some cases already found wanting, such as the multilateral nuclear force. But nothing was more unreal than the shying away from all commitments, all binding decisions for just as long as possible. This was true, above all, in Vietnam. Some part of all this was native to the man and would recur, but some part of it was peculiar to the circumstances.

What was real?

The appointment in December, 1963, of Thomas Mann as czar of Latin American affairs and the concurrent decision to conduct a major overhaul of U.S. policy and programs in the Hemisphere. Though Mann was never the Texas crony of the President that he was originally thought to be, the minds of both men ran together up to a point. He would be the only major, distinctively Johnson appointment for almost two years, and he was to give a new cast and a new coloration not just to Latin American affairs, but later, as he moved up to be Under Secretary of State for Economic Affairs, to the whole range of foreign economic policy.

The quick plunge into the revamping of foreign aid. In late December, Johnson turned a quiet intragovernmental foreign-aid committee initiated by Kennedy and then underway into a splashy Johnson reappraisal by the simple device of announcing its existence publicly. In a series of afterthoughts, he expanded the committee to include Peace Corps Director Sargent Shriver, the late President's brother-in-law, to furnish that necessary extra dash of continuity, and later, former World Bank President Eugene R. Black, who was to become a Johnson fixture as a permanent good housekeeping seal of approval for almost everything the President did in the field of foreign economics, where the good word and sound counsel of a distinguished banker of international, as well as national, repute would add strength and luster. As it turned out, this particular aid review was too slapdash to have lasting impact, but it was the forerunner of a more considered reappraisal which would produce truly significant changes in the U.S. foreign-aid approach in early 1966.

What else?

An instinctively rough response when the President feels that he is being crowded.

An equally strong instinct, indeed a profound preference for quieter diplomacy, for shoving things under rugs, for the second-hand, once-removed approach, and for clandestine action when action seemed indicated in cases where the risks were large, the prospects unpromising, and where U.S. prestige and the power position of the President were not, or need not be, directly engaged, as in Cyprus, Brazil, Chile, Laos, the Congo.

A set of high standards for the fealty of those nations who presumably "sit on the same side of the aisle," manifested, on the one hand, in an exuberant embrace of Ludwig Erhard and on the other, in the harsh words directed at those faithless friends, notably Britain and France, who had the temerity to trade with Fidel Castro.

And finally, above all, a preoccupation with "programs for peace."

Peace—*"That Little Old Five-Letter Word"*

The diplomats struggled to comply, but the cupboard was bare of promising initiatives and the atmosphere of East-West relations in recent months had hardly been encouraging. In retrospect, it seemed that the partial nuclear-test ban reached in July of that year had been a high-water mark. There was no end of follow-up measures on paper: a nonproliferation pact to end the dissemination of nuclear weapons by those who had them to those who didn't; a variety of proposals for mutual cutbacks of armaments, starting with the "bonfire" scheme, calling for the big powers simultaneously to destroy obsolete warplanes to discourage their distribution to littler nations; mutual trimming of defense budgets; open-skies inspection of each other's territory by the U.S. and Russia; and, of course, an extension of the limited ban on surface, water, and atmospheric testing to include tests underground, a measure blocked by Soviet refusal to permit on-the-spot verification of suspect seismic readings.

But the Soviets had been, if anything, less accommodating in Kennedy's last months; there was a nasty row building up over U.N. financing; disarmament probing was getting nowhere; and in November, the Russians abruptly began putting the squeeze back on Berlin in the face of clear allied warnings that interruption of access to that encircled city would not be tolerated. Dean Rusk, in company with most of the West's Kremlin-watchers, had been "frankly puzzled" by this Soviet behavior, and mystification about Moscow's intentions had not cleared up by the time Johnson became President. "There was a lot of talk about *détente* after the test ban," a prominent Soviet authority in Washington recalled some time later, "but it was already beginning to look more and more illusory before Kennedy was killed."

Still, the change of men in the U.S. Presidency had ushered in a spell of watchful waiting, with both sides cautiously avoiding precipitous moves or abrupt changes from established policy; both wished to betray no hint of weakness to the other, but both likewise wished to display their devotion to peace. Few U.S. experts saw much prospect for new American initiatives until after election day on the assumption that until then, almost everything the new President did would be rendered suspect by his electoral pursuits. Though there was instant, inevitable talk of summitry, and although Johnson would doubtless have welcomed an opportunity to do constructive business with his Soviet counterpart in the grand setting of a heads-of-state encounter, he was wary of an empty exchange that might only heighten tensions and sensitive to the danger that a hasty overture could all too easily be misread as a sign of insecurity; the danger of miscalculation by the enemy was a constant concern.

But "continuity" clearly called for something more than caution and a cold shoulder to the Soviets. Some of his advisers, moreover, were telling him that deep down there was strong clamor within the Kremlin hierarchy for wider *rapprochement,* to ease the burden of heavy defense spending and thus permit diversion of more resources to urgent economic and agricultural needs, and that this clamor ought to be encouraged constantly. Besides, by the end of December, Nikita Khrushchev was mounting an intensive "peace offensive" of his own, plugging "peaceful cooperation, good neighborliness, and friendship" between the people of the United States and Russia; and Lyndon Johnson is not a man who likes to be outdone at anything. So at the turn of the year, peaceful coexistence was everywhere in the air. Khrushchev was talking up a proposed nonaggression pact. He and the new U.S. President had exchanged warm New Year's greetings, in which the Soviet leader had taken the occasion to hail the "significant improvement . . . in the development of Soviet-American relations" in the past year. He pronounced the partial test-ban agreement a "good beginning and demonstrable evidence of the fact that given a realistic assessment of the actual world situation, cooperation of governments in resolving urgent international problems and achieving mutually satisfactory agreements is entirely possible."

He added, "We would like to hope that the coming year will be marked by further significant successes."

Responding to this, Johnson declared: "I, myself, am wholly committed to the search for better understanding among peoples everywhere . . . The time for simply talking about peace, however, has passed—1964 should be a year in which we take further steps toward that goal. In this spirit I shall strive for the further improvement of relations between our two countries."

And strive he did, even more intensively, at the outset, than was recommended by some of his more conservative counselors, including, by some accounts, Dean Rusk and McGeorge Bundy, who were chary of appearing overeager. But Lyndon Johnson, as he was to demonstrate two years later in the great Vietnam peace offensive, can strive only mightily; besides, as he was often heard to say, his father brought him up on the political principle of keeping open the channels of communication. So he moved quickly, in December, to pick up the personal correspondence that Kennedy and Khrushchev had been conducting ever since the Cuban missile crisis; the direct, personal touch, he reasoned, offered added insurance against misunderstanding, as well as increased intimacy and an opportunity to exchange views informally and in tight secrecy.

At Adlai Stevenson's urging, and with the speech-writing assistance of Dean Acheson, Johnson also addressed the United Nations in mid-December, putting heavy emphasis on disarmament; on common East-West efforts at economic development; on U.S. yearning "to see the Cold War end once and for all"; and, above all, on "the greatest of human problems, and the greatest of our common tasks . . . to keep the peace and to save the future."

In his first State of the Union Message, on January 8, 1964, Johnson got his loudest applause with a show of defiance—"We intend to bury no one, but we do not intend to be buried." Yet this message, too, was pitched toward peace, and arms control, and food for the world's needy, and peaceful exploration of outer space, and "new means of bridging the gap between the East and the West." It included a specific initiative: "We are cutting back our production of enriched uranium by 25 per cent," Johnson declared. "We are shutting down four plutonium piles. We are closing many nonessential military installations. And it is in this spirit that we today call on our adversaries to do the same."

Although it was not known at the time, this public appeal had been reinforced in the private Johnson-to-Khrushchev correspondence, and in April, the President was in a position to announce the first small breakthrough in his peace-promotion campaign and the only success of this sort that he was to have in more than two years in the Presidency. In a major foreign-policy address in New York City, he announced a further reduction in U.S. production of enriched uranium timed to coincide with an announcement from Nikita Khrushchev that he was doing the same. No provision was made for verifying the cutbacks, which both countries obviously had intended to make in any event simply because they were surfeited with the stuff. But the parallel actions could at least be counted as a small easing of the arms race, even if they could not qualify as an honest exercise in arms control.

Less successful, but significant in its way, was a quiet venture into the never-never land of "preventive" diplomacy; it did not bear fruit, but it did reflect the zeal with which Johnson was pursuing the effort for peace. In the course of his secret correspondence with Khrushchev, the President, in mid-January, offered a compromise proposal for heading off the collision then threatening between the United States and the Soviet Union over the complex question of who should have to pay how much for United Nation's peace-keeping in cases when one or another member did not approve of the conduct of the operation or its purposes. The Russians had refused to pay their assessed share of the U.N. operation in the Congo. Legally, they insisted, they weren't required to; politically, they felt, they had suffered indignity enough by having the Soviet diplomatic mission escorted out of the country by U.N. police. The Russians were also delinquent on payments to Middle East peace-keeping. The French, using their own law and logic, were likewise in arrears on the Congo, and the world organization was sliding toward bankruptcy, both financial and political. The United States had embedded its position in the concrete of Article 19 of the U.N. Charter and had constructed a splendidly rational legal argument that special assessments for peace-keeping purposes, if voted by the requisite majorities in the General Assembly, were just as binding as the regular budget assessments. Though the World Court had upheld the U.S. position, enthusiasm for it among the small-nation majority of U.N. members was slack, and the United States was in danger of losing if the matter came to a vote; this would have cooled Congressional support for the United Nations considerably; and if the United States won, the almost certain Russian defiance of the verdict would have brought on a paralysis of the organization for which the United States would almost as certainly have been blamed. So Johnson proposed a compromise worthy of a former Senate parliamentarian; it would have amounted to creation of an appropriations committee with considerable, if not absolute, authority to raise money for peace-keeping and with membership weighted to give the big powers added protection against the whim of an unmanageable Afro-Asian small-country majority. Khrushchev had hinted to Johnson that he might be in a conciliatory mood on the question (perhaps because neither side was sure how the vote would go in a show-down), and Johnson, like Kennedy, had firmly embraced the principle that all positive signs of conciliation should be seized upon; public polemics or even private debate for the sake of proving a point was, in Johnson's view, a waste of time.

So Adlai Stevenson was instructed to follow up the Johnson-Khrushchev exchange in direct discussions with his Soviet counterpart at the United Nations. Right up to the moment late that year when the United Nations was forced to close shop in order to avoid a shattering clash, there was hope that something still might come of this Johnson effort. Ultimately, however, the Russians apparently concluded that they had the votes, because their stand suddenly stiffened; still later, the United States was to reach the rueful conclusion that the Russians probably did have the votes, for in the fall of 1965, it was almost the first order of business for Ambassador Arthur Goldberg, Stevenson's successor, to abandon the Article 19 crusade entirely.

Lyndon Johnson, however, was never to abandon his effort to keep the door open to the Soviet Union and to the Eastern European satellites; the spirit that animated his efforts in the early days was to remain intense. Concern with Soviet reaction influenced his every Vietnam move—though not enough, some would argue. Long before his 1966 proposals to ease trade with countries behind the Iron Curtain, he was pushing other contacts, economic as well as cultural, talking up the need to encourage greater satellite independence from Moscow—"Even old Khrushchev recognized those governments had gotten too big to spank," he once declared.

Johnson did more than talk up disarmament; he did his best to give a new and, he hoped, intriguing twist to U.S. proposals at a new round of arms-control negotiations with the Russians that started in early 1964. And he did so against the built-in negativism of the bureaucracies, where resistance to disarmament proposals runs strong; the Pentagon is one obvious center of conservatism on this issue, but elements in State are also ever wary of proposals that might cause disquiet among allies, or stir controversy. "There were at least six vested interests working at cross-purposes on that particular go-around," recalls one White House staff man. "It was then the President discovered that if he wanted to have a disarmament policy with any real prospect of getting anywhere, he had to go in after it himself."

The Johnson technique, according to associates, was to become a familiar one, for he carried on a continuing struggle to bring his power to bear on bureaucracies immobilized by intramural differences. He handed the assignment to one man with unique and practical qualifications for the job—Theodore Sorensen, a proven expert in the skillful application of White House pressure. He was all the more effective in this instance; because of his dedication to the late President, he was that much more effective as envoy from a Johnson White House to a Kennedy bureaucracy.

At the same time, Johnson was clearing ground for possible breakthroughs toward *rapprochement* with the Russians in other ways. As one long-time intimate of the President put it then, "This is not a man who would go off on a foreign adventure until he has the heartland in good shape"; by "heartland" he meant the allies. The first step in this effort was fortuitous; John F. Kennedy had already set up a meeting in Washington with the man who was to become Lyndon Johnson's favorite foreigner—West Germany's brand-new Chancellor, Ludwig Erhard. Like

Johnson, he was a caretaker awaiting election in his own right; like Johnson, he was in need of the political prestige that comes from huddling with a fellow head of government. The briefing book was all prepared for Kennedy; it had only to be turned over to Johnson. There was a brief contretemps on where the meeting should be held, with Lady Bird reportedly favoring the dignity of Washington, with Rusk and Bundy urging whatever came naturally, and with Johnson leaning toward the LBJ Ranch with all those *Landsleute* close at hand to make the Chancellor feel at home, and all the opportunities for barbecue and ranch-house horseplay to convey intimacy, informality, rapport. For both men, it worked out almost perfectly, even if some critics were square enough to suggest that it was overdone. Moreover, Erhard proved a lot more tractable and somewhat more flexible than his proud, prestigious, iron-willed predecessor Konrad Adenauer on the question consuming Johnson's interest—what could the West offer Russia in the broad field of European security? There had been no end of offerings in the past, and there was no end to British enthusiasm for fresh efforts to negotiate for troop pull-backs and denuclearized zones in Central Europe, to begin the process of German reunification, to establish a new and less precarious status for West Berlin; inevitably, however, one ally or another had disagreed violently with the terms—in some cases, so violently that selected bits and pieces were leaked expressly to destroy whatever it was the allies were trying to agree upon.

Now Johnson was persuaded to give it another try. A special working party was established in Washington at the ambassadorial level, in an effort to concert the thinking of Britain, France, West Germany, and the United States in a low-key atmosphere. The outlook was not alluring; *détente* was in the air and, perversely, nothing is so calculated to demolish allied unity as the absence of a blatant Soviet threat or a fixed negotiating deadline. But it was a sensible arrangement, serving, as it did, as an earnest of Johnson's good intentions, without much danger of the whole thing getting out of hand. The British were satisfied, because they could point to continuing peace efforts and comfort themselves with the thought that if a peace package could somehow be put together, they would have an overwhelming argument for submitting it;

the French could pretty much count on the probability that nothing would be agreed upon; Erhard, who was confronted with a socialist opposition that was showing growing flexibility in its policy towards the Communists, could likewise point to continuing efforts toward *rapprochement* and take comfort in the thought that any package that could be agreed upon by everybody would probably be rudely rejected by the Russians; moreover, the Germans found safety in the package approach because it would make it more difficult to extract individual features—a procedure which, if carried out, would most likely be harmful to German interests.

The procedure suited Johnson's interests too; it combined movement with a bare minimum of commitment—and all in the interests of allied unity in pursuit of peace. "We don't think the prospects are worth a damn before the election," said a State Department official at the time.

As it turned out, the prospects were not worth much even after the election; indeed, the election was not the important element in Lyndon Johnson's inability to concert allied strategy for peace, or anything else. Vietnam was to become the vital element, but long before that conflict grew into a big and controversial war, there was overwhelming evidence that it would take a far stronger and perhaps somewhat subtler lead than Lyndon Johnson was able or willing to provide to impart a larger sense of common purpose in the Atlantic Community. The strength of the pack was recognized to be the wolf (or, more properly, the biggest wolf), to paraphrase Kipling's Law of the Jungle; but there was precious little acceptance of the rest of Kipling's verse—that "the strength of the wolf is the pack." French recognition of Communist China may have given Johnson his first measure of the degree of allied nonsolidarity. But a better measure of the Alliance malaise was to be provided indirectly by Fidel Castro.

Cuba had provided John F. Kennedy with his worst and his finest hours. But when it was all over, Cuba was still there, still Communist, still an open sore in the Caribbean, and still an open sore in American domestic politics. There was a moment of frenzy in the first weeks of the Johnson Administration when Castro shut off the water supply for Guantanamo, and there was ·

a demonstration of Johnson restraint in the face of strong urging to seize this pinprick as provocation for moving in on Castro in force. The U.S. military was ready to march, and there were some who were initially fearful that the new President might buckle under the Pentagon's pressure, but they were reassured by his stout resistance to the use of force. The President was acutely aware that the world, as one aide put it, was "watching . . . sensitively his every move" in search for clues to his future conduct of foreign affairs. He knew that the Russians would be all the more in need of showing *their* mettle if the President made a violent display of his, and that if the missiles could not be found to be provocation enough to justify a U.S. invasion, the turning off of a water tap hardly qualified. Moreover, though Barry Goldwater was loudly proposing that U.S. Marines rush out and turn the water back on, Johnson estimated, correctly as it turned out, that this would probably fade as a campaign rallying cry for the Republicans. So he quietly turned off the tap at the U.S. end of the line, and set about providing Guantanamo with facilities for producing its own water.

But Johnson was unable to shut off so easily another Cuba-connected controversy. The economic embargo, which the U.S. had asked all right-thinking nations to join against Cuba, was being flagrantly flouted by America's oldest ally, France; by her closest ally, Britain; and by some other supposedly friendly nations as well. It was to be a relatively minor, transitory clash of wills that illuminated a fundamental and enduring element in Lyndon Johnson's approach to the world.

Selling Buses from the White House Steps

For Fidel Castro, 1963 had been a banner year because of the Cuban sugar crop; he had piled up nearly $100 million in foreign exchange, and his buyers were busy spending it, in the first months of the Johnson Presidency, on buses from Britain, trucks from Spain and France, locomotives from France and other European countries, and fishing boats from Europe and Japan. It had been a busy year for Castro subversion too; in February, an OAS team produced elaborate evidence of a Cuban plot to overthrow the constitutional government in Venezuela.

The U.S. was in a bind. It had whiplashed the Latins into taking a stand against Cuba, into cutting off trade and diplomatic contacts, into viewing Castro as an active menace; and it was seeking, through diplomacy, to encourage all non-Communist nations to halt trade, keep the ships out of Cuban ports, and close down airline service to Havana, as well. The objective was strictly limited—to cut Castro's capacity for mischief, first of all; perhaps ultimately so to weaken his regime that there would someday be a chance he might be overthrown. It was pale stuff for a U.S. public thirsting for quick, decisive action; though Khrushchev had privately assured Dean Rusk that Soviet troops had all been withdrawn, many citizens and leading politicians still wondered whether those 82 Soviet intermediate-range ballistic missiles had really been pulled out. So there was a tendency in the State Department and elsewhere to make as much as possible of the U.S. embargo, as at least a palliative, if not a cure, for Castroism, and a companion violent reaction when the embargo was breached most dramatically by the sale of 450 British buses to Castro—financed with British Government credit. The political heat this generated for the Administration was serious enough; but it might well have abated, had not the British Tory Government, once challenged, proceeded to make a positive virtue of their Cuban trade for the benefit of their domestic public opinion, ever sensitive to any sign of knuckling under to the Americans. Thus it was that when British Prime Minister Sir Alec Douglas-Home visited Lyndon Johnson in February, he did not content himself with arguing out the matter privately. He made a light-hearted reference to it in his toast at a White House dinner ("Occasionally we may, perhaps, send buses to Cuba, but never will anything interfere fundamentally with the friendship and delight which we feel in the company of a great ally and a great partner.") and followed that up the next day with a public reassurance from Washington to his constituents back home that he hadn't sold out on the issue of Cuban trade.

Lyndon Johnson did not feel "delighted." This struck him—as comparable incidents were to continue to strike him—as a violation of the code; in any political arena with which he was familiar, the rules, whether written or unwritten, are abundantly clear, and one of them is that you don't use another man's home grounds for attacking him; in the Senate there are rules governing what one member can say about another and retain the floor, and unspoken understandings as well, based on the sensible theory that since all are more or less equally at the whim of their electorate, there are limits to what ought to be said or done that might complicate the problems of a colleague back home.

From all available evidence, Johnson applied this code more or less literally to the world at large; not the least of his reasons for putting off the visit of Pakistan's Ayub Khan was to be expressed to intimates in just those terms—that he saw no reason to give Pakistan's President a platform in Washington for propounding policy hostile to U.S. objectives in Vietnam. Canada's Lester Pearson provoked the same short-tempered response when he offered unsolicited guidance for the conduct of the Vietnam war and chose Philadelphia as the place from which to do it, just a day before he was to meet the President at Camp David; when they did meet, Johnson reportedly spent a good deal of their time together on the telephone. Harold Wilson was to follow his predecessor's footsteps into the Johnson doghouse by blasting U.S. policy for NATO just 10 days before he was to meet Johnson in Washington; when they met, Johnson grabbed the offensive, reminded Wilson of Home's indiscretion, and let him know in blunt terms that he didn't take kindly to those who caused him political trouble. Wilson was later to confide to a visitor that he had come to the conclusion that the only hope of exerting constructive influence on Lyndon Johnson was to do it privately.

Around the White House, this Johnson reflex was well recognized, and the kind of *gaffe* that provoked it came to be called "selling buses on the White House steps." It was not all a question of a political mutual-protection compact, either. In part, it was the first manifestation of a Johnson conviction directed specifically at NATO; the United States, he felt (and he thought Congress felt), was doing more than its share in the Alliance and not getting its money's worth in return; open displays of defiance or disunity could, therefore, only complicate his position in Congress and in the eyes of the American public. There is always quick Congressional reaction when U.S. actions do not seem to have wholehearted allied support, with Congress either berating the allies or questioning the action. In the case of the Cuban trade, Congress had tacked an amendment onto foreign-aid legislation making it all but mandatory for the President to halt assistance to any nation which did not take steps within a fixed period to sever shipping and air contacts with Cuba. This was irritating enough; it became more so when the Administration dutifully halted a $7,000 remnant in military assistance to Britain and was promptly assailed by Senator Fulbright for using a "stuffed club" to clout allies in foolish pursuit of a useless embargo against a Communist regime which was no more than a "nuisance" anyway. Since the club had been stuffed by Congress, this fired Administration anger all the more, and Dean Rusk took sharp issue, alleging that Castro was indeed a "menace." A massive diplomatic campaign was mounted not only against the allies but through U.S. business contacts, aimed toward businessmen in allied nations as well. And Johnson's rage was visited once again on an Englishman in a 15-minute tirade directed against Foreign Minister R. A. Butler when he came to Washington in April. Before that, in a secret session of the NATO Council in Paris, Under Secretary of State George Ball gave the allies a good measure of the Presidential mood. In a long discourse on Cuba, Ball assailed the British in terms not normally employed in what is supposed to be a "special relationship" and in the process joined the issue squarely.

"I must say, quite frankly, that continued sales of critical commodities to Cuba, sanctioned and even guaranteed by governments of the Alliance, will produce a cumulative irritation and discontent in my country," Ball declared, adding: "As the situation is viewed not merely in my country but particularly in Latin America, a government decision to guarantee credits to assist the Cuban acquisition of needed equipment appears as a political act in favor of the Castro Government. Is it, in fact, the intention of the members that a single nation should be able to frustrate a serious policy affecting the defense of free world interests in a vital area of the world?" Ball demanded, concluding: "This seems to me a consideration of great seriousness since it goes to the heart of our ability to build a solid and effective Alliance."

In late April, with White House approval, an expurgated version of this closed-door discourse, with the specific reference to "a single nation" deleted, was delivered as a public speech by Ball. None of this had much effect on the allies—France, a few days later, was to nail down a deal to sell locomotives to Castro. But it gave Lyndon Johnson a reading on the state of the European "heartland" in the spring of 1964 that could hardly encourage him toward a new initiatives in company with his Atlantic allies.

He was keeping the lines open, anyway; secretly he sent his old friend, Robert Anderson, formerly Eisenhower's Treasury Secretary, to talk to De Gaulle; later in the first year, George Ball was to make two pilgrimages to Paris and encounter the same cordial but uncooperative response on everything from NATO to Vietnam. Johnson's view of the French President, as expressed to visitors, was philosophical. He seemed to have marked De Gaulle down as he would a recalcitrant Senate committee baron for whom he did not, for the moment, have a handle and therefore had no reason to bother his head about; it reminded him of his baseball-playing days, he would explain; he was feared as a power hitter, and rival pitchers would try to dust him off, "but [he] would just lean back and let the ball go into the catcher's mitt."

Britain's old-shoe Tory Government, scuffed by scandal and showing its age in other ways, was to be discarded in October, in favor of Labour's Wilson, by a hair-breadth margin; Erhard was looking ahead to elections in 1965. The Atlantic Alliance, in short, was not ripe for remodeling or ready for fresh initiatives, which was probably just as well. For Lyndon Johnson was not ready, either. He had some urgent alliance remodeling he wanted to do, but he had a different alliance in a different Hemisphere in mind.

The Mann Story

On December 14, 1963, just three weeks after assuming office, the President announced plans for a sweeping overhaul of U.S.

activity in the Alliance for Progress and U.S. policy in Latin America and named as his czar for the Hemisphere a Texas lawyer and long-time diplomat then serving as U.S. Ambassador to Mexico, Thomas C. Mann.

"Next to keeping the peace—and maintaining the strength and vitality which makes freedom secure—no work is more important for our generation of Americans," the President said in a letter to Mr. Mann, "than our work in this Hemisphere."

Though Lyndon Johnson had more than one complaint with the conduct of U.S. policy in Latin America, his main complaint was fundamental and indicative of the whole Johnson approach to the interplay of foreign aid and foreign politics.

It was basic, in his view, that one man have all the levers of influence, political as well as economic, at his finger tips; in some instances this was to be the President himself, or a special emissary, be he Robert Anderson, Ellsworth Bunker, or George Ball. In Latin America, it was to be Tom Mann (or his successors), holding down what had always before been two jobs. One was the top Latin American post in the State Department, that of Assistant Secretary of State for Inter-American Affairs. The other was the top Latin American job for the Agency for International Development, which, under Kennedy, came to be called the U.S. Coordinator for the Alliance for Progress. Now, Tom Mann was to take over both those titles, and a third one, of Special Assistant to the President "to coordinate our policy in Latin America," thus acquiring a direct channel to the White House while still operating under the authority of the Secretary of State.

"We expect to speak with one voice on all matters affecting this Hemisphere," the President said in a news conference a few days later, adding: "Mr. Mann, with the support of the Secretary of State and the President, will be that voice." Not satisfied with this resounding send-off, the President shortly thereafter called in the Latin American ambassadors and, with Mr. Mann present, bestowed upon him so sweeping a Presidential blessing that some of the envoys present were frankly astonished. "I have never seen such a delegation of authority," said one of them afterwards in recalling the way that Mr. Johnson had let the assembled Latin envoys know in no uncertain terms that Tom Mann was "his man for this Hemisphere."

This, of course, was precisely the reaction the President had hoped to create. His reading of the Latin mentality and method, old associates contended, had led him to conclude that the profusion of Latin American experts operating in free-wheeling fashion under Kennedy had made it too easy for Hemisphere leaders to play one branch of the government, or indeed even one wing of the White House, off against the other. There was something to be said for the argument; so rich in variety was the range of Latin hands under Kennedy that Latins of all stripes could find a sympathetic hearing somewhere. For the Venezuelans and other Latin liberals, there was Arthur Schlesinger, Jr., working out of the White House, as well as Richard Goodwin. For the archconservatives there was the late DeLesseps Morrison, serving as Ambassador to the Organization of American States; as Mayor of New Orleans, a major commercial link to the Hemisphere, he had knit close ties with most of the strongmen of the Central American republics. At State there were the careerists, mostly conservative; and at the head of the Alliance for Progress programs was Teodoro Moscoso, a dedicated, progressive, reform-minded Spanish-born Puerto Rican. The whole Latin American program needed pulling together, and nobody recognized it better than Kennedy. In August, 1963, he had voiced his despair at the enormity of the job ahead for his cherished *Alianza,* conceded it had "failed, of course, to some degree because the problems are almost insuperable" and conceded, too, that he was still "not sure that we are giving enough attention to Latin America." Before his death, he had plans under way to give it more attention, quite probably to give it the sort of organizational shake-up Lyndon Johnson was to give it, and to hand the top job to his brother-in-law, Sargent Shriver. There was, then, little argument with the concept of "one voice." The argument, which began before Mann's appointment was announced, and was to last for as long as Tom Mann remained a leading figure in the Johnson foreign-policy-making machinery, was strictly over Johnson's choice of Mann.

It was, from the start, a highly charged argument, partly because this was Johnson's first appointment in the foreign field, and the tendency was strong at that stage to read profound meaning into every Johnson move. But it was also an argument founded in large part on fallacy. What a lot of the liberal, left-of-center critics in Washington and in Latin America were quick to conclude was that because Tom Mann was a Texan, he must be an old Johnson crony, that he must also be a Johnson Trojan horse, implanted in the State Department as the President's faithful agent for a Texan, Mexican-oriented, conservative, pragmatic Latin policy, and that this must be only the beginning of the Texanization of American foreign policy. The critics were only partly right and there was rich irony in where they were wrong. Lyndon Johnson came to know Tom Mann when in early 1961, as Vice President, he was asked by John F. Kennedy to try to talk Tom Mann into staying on in the job of Assistant Secretary of State for Inter-American Affairs, to which he had been appointed by Eisenhower. "He struck us as the most likable and most liberal of the Eisenhower assistant secretaries," one of the Kennedy recruiters had observed at the time. But Mann, for personal reasons, wanted to return to Texas, and it was Johnson who helped persuade him to take the Mexico City assignment, which would at least place him close to home. In December, 1963, it was Dean Rusk who first proposed Mann for the job Johnson gave him and for his subsequent promotion to the No. 3 post in the Department. As for the theory, also widely circulated, that Mann's direct link to the White House would undercut Rusk's authority, the word from the Secretary's associates at the time was of a quite different concern. Rusk was an old Asia hand, with little background in this Hemisphere. "Frankly, Làtin America doesn't interest the Secretary," one of his aides declared, shortly after the Mann appointment. "His real worry is that Mann will be too much of a stickler for protocol, that he won't take full advantage of his capacity as a direct adviser to the President." Some of the criticism, however, was more soundly based, and it came down, in the last analysis, to a mystical element called charisma, a vital ingredient in the Anglo-Saxon approach to the world of Latin American politics. Roosevelt had it and got by with little else. Kennedy had it, but he added real sub-

stance as well to U.S. policy in this Hemisphere. Johnson inherited the substance, which was growing stale, but he didn't have
charisma and neither did Tom Mann. Mann was, by almost
unanimous consent, able, industrious, tough-minded, knowledgeable; but he was also uncommunicative beyond the bare needs
imposed by efficient management, intellectually uninspiring, un-
colorful, mechanical, and pragmatic. He not only didn't have
charisma, he didn't believe in it. He had been raised in Laredo,
where Spanish is the common tongue, and politics had been
largely an autocratic family affair; in Laredo, power had been
handed down through several generations, juries were rigged, and
as a young lawyer, Mann had fought the system in a fashion that
his liberal critics would have applauded. But he had concluded
later in life, as he had often explained it, that total hostility
didn't pay, that he could have been more constructive had he
gone along with the system and tried to improve it. He helped to
draft the celebrated "Blue Book" denouncing the Perón
regime in Argentina, watched Perón's popularity soar on the
wings of Yankee intervention, and concluded again that discre-
tion might have been the better part of valor. He had gotten in
hot water in the State Department, even gone over the head of
his superior to put through a loan to Brazil, seen inflation devour
it, and concluded that a harder line would have been a favor to
Brazil.

He was, in short, a hard-liner by 1963 and Lyndon Johnson's
kind of man. Johnson defended him often and vehemently after
the appointment was made as "the kind of fellow who can deal
with David Rockefeller or the Export-Import Bank and not make
them mad, and without kowtowing to them. He doesn't put in his
money until they have made their obligations. He is not a
shover." As Johnson saw it, this was precisely what the *Alianza*
needed—a banker's cold eye, a pragmatist's readiness to live with
the realities, and a top management man. And a case can be made
that it was what the *Alianza* needed. The question was whether
with the Kennedy charisma gone, Tom Mann plus Lyndon Johnson wasn't too much. As one ambassador from an important
Latin American country put it, shortly after Kennedy's death:
"There is not much you can do in a tangible way for the great

mass of Latin Americans of this generation. If the Alliance for Progress is successful, we may do something meaningful for the next generation. In the meantime, this generation must at least have hope, and inspiration, and a real belief that things will get better for their children if not for themselves. You have to have the ideology, and you have to keep saying it over and over and over again."

That, essentially, was the case the liberals were making against Tom Mann—that Kennedy had kindled a fire, and that Lyndon Johnson must be extra careful not to extinguish it. A quick campaign materialized, when word of Mann's choice began to circulate privately, to talk the new President out of it. And one of its spokesmen, as it turned out, was to be Lyndon Johnson's running-mate for Vice President. Hubert Humphrey, then a Senator with an active, long-standing interest in Hemisphere affairs, believed fiercely in the ideology of the *Alianza,* and his fears about its future were expressed in detail some months later in an article in *Foreign Affairs,* in which he declared that "in view of the criticism leveled at the Alliance, the persistence of political instability in many countries, and the ever present Communist threat in others, some will be tempted to abandon the original emphasis . . . on radical economic and social reform. Some will be tempted to return to less venturesome, more conventional goals, to place less emphasis on reform and more on working with the established groups to minimize political instability. Indeed there are those who believe we should abandon our identification of the Alliance with 'peaceful revolution,' with rapid reform of the economic and social structure of Latin American societies. I believe this would be a grave mistake."

This was the concern of many of the more liberal authorities on Hemisphere affairs. They feared, as did Humphrey, that Americans would take the Marshall Plan timetable for an already industrialized Europe, apply it to Latin America, and conclude prematurely that the *Alianza* was a flop. Humphrey found himself under considerable pressure to intercede against the Mann appointment and reportedly prepared a memorandum, which in one early version specifically counseled against the choice of Mann. But by the time Humphrey's rendezvous at the White

House rolled around, it had become increasingly apparent that the President's mind was fixed. So the Minnesota Senator edited out of his memo any mention of Mann by name, although he left in it a definition of what sort of alliance administrator the President ought to name, a definition that would have seemed to argue against Mann. His idea was to make the case against Mann orally. But Lyndon Johnson has a good nose for impending dissent. When Humphrey arrived at the President's office, there with Johnson was Tom Mann. Johnson did not wish to argue—he wished to convince. The irrepressible Humphrey read his memorandum anyway. It was a losing gesture, but the spirit that animated it was to dog the footsteps of Johnson and Mann for months to come. Everything that either of them said or did was to be weighed and watched with a fishy eye by the vocal advocates, in this country and in Latin America, of democracy, and constitutionality, and progressive reform, and all the other ingredients of the great social revolution which was then, and still remained by the end of 1965, to a very large extent an abstraction which could be admired and even advanced here and there, but could not realistically be expected to materialize for years to come.

Both Mann and Johnson would continue to deny that they were long-term friends, which was, from the beginning, beside the point. The point was that on Latin America (but not, as it turned out, on some of the broader economic issues with which Mann would be dealing after his elevation to the Under Secretaryship for Economic Affairs), the two men were *simpatico*. Mann knew the business crowd in Texas and their recommendation of him to Johnson had considerable influence in his choice. Neither man was blind to the urgent need for social and economic reform in Latin America, any more than either one had been blind to the needs of the Texas *vaqueros*. But both were more interested in where the power lay than where, in the best of all possible worlds, it ought to lie. With this approach, it became reasonable not to play around with revolutionaries, however noble their stated purpose, if they were too weak to tackle the entrenched, military-backed oligarchies without falling prey in the process of the struggle to infiltration or outright takeover movements by the better disciplined, better organized cadres of the Communists. They would not have to compare notes for long, then, to concur on how to tackle most of the Latin crises that were to confront them, from Panama and Rio de Janeiro to Santo Domingo, in the months ahead. And those who would argue that Tom Mann was exercising strong—and ultraconservative—influence on Lyndon Johnson's Latin American policy were to be given early evidence to the contrary when the rioting broke out in Panama. It was Johnson's fate that his performance in this first foreign test would only compound the impression that his was a retrograde Latin policy; but if it was retrograde or even merely overly rough at the outset, it was not because of the actions or advice of Tom Mann.

Panama—"A Pistol at Your Head"

"They were killing people and some thought we should write a new treaty right off, or at least agree to do it. But you can't say 'I'll give you a blank check' when there is a pistol pointed at your head."

That was the heart of the matter, as Lyndon Johnson saw it, when unruly students (American as well as Panamanian) touched off bloody rioting on the fringe of the Panama Canal Zone in the first week of January, 1964, and the Panamanian President, Roberto F. Chiari, seized on the occasion to demand an end to the 62-year-old treaty arrangement governing U.S. operation of the Panama Canal. Johnson had been in office a little more than one month; his man for Latin America, Thomas Mann, had been in office for only three days. Now they were confronting their first test in the Hemisphere; U.S. troops had been sniped at and had suffered casualties; important figures in Congress were calling on the United States to stand firm; a treaty, after all, was a treaty, and a show of weakness would be bad for U.S. prestige throughout the Hemisphere.

Johnson needed little convincing on this count. He had put through a hurried phone call to Chiari, and though the din of the demonstrators in the background made conversation difficult, the Panamanian President made his point emphatically, for he was under heavy pressure too. Indeed, the hot breath of the rioters, which Johnson took as an affront to his prestige, was at least as much a challenge to Chiari; with May elections coming in Panama, he could do no less, he thought, than insist that the United States agree not just to talk things over, but agree in advance to negotiate a new treaty, to replace the archaic arrangements which had in effect given the United States all the prerogatives of sovereignty "in perpetuity" within the 10-mile-wide Canal Zone slicing across Panama.

So it began badly, and while it was to take an astonishing turn for the better before the year was out, the first few weeks of the Panama crisis did little for Lyndon Johnson's good name in Latin America, for all his emphasis on making the right impression from the start. Criticism of his performance boiled down to the charge that he should have been bigger about it, and it was based in large measure on the tawdry history of U.S. relations with Panama going all the way back to Panama's creation in 1903. The creation of the country had been incidental to the aims of President Theodore Roosevelt, when he used U.S. troops to support a revolt against Colombia which led to the establishment of present-day Panama. His basic objective was to set up a servile state athwart the narrow isthmus that binds the two halves of the Western Hemisphere, and thereby establish a secure route for a canal link between the Atlantic and the Pacific. For the next 62 years, the United States had remained consistently more concerned with the canal than with the country through which it ran. The shipping short cut became not only increasingly important economically, but a vital strategic asset as well; it had also become a private fiefdom of the U.S. Army, whose operations in the Canal Zone created a cozy colony of Americans with a sense of superiority, special privileges, and a standard of living that could only inflame the Panamanians just across the Zonal border. So essential had the Canal and all its workings become to U.S. security—or so, at least, it was said—that no President since Theodore Roosevelt felt comfortable in tinkering with the terms. Politically, the Canal had become a sacred cow; in such citadels of conservatism as the American Legion, a resolution upholding the divine right of the United States to maintain the status quo in the Canal Zone was an annual ritual, and Legion commanders made regular pilgrimages to Panama as the Army's honored guests.

But Panamanian nationalism did not stand still; grievances ranged from economic to political, and they were regularly fanned by far-left agitators eager to exploit the grievances for a better financial deal, or the clamor for the removal of such symbolic irritants as the lavish display of American flags at Zonal installations.

All this had begun to blow up ominously before Lyndon Johnson became President; the Panamanians had been angling for a new treaty, with a time limit, more generous financial terms, an end to work rules discriminatory against Panamanians, and a new formula for flag-flying; slowly, grudgingly, the U.S. had been giving ground. Back in 1936, the United States surrendered the right to intervene in Panama itself or to grab additional territory for the Canal—a right that offers some measure of the sort of bargain Teddy Roosevelt struck at the start—and in 1955, the annuity paid to Panama was raised substantially.

In 1960, after prolonged negotiations, the U.S. Government tossed Panama another bone; it was agreed that the United States would fly the Panama flag alongside the American flag in one designated spot in the Canal Zone. In late 1962, the then Panamanian President Chiara met with President Kennedy, and in January, 1963, it was announced that side-by-side flag-flying would be extended to all sites in the Zone where the American flag was normally flown by civilian authorities; some relatively minor concessions were made dealing with labor problems, the use of Panamanian postage stamps in the Zone, and other matters having to do with Panamanian prestige. But neither on this occasion, nor in a meeting later in 1963, where the United States made a few more concessions to Panama, were the really basic issues—sovereignty, the perpetuity of the U.S. Zonal rights, and the negotiation of a new treaty—tackled head on. No more than his predecessors did John F. Kennedy wish to court political trouble at home on the prickly Panama Canal question. Meantime, however, U.S. employees in the Zone were getting increasingly nervous; families had lived there, and enjoyed their pre-

ferred status, for two or three generations, and they saw in the
relatively insignificant concessions to the Panamanians the beginning of the end of their position of privilege.

The 27,000 or so U.S. civilians working in the Canal Zone
seemed to read especially dark portents into the matter of the
flags. There were, at the time of the Kennedy-Chiari flag-flying
compact in January, 1963, nearly 50 flag sites, including 18
schools for American children. Rather than erect another flagpole
for the Panamanian flag in all these places, the U.S. authorities
decided to implement the two-flag policy largely by progressive
elimination of places where the flag of either nation would be
displayed; the schools were included on this list. The whole
policy was applied progressively over the course of a year, to give
the least offense to anybody.

And so it was that on January 2, 1964, when the Canal Zone's
schools were about to open up after the Christmas holidays, the
powers that be had decreed that at Balboa High School there
would be no American flag in its familiar place; thus did the
inexorable processes of diplomacy and bureaucracy set the stage
for the first international challenge to America's new President.
On January 7, a gang of teen-age students got up early and ran
an American flag up the Balboa High School flagpole. The U.S.
Governor of the Canal Zone saw the evidence of this violation
of a solemn international agreement flapping in the breeze from
his office window and ordered school authorities to strike the
colors. Later, however, the students brazenly ran up another
smaller flag, and this was allowed to fly for the rest of the day,
apparently on the theory that the students deserved to have their
fun. Given the incendiary state of relations between the Zone
and Panama, the inherent instability in Panamanian politics,
and the not inconsiderable capacity of left-wing extremists to
exploit any anti-American issue almost anywhere in the Hemisphere, the illicit flag was all that was needed to touch off a con-
flagration.

It started off almost harmlessly, with a group of Panamanian
students marching into the Zone for a brief demonstration; on
their way back, however, they got tangled up with a more mature
mob, which had apparently assembled in connection with a pend-

ing labor dispute; the two groups mingled and milled about, and at this point agitators went to work. "There were a lot of Molotov cocktails appearing pretty fast," Dean Rusk reported a few days later, noting that there were also "a good many snipers who appeared who perhaps had to have had arms in known localities available to them." It did not make Lyndon Johnson's political problem any easier when Chiari saw fit, in the interests of his own political situation, to put almost all of the blame for the ensuing rioting and bloodshed on the Communist agents. (There were certainly some Communist and Castroite agents involved.) But Panama was now suddenly subject to the "another Cuba" syndrome, which could not have been expected to encourage conciliation on Johnson's part. Nor was compromise made easier when the hard-pressed Chiari Government felt compelled to rupture relations with the U.S. Positions were hardening; and what followed—the frenzied OAS interventions, the stiff-necked posturing on both sides, the semantic nit-picking—might have qualified for high comedy had there been less at stake.

The United States was insisting that law and order be restored as a prerequisite to any solution of the basic quarrel, but there was grave reason to wonder whether Chiari was capable of complying, even though he had even less interest in disorder than did Lyndon Johnson. Congress was up in arms about a Communist plot—which was fully as worrisome to Chiari. The best hope for quieting the agitators, Chiari was arguing, was some concession on the crucial treaty issue. That might well have solved his problem, but Johnson was adamant about not bowing to mob violence. Yet, even though Chiari was making use of the disorders and the Communist menace as a talking point, it is hard to believe that he was inciting violence, part of which, after all, was directed as much against his government as against the Yankee despoilers.

Johnson was in a bind; he could not see clearly where the real elements of power lay or envisage a suitable compromise as a logical consequence of the forces then at work, or even see how to rearrange the power structure to produce a satisfactory compromise. Those were the things he instinctively looked for, and, at the beginning of the Panama crisis, they were simply not to be found. So Johnson dispatched Tom Mann to reconnoiter on the spot and otherwise lay low while a team of OAS mediators went to work. On January 15, there was a brief moment very early in the morning when it seemed as if an agreement had been reached to restore diplomatic relations between the United States and Panama and to initiate negotiations. But just as quickly, this prospect was shattered by a semantic quarrel over whether preconditions were being imposed by the Panamanians; the issue boiled down to the question of whether the United States would agree in advance to negotiate a new treaty, or would simply agree to discuss terms of a new treaty with no prior commitment to come up with one unless compromise could be found. The argument centered, as these things so often do, on just a few words— the United States wanted to "discuss" and the Panamanians to "negotiate," and by the time both had gotten through setting forth what they thought they had agreed upon, it became apparent that they hadn't agreed on anything. There the dispute rested, just barely below the boiling point, until a second OAS mediation team managed to bring the United States and Panama once again to the brink of agreement. The tentative end-product gives some measure of how wide the gulf was between the two sides, how sensitive were the political considerations both for Lyndon Johnson and for President Chiari, and how thin any agreement would have to be stretched in order to cover up these differences. The formula called for a three-way stretch: the OAS would announce a brief statement of agreement between Panama and the United States, and then Panama and the United States would issue separate interpretations of what the agreement meant. The hope was that each country would issue an interpretation acceptable to the other, to avoid the kind of bickering that had broken up the first compromise effort. Chiari wanted to be able to tell the Panamanians, and in particular the small number of the powerful, behind-the-scenes political elite with which he had to deal, that he had in fact opened the way for a new treaty and a wholly new arrangement with the United States over the Canal. Lyndon Johnson wanted to be just as free to reassure his public and U.S. political powers that he had not yielded under crude threats or the pressure of mob violence to any agreement which threatened U.S. interests. On Thursday, March 12, the oas thought it had found just the right words to satisfy all concerned. The United States had at least tacitly accepted President Chiari's proposed "interpretation" of the joint declaration, and word was expected hourly that Chiari had approved what the U.S. Government intended to say. Announcement of the accord was tentatively set for 6:00 p.m., and at the White House an alert was on that a news development of primary importance was imminent. At the State Department, Tom Mann was getting ready to hold a background briefing to set reporters straight on what the United States had and had not done. But nothing was heard from President Chiari that night, and over the course of the next four frantic days, Lyndon Johnson was to give Latin Americans and the rest of the world—not to mention the U.S. diplomatic community—their first inkling of what to expect when the new President of the United States sensed that he had been pushed, crowded, trod upon, or even just trifled with.

After what must have been a lengthy internal debate in the ruling councils in Panama City, President Chiari on Friday finally notified the oas mediators that he would accept the three-piece truce arrangement, but with one seemingly slight exception. The joint Panama–U.S. declaration, to be issued under oas auspices, spoke of projected "discussions and negotiations" on a new agreement to eliminate causes of conflict between the two countries. This was supposed to paper over the semantic chasm between discussing and negotiating, and it enabled the Panamanians to stress their preferred word, and the United States to do likewise. Accordingly, the U.S. "interpretation" was to refer only to discussion and Chiari suggested that the United States use almost any other word—such as "look at," "review," or whatever—if it could not bring itself to mention the word "negotiate" because of its implication of commitment in advance to a successor treaty.

President Johnson's reaction was explosive. "He went through the ceiling," an associate recalled later, adding: "His attitude was, Who do they think they are? How do they dare to rewrite my statement?" The President's patience was especially strained by the fact that the United States had by that time lost a good deal of its interest in what the Panamanians said in their description of the agreement, on the theory that the Mann backgrounder could be counted on to keep the record straight. That Friday night, all hope for the three-way formula seemed to be dead.

But the OAS did not give up; it desperately wanted an agreement, in part because the Organization's prestige was deeply committed, in part because the crisis itself was serious and another diplomatic failure threatened a new outbreak of violence, and in part because Latin diplomats were assembling for a gala commemorative meeting the following Monday to celebrate the third anniversary of John F. Kennedy's first formal presentation of his plan for the Alliance for Progress to a gathering of Hemisphere envoys at the White House. So on Saturday, March 14, the OAS in some desperation decided on a new strategy of simply making public the joint declaration with no interpretation from either side mutually agreed upon in advance but with, of course, the approval of both. Once again, however, there was difficulty getting a straight answer quickly from Panama; and U.S. officials, plainly inhibited by the President's display of irritation seemed, at least to the OAS representatives involved, to be almost equally incapable of giving a clear statement of U.S. views. The OAS mediators insist their plan was well known to the State Department and never flatly opposed; Department officials, while conceding there may have been grounds for honest confusion all around, also maintained that they manifested clearly their opposition, if not to the new OAS strategem, at least to the haste with which it was being pushed.

The OAS, however, was not to be denied. A press conference was called for 6:00 P.M., Sunday, and at approximately 6:25, the go-ahead arrived from Panama. Once again U.S. concurrence was solicited and once again there is a sharp difference about what position the United States took. Tom Mann did the talking, and the OAS officials he was talking to insist he neither opposed nor approved but simply left the decision to the OAS, arguing that it was "your business." Reconstructing that exchange, U.S. officials say only that if the OAS was under any illusions that it had American backing for its compromise declaration, it was "engaging in wishful thinking."

Whatever the case—and the records themselves do not furnish a definitive answer—the OAS issued its statement in the name of both Panama and the United States. That took place at about 6:45 P.M. At 9:00 P.M., Johnson summoned Rusk and Mann to the White House for a decisive and secret meeting.

Meantime, the President had turned for advice and backing to his old friends in Congress and discovered, in a meeting with legislative leaders, that he was on very thin ice. Some, such as Fulbright, Mansfield, and Humphrey, leaned toward discussions or negotiation or whatever on a new treaty, without too much quibbling about semantics—but with no guarantee in advance that a new treaty would in fact be concluded. But Johnson's old friend Richard Russell of Georgia, together with prominent Republicans, was against any discussions, and Everett Dirksen, leader of the Senate Republicans, held forth at length on the dreadful example that would be set for "every little country in the world" if the United States was to budge at all.

At some point during the evening, Johnson also received reports that Panamanian officials in Panama City and Panamanian radio broadcasters were giving their own interpretation of the OAS announcement in what struck the President as extremely free-wheeling style.

He felt that he was being shoved around—and by a country which he had publicly demeaned, at one point in the Panamanian crisis, as no larger than the city of St. Louis. As something of a connoisseur of compromise, it must also have occurred to him that the OAS formula simply strained too hard to stretch across the gulf then separating Panama and the United States, given the domestic political pressures at work in both countries.

According to some of those who were close to him at the time, he was also acutely conscious that any new arrangements that might emerge as a result of the controversy would undoubtedly require confirmation by the Senate. Therefore, what might be described as the "legislative history" of any new Canal treaty would have to take into account its origins, the degree of pressure exerted by Panamanian mobs, for example, and the general atmosphere prevailing at the time. The President reportedly did not consider the genesis of the agreement then taking shape to be auspicious.

The precise details of the debate at the White House that night are not known publicly, but according to one participant, "it was rough." And according to another account, the climax came when President Johnson turned to his brand-new Latin American czar, who was to take much of the brunt of later criticism against Johnson's "hard line" on Panama, and said, in almost so many words: "I'm sorry, Tom, but I'm going to have to pull the rug out from under you."

At 11:00 P.M. that Sunday, the White House Press Secretary summoned reporters and announced, squarely in the teeth of the OAS declaration only a little more than four hours earlier, that there was as yet "no meeting of minds."

That would have been quite enough to rock the OAS, but there was more. Monday morning, the President addressed the Aliance for Progress rally, and his advance text was unstinting in its praise of the *Alianza* and in its pledge of U.S. devotion to the Alliance for Progress and all its works. But Johnson did not stick to the script. "Let me now depart for a moment from my main theme to speak of the differences that have developed between Panama and the United States," he interjected. "Our own position is clear," he said pointedly, "and it has been from the first hour that we learned of the disturbances." The President said the United States would meet with Panama "any time, anywhere, to discuss anything, to work together, to cooperate with each other, to reason with one another, to review and to consider all of our desires and all our concerns but we don't ask Panama to make any precommitments before we meet, and we intend to make none."

And the President then added: "As of this moment, I do not believe there has been a genuine meeting of the minds between the two Presidents of the two countries involved." Thus, from the President himself came the *coup de grâce* to the OAS mediation effort. This was thunderbolt enough to the assembled Latin diplomats. The President's next remark, however, shook some of them even more profoundly. "Press reports indicate that the Government of Panama feels that the language which has been

under consideration for many days commits the United States
to a rewriting and a revision of the 1903 Treaty. We have made
no such commitment and we would not think of doing so before
diplomatic relations are resumed and unless a fair and satisfactory
adjustment is agreed upon." Thereupon Mr. Johnson took up
again his main theme and concluded with a soaring endorsement
of the *Alianza,* complete with a quote from William Butler Yeats.
But judging from the immediate reaction of the Latin Americans
there assembled, his audience had ceased to listen. One of the
oas mediators later angrily voiced the sentiments of a good many
of his colleagues: "How policy can be built on radio accounts of
statements to the press which Panama has denied publicly?—
That's what surprises me. Panama is still saying that it accepts
our joint declaration as it stands." Ever sensitive to any occasion
and long on ceremony, many Latin Americans were a long time
forgetting or forgiving Lyndon Johnson's intrusion of the Panama
question in what was to have been a poignant rededication of
heart and energy to the high principles of John F. Kennedy's
Alliance for Progress. Quite possibly, what Lyondon Johnson had
to say was somewhat more real, and certainly more candid, than
what the Latin Americans had in mind for that occasion. But the
need for the President to say it became even less compelling almost immediately. The five-man mediation team quickly reported
on its performance to the full oas Council and just as quickly received what amounted to a ringing vote of confidence from most
of the Organization's members. The U.S. Government began to
have some second thoughts. The following Saturday, President
Johnson arrived unannounced at the office of his Press Secretary,
George Reedy, and interrupted a routine press briefing. "Is it all
right with you folks if I monitor your press conference?" the
President asked, and then proceeded, without a pause, to shower
the oas and Panama and President Chiari with praise and bon-
homie. In a statement which he said he was sending to President
Juan Bautista de Lavalle, Chairman of the Council of the oas,
Johnson took great pains to reiterate U.S. willingness to seek a
solution to the Panama problem; he talked feelingly of the long
record of cooperation between the two countries, including
Panama's quick action to declare war on the Japanese at Pearl

Harbor; and he offered to send an ambassador to Panama City as soon as Panama was ready to restore relations; finally, the President also volunteered the services of a special U.S. representative to help seek a solution to the Canal question and other issues. Most important, while Mr. Johnson was careful to sidestep the dread word "negotiation," he was also willing to depart from the word "discuss."

Graciously, Johnson made a point of emphasizing U.S. willingness to "review" all problems and all difficulties. "I don't say discuss, because that is a sticky word," the President said, adding, "some of them do not quite understand what it means. But I say review. We are glad to do that."

Whether Mr. Johnson was aware that that concession would probably have been sufficient to bring at least a temporary, patchwork truce a week earlier—or whether he was indeed conscious of the semantic distinctions but had decided that he had made his point and it was time to soften his stand—may never be clear. Johnson insisted that as far as he knew, the U.S. position at the beginning was exactly as he stated it at his impromptu Saturday press conference on March 21.

But he also conceded, "I am not sure that I know all that went on" in the frenetic round of U.S. diplomacy that had been conducted in his name the preceding weekend.

In any event, the Saturday press conference marked a major turning point. Not too many weeks later, a reconciliation of sorts was reached between the U.S. and Panama, and the whole crisis was successfully put on ice through quiet, patient diplomacy, under the guidance of one of Johnson's favorite troubleshooters, Robert Anderson. Panama was to become, by any reckoning, a plus for Lyndon Johnson. It was his fate, however, for Panama to have been a minus when it was making news, and when Latin Americans were making up their minds about a new American President whose approach to the Hemisphere was already, in their eyes, suspect.

The Covert Crisis Manager

Panama produced a stark impression of Lyndon Johnson—impetuous, erratic, short-tempered, unyielding, and easy prey to domestic political pressures. Yet even while Panama was putting the new President under the hot glare of publicity, quite different kinds of international crises were crowding in upon him and creating quite the contrary impression among those who had an opportunity to watch him at work behind the scenes. There they saw a cautious, prudent, and more malleable man, eager to shun the spotlight, anxious to conceal his hand and that of the United States whenever possible, fully aware that a *sub rosa* role would earn him few plaudits if things went well and leave him open to all manner of criticism if things went badly.

Both Johnsons were real, and neither one was as contradictory of the other as it might appear. As Senate manager, Johnson was never much of a man for taking the floor; he did his best work in the lobby, roaming the aisles, stalking the corridors; he was most effective when his prestige and power were least engaged— publicly and inescapably—and it was no different in his dealings with the world at large. It was prudence that made him refuse to be pushed or rushed in the Panama affair; the only difference was that it was more difficult to work to his own clock in full public view. It is therefore worth examining some of his first flings in foreign affairs where almost all the Presidential maneuvering was going on behind the scenes—in Cyprus, in the Congo, in Brazil and Chile, and in Laos—for the basic technique was to remain the same in Vietnam, in Kashmir, in Indonesia, and whenever Lyndon Johnson was allowed the luxury of a little time and some degree of privacy.

As described by long-time and close associates, Lyndon Johnson prefers to approach a problem, whether domestic or foreign, as one might approach a porcupine. "He creeps up on it, it's really great fun to watch," one of the Kennedy "professors" once observed with the detachment of an academician. One of the White House Texans, who had watched the President at work close up and for a longer period of time once put it this way:

"Johnson likes to get up and walk around the problem and keep walking around it and examining it and poking it and looking at it from every angle. He believes absolutely that you don't move, you don't show power, until you are ready to use it. And then if you do decide to use it, you don't just do this," he said, lightly patting his kneecap. "What you do then," he declared, leaning forward and clawing the air with both hands, "is go for the jugular."

In July of 1964, Johnson was to give a vivid demonstration of what "going for the jugular" meant to him—and to defend it in almost those words—by a one-shot air attack against torpedo-boat pens and other installations in North Vietnam, in reprisal for a North Vietnamese torpedo-boat attack on U.S. warships in the Gulf of Tonkin. Later, in Vietnam and in the Dominican Republic, the "jugular reflex" was displayed and defended by the President in defiant terms when he thought his honor or political position was at stake. "They thought they could frighten the President of the United States," he said after Vietcong terrorist attacks had brought retaliatory U.S. air strikes to the North, adding: "They just didn't know this President." Yet this tough talk is misleading, too, for early in his Presidency, Johnson displayed a positive preference for working behind the scenes in a series of complicated, if less dramatic, international imbroglios where U.S. interests were gravely threatened, even though the challenge to the United States was indirect.

Just such a challenge to U.S. interests came quietly, on January 25, 1964, while the Panama crisis was burning briskly in the public prints. The Cyprus crisis came to Washington in a quiet meeting between the British Ambassador and Under Secretary of State Ball; the United States, at that point, was already well aware of deep trouble on the island of Cyprus, where a patchwork agreement giving Cyprus its independence in 1960 was rapidly coming unstuck. It was a complicated agreement because Cyprus is a complicated island, composed, in a ratio of four to one, of Greek Cypriots and Turkish Cypriots who have been conducting a running feud for centuries. When Cyprus was seized by the postwar urge for independence, the British resisted for six years and then agreed to an almost unworkable compromise that provided for a Greek president and a Turkish vice president, with each of the two communities empowered to veto proposals advanced by the other. In late 1963, as this system proved less and less workable, the nation's President, Archbishop Makarios of the Greek Orthodox Church (described by Dean Acheson, who was to play a major role in Johnson's Cyprus policy, as a "political priest with considerable gifts of demagogy, and ruthlessness"), proposed constitutional reforms, which were by nature unacceptable to the Turkish elements, and then began doing a little reforming on his own. Bloodshed had broken out, the two groups were massacring each other, and the U.S. Government was not unprepared for the visit by the British Ambassador in January.

What the British were proposing, however, was, in effect, for the United States to plunge deeply into a Mediterranean controversy from which it had mercifully been able to stay out of until then; Britain, Turkey, and Greece had responsibility under the Cypriot independence agreement for keeping the peace and upholding a "treaty of guarantee" of the settlement that set Cyprus free of British rule. But civil order was deteriorating rapidly, and now the British were saying they could not carry the burden of maintaining order alone; what they wanted was an international force and the usual recourse to the United Nations did not recommend itself, partly because of the opportunity that would open up for Soviet obstruction, partly because the U.N.'s Afro-Asian majority would have probably favored Makarios and his Greek Cypriots at the expense of the Turkish Cypriots and might, in the end, have provoked desperate measures by the Turks to rescue their Cypriot kinfolk from Greek Cypriot subjugation. So the British thought was that the NATO allies should take up the responsibility of policing Cyprus with forces drawn from their NATO contingents—forces which would thereby have automatically included U.S. troops.

The stage was thus set for yet another U.S. military involvement, at a time when it already had commitment enough in Vietnam and around the world. The strategy accepted by Johnson was an ingenious one. He and his advisers felt strongly that the U.S. could not stand aside; they wanted an American voice in whatever was going to be done, because American interests were vitally involved. At the end of the road was nothing less than the prospect of war between Greece and Turkey, which could only shatter the cohesion of the NATO Alliance. Clearly, the British were determined not to try to go it alone, not to try to maintain order by increasing their own forces on the island, which they had every legal right to do. Yet the United States could not expect to have a hand in developments unless it was prepared to supply troops. So Johnson decided to make the offer, but within a framework that made it more than likely that it would be rejected—which indeed it was. The original idea of a NATO force collapsed and with it any further obligation on the part of the United States to furnish combat forces; ultimately the policing was turned over to the United Nations.

Not all, or even much of the ins and outs of this tangled controversy need to be set down here. It is enough to note the Johnson reflex, when the matter was first brought to him in January; he turned to Ball, who had been engaged in the first serious talks with the British, and invested him with sweeping authority to try to organize a peace-keeping force and do whatever else he could to promote a peaceful solution. "You have my confidence," the President said to Ball, dispatching him on a tour of London, Athens, Ankara, and Nicosia in urgent search of a solution. As officials involved saw it from the inside, it was to become a "beautiful exercise," as one of them put it, in striking a balance between the President's role as decision-maker and the effective execution of his decisions. Johnson made himself intimately familiar with the issues, conducted lengthy correspondence with most of the major figures involved, took the initiative to invite the Turkish and Greek Prime Ministers to Washington for a little reasoning together, and on at least one occasion was personally instrumental in forestalling the ultimate calamity of a Turkish invasion of the island by writing a stiff warning to Turkish Prime Minister Inonu, insisting that the Turks do nothing without consulting the United States. "I put it to you personally whether you really believe that it is appropriate for your Government, in effect, to present a unilateral decision of such consequence to an ally who has been such a staunch supporter over the years," Johnson wrote.

This was in June, and much earlier, in February, the Turks had also assembled military and naval forces and threatened to invade. On that occasion, Ball had had much to do with staying the Turkish hand. It would have been too much to expect, for all the complicated maneuvering, that a settlement could have been reached, and the main U.S. effort was directed towards damping down the crisis to the point that a serious effort toward compromise might be possible. The Greek Government lacked the political force to control the Archbishop, and it was never entirely clear in turn, whether the Archbishop could control the extremists within his Government. Nobody seriously expected the deep and ferocious hatreds that were at work on both sides to be brought under control quickly, let alone assuaged by diplomacy.

"This came to Johnson as a war-or-peace issue," one of his advisers said at the time, "and his main effort was to keep it from becoming a war." What distinguished Cyprus from Panama—or the Dominican Republic, for that matter—was that it never deeply engaged the interest of Congress. When it did stir political pressure, mostly from the Greek community in the United States, Johnson was in a position to take a hard line and did, according to those in a position to know. Because the President's personal prestige was not openly involved to any great degree, his role was reserved to those critical moments when a White House decision was imperative; the rest of the time, authority was delegated at first to Ball and later to Dean Acheson as special presidential emissary in search of a political solution. In an essentially disorderly and at time profoundly critical situation, it was, therefore, a remarkably orderly performance by a President and an Administration which had been working together for only a few months.

Elsewhere in the world, the United States was edging more deeply into that murky political no man's land of unacknowledged and unacknowledgeable activity designed to influence the course of events, either militarily or politically, without attribution to the United States. Partly it may have been coincidence, but partly it was a Presidential penchant in 1964 for damping things down, moving without public commitment, struggling to keep lids on all over the globe until after election day.

Though Vietnam was soon to become the great Johnson preoccupation in foreign affairs, in the spring of 1964 the attention of a good many Southeast Asian experts, and of the President as well, was centered on neighboring Laos, where the Pathet Lao guerrilla forces, once thought to be under rather strict control by the Russians, who had been their major suppliers, were now violating the 1962 truce more flagrantly than ever, moving out from territory they had held and grabbing for more.

For Johnson, this was a direct test, for Laos had long been regarded as a barometer of the intentions of Hanoi as well as those of Peking, both gaining increased influence and control over the Pathet Lao elements. So what the Pathet Lao did or did not do could be taken as a measure of the militancy of the North Vietnamese and the Communist Chinese, and what the United States did or did not do to help salvage Laos from total Communist takeover would also be read carefully in the enemy camp as a token of toughness or weakness on the U.S. side. The last thing Lyndon Johnson wanted to do was to commit troops to Laos; though Kennedy had seriously considered it in his day, he had managed to stem the tide merely by moving U.S. forces into adjacent Thailand. As the Pathet Lao forays became more bold, the United States was once again confronted with the question of how to deter the Communists without committing its own forces in a tiny land-locked nation bordering China as well as North Vietnam and quite capable of absorbing huge numbers of U.S. troops without offering the opportunity of a decisive military solution. Even the once-used resort to a kind of gunboat diplomacy, bringing U.S. troops into Thailand, seemed unlikely to work a second time. Inevitably, perhaps, air power was suggested as an answer, but once again Johnson did not wish to commit U.S. aircraft openly to the Laotian fighting—above all, not in an election year when he was picturing himself as the prudent man of peace. From this line of reasoning, the solution suggested itself: airpower not openly acknowledged as American. Thus it was that in June, 1964, there was a sudden uproar in the Communist press that U.S. airplanes were attacking Pathet Lao forces and installations in Laos. The U.S. Government denied it, of course, for as long as possible —that is, until an American reconnaissance plane and a fighter escort were shot down. Even then, the flights were passed off as reconnaissance operations to check for violations of the 1962 agreement, and the fighter escorts were said to be along simply to provide protection. When one of these escorts blasted Pathet Lao headquarters, it was attributed to a pilot's mistaken impression that he was attacking an anti-aircraft installation. The facts were, however, that the U.S. Government had organized an air war in Laos against the Pathet Lao on a modest scale, with only intermittent attacks at selected targets. But it was nonetheless a systematic aerial operation designed in large part to discourage the Pathet Lao from further incursions and demonstrate U.S. resolve to resist.

Under the semaphore system of diplomacy, which had played so large a role not only in Southeast Asia but in Cuba, Berlin, and other trouble spots in recent years, the theory was that some show of American military strength was needed in order to convince the Communists that the United States was not incapable of taking strong action, even in the middle of an election year. There is some reason to believe that the message got across in Laos, for the Pathet Lao land grabs slackened off. But the real import of the message apparently did not get through to Hanoi, for even then the powers that be in North Vietnam and in Peking must have been planning the massive escalation of their war effort in South Vietnam, which was to unfold in early 1965.

June, indeed, was a bumper month for covert activity—and a bad one for credibility—for even as the U.S. Government was proclaiming "Look, no hands" in Laos, it was being charged, again with uncomfortable accuracy, with running covert military operations in the Congo on behalf of Moise Tshombe, the one-time leader of the secessionist Katanga province who had worked his way back to political prominence, this time as head of the whole Central Government. Tshombe, while certainly one of the ablest Congolese politicians, was also anathema to much of the rest of Africa, where Tshombe's role as leader of Katanga and ally of the European mining interests had marked him as a traitor to the cause of African nationalism. So there was no end of willing hands in Algeria, Egypt, and in the African countries neighboring the Congo; they were more than ready to fuel the fires of rebellion which had burned briskly even in the best of times since the Belgian Congo gained independence in 1960. Tshombe's predecessor had done little to build up an effective police force—and Tshombe himself had always found it much more effective to hire white mercenaries to lead his forces in Katanga. There was no real force of law and order to replace the U.N. peace-keeping units which were pulled out of the Congo, largely for lack of financial support from the U.N. membership, in June, 1964. Dissident groups, some tribal in their motivations, some bank-rolled by assorted Communists, both Russian and Chinese, barely waited for the U.N. troops to pull out before beginning their rampages. The authority of the Central Government was practically nil. Were it to be destroyed entirely, there was serious danger not only of ever widening bloodshed, but of total disintegration of the Belgian Congo as a country. So, as quietly as possible, the United States moved in to help with military assistance of various kinds. In Washington there was little enthusiasm for the mission, for it raised some delicate questions at the outset. Nobody wanted to be seen publicly showering military aid on Tshombe because of what this would have done to the U.S. image elsewhere in Africa. But Tshombe needed officers for his troops, so the first thing the United States did was to look pointedly in the other direction while Tshombe began recruiting new white mercenary cadres. "We didn't give our approval, but we didn't disapprove either," one U.S. diplomat explained it at the time, "and in Africa not disapproving is the same thing as saying go ahead." Then, suddenly, Peking Radio was on the air, in mid-June, 1964, charging that American aircraft were fighting in the Congo. This was roundly denied, but later public acknowledgment was made that U.S. transports were being used to move Tshombe's troops from one trouble spot to another, and there was good reason to believe that Americans, recruited by the U.S. Government, were pitching in as pilots on Tshombe's behalf. Ultimately, of course, Lyndon Johnson would have to make a much more dramatic decision to help fly in troops to rescue hostages being held by Congolese rebel forces in Stanleyville, and thereby stir a storm of African anti-Americanism. The unrest in the Congo was to worsen (dramatically) at the turn of the year, before the Central Government was finally able to restore some semblance of law and order, but there were some who would argue that it might not have survived at all, had the U.S. not lent a discreet helping hand with Tshombe's initial military problems.

In the Western Hemisphere, as in Asia or Africa, public attention focused on what was glaringly apparent. In Asia, it was the debilitating game of military musical chairs played out in Saigon. In Africa, it was a succession of impenetrable crises, in Zanzibar and throughout East Africa. In Latin America, the North American mind was riveted to Cuba and Panama. But the big Latin dramas were unfolding, relatively unnoticed, in that part of the Hemisphere that matters the most and is the most remote. The Caribbean countries of Latin America may be closer, but half of the Hemisphere, as it is normally spoken, of, is Brazil, and in Brazil there was a slow, steady, relentless drift towards catastrophe for that country, for Latin America, and for anybody who happened to be President of the United States at the time that it happened. In the first year of the Kennedy Administration, Janio Quadros had taken office as President of Brazil after a landslide victory, and seven months later had walked off the job for reasons that were never very clear; his Vice President, Jão Goulart, the leftist opportunist who was in line for the Presidency, had taken this inopportune moment to be in Communist China, and the military did its best to block his path. But he got there anyway—after agreeing to a compromise that was supposed to reduce his power—and then quickly set about building his power up again. At the end of 1963, Brazil was ready for revolution and the only question was where it would come from —the Communists and extreme leftists and fellow travelers who had been given very nearly a free rein under Goulart, or the conservative military elements who were getting increasingly nervous about the Communist infiltration of the Goulart Government. By the end of 1963, Goulart had made such a mess of the economy as well as the government itself that officials in Washington were beginning to talk quite seriously of at least a violently nationalistic, anti-American, nonaligned Brazil, and conceivably even a pro-Communist Brazil, a situation which would have made a mockery of the Alliance for Progress and of everything else that the U.S. Government was trying to do in Latin America. Yet open intervention in the Brazilian political struggle then raging behind the scenes between military elements as well as the politicians would almost certainly have aggravated the trend. Brazil desperately needed economic help, but the United States had felt, with some justice, that there was no effective way to help a Brazilian economy ravaged by inflation and mismanagement. So there was not much to be done, overtly, and there is little that can be said about what may or may not have been done covertly. What is clear, however, is that when the lid finally came off, in a three-day revolution at the end of March, 1964, the U.S. Government was not an idle bystander. Nor was it, to be sure, an active, open participant, although as the revolt developed, Lyndon Johnson was under heavy pressure to throw U.S. weight behind the generals who were struggling to overthrow Goulart. The President was presented with strong arguments for a display of gunboat diplomacy. According to some of his advisers, he was, as one of them put it, urged to "move the fleet, and show the flag." Johnson did not move in any open way, even though he would surely have come under the strongest sort of criticism if Goulart had prevailed, for that would have meant an even deeper Brazilian turn toward the left, given the nature of the military showdown. Instead, the United States showed its sympathy in subtler ways, and though the ways were not visible and could not be positively identified, there is reason to believe that U.S. money was thrown heavily onto the scales in favor of those forces opposing Goulart. At a time when military coups were thought to be dimly regarded in Washington, there is every reason to believe that Washington gave the Brazilian military as much encouragement as it could discreetly give.

And Johnson wasted little time giving the anti-Goulart revolutionaries a quick blessing by diplomatic recognition of their regime at the earliest moment consistent with diplomatic niceties —and somewhat earlier than some of his advisers were recommending at the time. Indeed, Tom Mann, who was hospitalized, was cautioning a delay of "a few days." Ironically, a "Kennedy professor," Lincoln Gordon, who was then U.S. Ambassador to Brazil and who later was to be appointed by Johnson as Assistant Secretary for Latin American Affairs (Tom Mann's old job), was probably decisive in urging quick recognition. "It was tricky," Johnson later told a visitor. "But what do you do? It could have been a disaster if it had gone wrong. When things go right, people forget." Elaborating, a White House staff man noted afterward that "Johnson would have been blamed if Goulart had won. But he doesn't like to plunge recklessly into things until he knows where they're headed, so while the thing was building up, we handled Brazil covertly."

Covert was also the word for the Johnson approach to Chile, even though all through the spring and summer of 1964, there was at least a strong chance that Chile might become the first nation in history to vote itself Communist. The threat was there in the person of fifty-six-year-old Salvador Allende, a wealthy physician who called himself a socialist, headed the Socialist Party, and was running as the candidate of a "Popular Front" coalition which included the Communist Party. If Allende could not be labeled as an out-and-out Communist, he would have certainly ushered in a regime that would have been wide open to Communist dominance, if not total Communist takeover. Allende had all the familiar earmarks of a Communist stalking horse; he was all for Castro and for Moscow and for Peking, and for outright seizure of foreign property, including the rich U.S.–owned copper mines. The Johnson Administration, accordingly, devoutly wished to see Allende's main opponent, Eduardo Frei, win and, from the evidence, was not quite prepared to leave it all to chance. Again, open support, indeed, any overt activity on Frei's behalf, would have almost certainly backfired. Again, Johnson could only lose; no one would give him much credit for Frei's victory, but a win for Allende in September, 1964, just before the U.S. elections, would have been counted a black mark against the Johnson Administration and the Democrats, whatever they did to help avoid it. Exactly what was done cannot be known, but there were all sorts of ways in which U.S. influence could be brought to bear, with campaign funds, with timely declarations of sympathy for specific Frei objectives, and in other ways which officials concerned were understandably unprepared to talk about. All that was abundantly clear was, as one Presidential aide put it, that "We helped Frei quietly, behind the scenes. Johnson didn't offer open support. That's not his way."

First
Impressions

A Kennedy legend springing from a classic Inaugural Address could survive a Bay of Pigs. It was Lyndon Johnson's fate from the very start to have international missteps of smaller magnitude become a part of his permanent record.

First impressions are not supposed to matter, of course; but in politics they can make or break a man. Which way opinion goes, and how far, depends on many things: the strength, or novelty of the impression; natural, personal appeal; the atmosphere in general, and in particular, the inclination of those who sit in judgment sometimes to grant the benefit of the doubt.

Lyndon Johnson came on strong. It was not just that he was so different from his predecessor—he was unlike any U.S. President the world had ever known. He dispatched special emissaries all over the globe. He welcomed diplomats in large bunches to the White House. He lavished tender care upon editors and publishers and network presidents. He swarmed all over Congress with telephone calls and private talkfests. He bestowed special attention on intellectuals. He all but suffocated the White House press corps with blandishments. He wined and dined the pundits as well as foreign visitors.

But he was also a little transparent and, to the conventional, a little eccentric. While he was switching off White House lights, for economy, Government limousines were moving from house to house, delivering handsome, king-sized Christmas cards and baskets of pralines. He fixed a sky-high starting figure for the federal budget, bemoaned the impossibility of cutting deeply into anything so bulky, then brought it masterfully under the magic $100-billion figure, a feat which shrewder observers knew he could and would bring off all along. A State Department duty officer thought it was a gag—but only for a moment—when his phone rang one Sunday morning, and a voice said "This is Lyndon." He assembled the top public-information officers of the government in the early days and advised them not of his plans and policies, but of his insistence that they get him more often, and more favorably, on page one. He met and talked and pleaded with the representatives of business, labor, the consumer, the farmer, civil-rights movements. His reach missed few lapels.

For those who had known him long, and understood him—for the men of Congress, especially, who had seen The Treatment—it was Lyndon-as-usual. As one long-time Senate colleague described it, "Johnson was shameless [in the Senate]. He'd be right out on the floor, in plain view of the galleries, nose-to-nose, shaking his finger, working 'em over, even when he had more votes than he needed. He wanted every last sheep in his fold."

But for others, the shock of the contrast was too much to absorb. For many who had been of the Kennedy era, and reveled in it, it always would be. Some would adjust. But there were many, in the beginning days, who deplored his style and manner and methods; and because they could only applaud his domestic policies, they found outlet for their antipathy in a predisposition to find in his conduct of foreign affairs nothing but the worst. Criticism came quickly, often prematurely; and the more he attempted to answer it, the more he accentuated the very deficiencies for which his critics in the news media, in the bureaucracies, and in the foreign embassies were criticizing him.

Thus was set in motion mutual antagonisms which make the first impressions of President Johnson—both his of the world and the world's of his—of enduring significance, for they interacted upon each other to fix the atmosphere in which he would be judged and misjudged for a long time to come.

Washington is an inbred society and a small town, with a rich concentration of intellect focused relentlessly on one subject—affairs of state. The elected politicians and the diplomats, the bureaucrats and the high policy-makers, the pundits and the commentators, the sages and elder statesmen, mingle and exchange information and rumors and judgments—endlessly. In this fashion, opinion is manufactured for export by diplomatic cable or television or the press or word of mouth, to the public at large, to the power centers in the universities and the corporations, to Wall Street and Main Street, to Foreign Affairs councils in Cleveland or San Francisco or Atlanta, to foreign capitals. The validity of the opinion often matters less than its rippling impact around the world and on the opinion-makers themselves. The group of opinion-makers is at its heart something of an international intelligentsia; it includes foreign diplomats and foreign correspondents. Its American component may or may not be East Coast–oriented, or socially elite, or Ivy League–educated, but it is largely liberal in inclination and always global in outlook. Supposedly sophisticated and rich in worldly wisdom, it embraces bureaucrats, diplomats, pundits, newsmen. It is not a group, on the whole, that could have been expected to have a natural affinity for Lyndon Johnson; it is not one with which a Texas practitioner of practical, elective politics could have been expected to have an easy rapport; it is one, in fact, for which Lyndon Johnson had instinctive contempt. But it is also a force—and the general impression of Lyndon Johnson that was permeating the thoughts of the opinion-makers in the early months of his Presidency was having a pernicious and unsettling effect on his conduct of international affairs, if only by generating misconceptions and excessive animosities.

He needed, for example, the good will and, indeed, the respect of his White House press entourage—and they called him "Hud" and "Jubilation T. Cornpone." He needed the same things from the pundits and commentators, and while he had the respect of some of them, it was grudgingly given, and tempered with resentment for the treatment they received. He needed the same things from the eggheads and while many worked in his cause, one of their leading lights was to call him "the first President since Roosevelt who enjoyed pulling wings off flies," and another, to the apparent horror of visiting British journalist Henry Fairlie, was to refer to the President of the United States as a "slob." He also needed respect and good will from the foreign diplomats, as well as the U.S. professional diplomatic community, and while the former grumbled over real or fancied indignities, the latter squirmed under the pressures of what one dedicated State Department hand referred to as "the politics of intimidation." Above all, he wanted and needed the allegiance of the Kennedy men— for longer, as it turned out, than anybody had supposed at the beginning—and while he felt compassion for some and dealt respectfully, by and large, with the top figures, the Kennedy contingent as a whole was never unaware of his jibes at the "stay-combs" (Johnsonese for "greasy kid stuff") and "socialites," and his graceless reminders that "the touch football crowd isn't making decisions around here anymore."

Johnson seemed equally outraged by the response of the Washington press. If Kennedy had canceled the White House subscription to the *New York Herald Tribune,* Johnson would do more than just renew it by way of restoring relations with this pillar of Eastern Seaboard respectability. He would have the publisher and the Washington bureau chief and their wives (and Billy Graham) all to dinner at the White House within the first few weeks, and the Trib's White House man to the ranch for a weekend. When that same correspondent was one of the first to knock the Johnson foreign policy, Johnson was livid, and almost unbelieving that The Treatment could be so ephemeral. He told one coterie of White House reporters that he would make "big men" of them—if they played ball. When it appeared to him that they weren't playing ball, he stormed at their bosses, as well as at them, and kept his staff hard at it, registering protests all over town.

With the press, it was not just a matter of the frequency of press conferences, or the open antagonism, mingled with contempt for "your cruel little press," as he once put it, or his scatological turn of phrase, or high-speed driving, or the cynical, practical, political twist he put on everything, although all this figures in it. For many, it was the sweeping simplicity with which he discussed crucial, complex problems; the impression (usually misleading) of abject ignorance of nuance or detail; the boundless self-interest implicit in almost everything he said; the self-aggrandizement; the bombast; the boasts.

Spasmodically, the Johnson feud with the press waxed and waned, depending on the Presidential mood; he was inclined to be amiable, considerate, and almost euphoric after a tough decision had been made. But it is probably fair to say that relations never really recovered from his first frenzied effort to take the press into his camp and his bitter disillusionment when it didn't work. As Senate Majority Leader, he had been less the center of all eyes and more conspicuously successful in achieving his aims, and he had apparently assumed that as President, coming to the job as he did, things would be even better. The resulting hard feelings were of interest chiefly to the press but important beyond that, for they helped establish the general atmosphere if in no other way than by driving the President to intemperate comment and unjustified defensiveness. (On one occasion, the President's preoccupation with the injustices—to him—of the U.S. press impelled him to pour out a bitter five-minute tirade on the subject to a visiting British Foreign Minister who had merely asked how the President would want him to play it with the waiting reporters on his way out.)

On other occasions, his diatribes at newsmen more indirectly became an element in international relations. In many of his private encounters with newsmen, Johnson may well have assumed that nobody was taking him literally since nothing was for attribution to him by those present; he may have been talking for relaxation as Eisenhower practiced golf shots. But lifted out of context in the inevitable retelling around town, the Johnsonisms were polished, and refined, and took on, in the process, deep meaning to those who had not heard him firsthand and had no feel for the circumstances, and to those who did not understand or like the man.

In the inevitable retelling, the "latest horror story," as the Johnsonism came to be called, was bound to seep out of the journalistic fraternity into wider circulation and reach the ears of those even less likely to understand, or forgive, or forget. What Johnson said about Ho Chi Minh (and about what he had done to Ho Chi Minh at the Gulf of Tonkin) might cause no problem— Kennedy's private commentary on Khrushchev after his Vienna encounter was scorching, too—and it cannot even be argued that Johnson's private appraisals of De Gaulle, Lester Pearson, Ayub, Shastri, U Thant, or the oas had serious consequences, even though they were common conversational currency. Mostly his targets would not or could not afford to take offense, or if they did, it wouldn't matter much. What did matter, however, was the general atmosphere engendered—the eyebrows raised, doubts planted, antagonisms generated, without any real relevance to Presidential action or policy. What mattered, whether Johnson cared or not, was the atmosphere.

The President's overpowering manner was part of it. So was his method, as he reached out for support from men of intellect and stature and influence.

Ever sensitive to comparisons with Kennedy, he was well aware that Kennedy had harnessed the energies and earned the approval of that amorphous, influential body of internationally oriented bankers, businessmen, lawyers, and professors whose members had formed the backbone of the Truman Administration, played a major hand in the Eisenhower Administration, and helped assemble the Kennedy Administration. It has been called the Establishment. Its luminaries have included John J. McCloy, James Forrestal, Robert Patterson, Robert Lovett, Arthur Dean, Eugene Black, Christian Herter, Lucius Clay—the mobile men who moved freely back and forth from corporate offices and law firms and banking houses into top government posts or offices or onto

Presidential advisory committees. While the original Establishment was getting long in the tooth by Lyndon Johnson's time, there was a new generation moving up, and its members or protégés remained imbedded in the bureaucracy. It was a force, and Johnson wanted all forces working for him. He also knew that Kennedy had captured the eggheads, and Johnson hankered for their support too, for he was ever conscious of seeming "regional"; and he wanted to be the great unifier, a President for all people; he wanted everything that Kennedy hadn't—business backing, for example, and the old South—and everything that Kennedy had; and he wasted no time setting out after it.

But to the extent that he wished to rekindle the love affair of the intellectuals with Kennedy, he was doomed to fail, just as he was doomed to fail with the press, and just as his early efforts to buffalo the world by overwhelming it were largely to produce, at best, increasing bafflement. To the extent that he wanted the same intimate connections Kennedy had with the Establishment, he was doomed to fail again. More devoted to ideas and ideology and institutions and the exercise of influence than to individuals, the hardy perennials of the Establishment, unlike the eggheads, rarely bestow upon any political figure the sort of unalloyed loyalty that Lyndon Johnson had always sought from his associates. The Establishment sees Presidents as its instrumentality, with Johnson, it would always have to be the other way around.

But to the extent that Johnson wanted help from the Establishment and from the eggheads or at least the appearance of support and a certain superficial harmony—which would have been more realistic—it was possible, for a time, to arrange a marriage of convenience. Leaving aside the egghead spectators—the intellectuals of the ivory tower, the poets and painters and playwrights— and enlarging the Establishment to include the new generation as well, one finds few in this wide grouping who could deny a fascination for the political prowess of Lyndon Johnson (while deriding his lack of grace) and few who could not be awed by the energy (while decrying his lack of intellectual sophistication). There were many who yearned to put his raw power to particular purposes, be they Medicare, or federal aid to higher education, or civil rights, or East-West trade, or disarmament, or a new China policy. There were some Washington eggheads-in-residence who made common cause from concern for their place in the sun.

The basis for accommodation was there, even among the Kennedy men. Though some drifted away to quieter cloisters, many stuck to their posts as a duty, and some of them were to become positively gripped by the political drama and intellectually engaged by the manner in which Johnson applied his unique talents to the practice of politics. McGeorge Bundy was one of those for whom the conduct of the Presidency and the obligation to serve (and the possibility of a higher office) counted more than the identity, or even congeniality of the occupant of the office, though Bundy was finally to accept the presidency of the Ford Foundation at the end of 1965.

Some responded to President Johnson's genuine need for brain power and flourished. One who did so for a while was Richard Goodwin, a talented speech-writer and imaginative initiator in Latin American policy-making for Kennedy, who had slipped (or been shoved) into the kind of Coventry that can so easily befall the innovator in government. Scintillating and ascerbic, he was a man of genuine cultivation, and his restoration by Johnson to a major role as Presidential speech-writer after the departure of Theodore Sorensen suited the purposes of both men for a time, though the grace of language Goodwin imparted to Johnson oratory often seemed out of tune with Johnson the man.

Ultimately, Goodwin also slipped away, though not completely; it was Johnson's habit to insist on retaining a call on the part-time services of all who served him if he could—partly out of need, partly because a clean break might be taken, somehow, as a mark against him. He was ever conscious of the appearance of things, especially where a genuine egghead or an Establishment figure was involved. He tried to replenish the egghead ranks, but while he was able to recruit such men as John Gardner as Secretary of HEW, and Charles Frankel, a Columbia University professor, as his Assistant Secretary of State for Educational and Cultural Affairs, he tended to implant his "thinkers" in their "natural" niches—education, culture, etc. When vacancies fell open, he searched the ranks of the bureaucracies and the career men for the can-do qualities he most admired.

In short, the estrangement between Johnson and the intellectuals, while it was to grow rapidly with the growth of the Vietnam war, cannot really be counted as an estrangement, because it was not even a very sound alliance from the start. Until November, the liberal left scarcely needed to be coaxed into the Johnson camp; Barry Goldwater was, after all, the alternative. It hardly needed to be coaxed into support for his domestic programs, for his were theirs. As for what could be perceived of his foreign policy, the egghead backing for it was never very strong; as for the Establishment, while it was to be called on from time to time to lend its weight to Johnson projects, its initial, pre-November allegiance was illusory, too. This was partly because the eggheads and the Establishment didn't fit into the Johnson scheme of things, and his beginning efforts to fit them in was as spurious as it was effusive.

Early in his Presidency, he set up a braintrust, composed of private thinkers of some renown from the business, university, and literary communities, headed by Professor Eric Goldman. Its stated mission was to generate new ideas and feed them to the government. But after it took a brief plunge into the poverty war and other aspects of the Great Society, less and less was heard of it. Other task forces, with impressive membership, were called on from time to time, not so much for new ideas as for embellishment of ideas already kicking around—on East-West trade, foreign aid, disarmament, education, and foreign economics. The point, in most cases, was political: to reinforce an argument for something the President wanted to sell to Congress or to a divided bureaucracy. The point of the Goldman exercise, as the President once candidly confided to a visitor, was "to keep the intellectuals happy."

And the real point of it all is that it didn't keep them happy, because Lyndon Johnson wasn't really trying.

They came to have the unmistakable impression they were being used and, in a sense, abused. "Dammit, I can't get a word in edgewise," one celebrated elder statesman exploded after a long session with the President, set up at Johnson's request, presumably for his own enlightenment. For intellectuals, and especially the academics and commentators who like to be listened to or at least engage in debate, encounters with the President were exercises in futility. At the very outset, Johnson did listen; but increasingly with the Great Persuader in the White House, argument tended to run all one way, and more than one important figure came away with the firm conclusion that he had been summoned, as others had been summoned before Johnson reached the Presidency, mostly for show, or to satisfy some inner relish for beckoning the mighty to the Johnson presence. This was not new; once, as Majority Leader, Johnson invited two of the most influential Senate liberals and a famed columnist to lunch to talk about Berlin—and spent the entire time in a monologue on Texas politics.

Nor were conditions for consultation with Johnson exactly ideal. A lunchtime invitation might—or might not—mean that food or refreshment would be made available; and if lunch had been specified, there was no telling when it might arrive, whether 1:00 P.M or 4:00 P.M. Johnson might give 10 intense minutes to the topic at hand, or sometimes more, but it was never certain at what stage the business at hand would be dealt with. He might simultaneously be sitting for a bust which he was having sculptured, taking or initiating phone calls (even with foreign dignitaries, he did this while his words were being translated until persuaded it was bad form), studying bills to be signed or vetoed, or reading priority cables; aides might walk in at any moment with drafts of letters or Presidential messages or decisions to be made. Visitors were also likely to come away with the impression that at least part of the purpose was for them to observe a can-do President can-doing.

And, indeed, the President did like to boast about whom he had seen. "Bill Fulbright was sitting in that chair right over there two days ago," he would say, by way of reinforcing his argument to his visitor of the moment; the point apparently was that if Fulbright was there, he must have been agreeing—or that his disagreement, at any rate, had been duly taken into account. He also liked to knock those members of the intelligentsia who disagreed with him. Handing the Dominican Republic back to Juan Bosch, the President was to say to register his lack of enthusiasm for the idea, "would be like turning it over to Arthur Schlesinger,

Jr." He would praise Walter Lippmann, especially in the earlier days before they came into conflict over Vietnam, but in a distinctly back-handed way. "He's a great man," the President once said, "because he agrees with me."

Agreement was the touchstone, and from this sprang the conclusion that Johnson didn't want to hear from those who disagreed; as time wore on, this was certainly less and less so—but the impression was to stick. So were some other impressions, which filtered down to the old hands in the government agencies, that the President was indecisive, leery of foreign policy, basically uninterested in it, and unwilling to do anything that might cut into his popularity. Both Lippmann and Acheson, among the sages, sought to persuade him to lead more lustily, take more chances, employ his power to enforce his will (though they rarely had the same course of action in mind).

In his encounters, Acheson and others found the President inclined to brood over past decisions, and castigate his counselors for offering proposals without assurances that they would work out. Their counterargument was that the U.S. President has more than enough power to make things turn out his way by application of sufficient energy and effort.

The complaint of many, in the early months of 1964, was that he was too preoccupied with Congressional reaction, too concerned with "consensus," too worried about appearances—and too talkative. Without pinpointing the Johnson Administration or mentioning that overworked word "consensus," Acheson was to voice, in a public speech in early 1965, the argument a good many students of the Presidency were making against Johnson, especially in the earlier days. "Agreement can always be reached by increasing the generality of the conclusion," he observed, adding: "When this is done, only the illusion of policy is created. The President gives his hierarchical blessing to platitude."

In the Senate, of course, a certain degree of "generality" in the conclusion may be required simply to round up enough votes. Similarly, in the Senate, a wise majority leader does not commit himself too tightly to a particular formulation—a key clause or section of a bill, or a proposed amendment. Who is to say what may have to be jettisoned to win passage at some later stage? It was no more than natural for the President to apply past habits and practices to the Presidency. But Dean Acheson had a stern warning on this point, too. "Flexibility of maneuver may be highly desirable in certain circumstances," the former Secretary of State said. "But when it leaves one's forces and commanders in doubt as to the nature and purpose of the campaign or who has responsibility for what, it can be a handicap."

Foreigners on the Washington scene were reaching the same conclusion; Johnson had charmed the Italians, Germans, and Japanese by amiable, uncontentious encounters with their heads of state. But, because they could see no policy lines vividly etched, the foreigners, like so many of the President's subordinates in his own government, concluded there must be no distinctive Johnson view, nothing he wished to initiate—that he was indeed uninterested. A high-ranking ambassador had reached the conclusion that Johnson probably never would move in the foreign field, except in ways that would shore up his domestic political position. "A feature of international affairs that has import on the home front might engage him," was this man's conclusion. Other diplomats who had wangled an audience found the President would light up a little over Latin America, was almost wholly uninterested in Africa, wanted more foreign nations to carry more of the load in Vietnam, was genuinely preoccupied with peace, would not object to easing the U.S. burden for defending Europe. But as one of their number expressed it: "It is tough to interest him in the amorphous areas where leadership is needed. He gets interested when it becomes immediate or affects Congress."

When De Gaulle proved unyielding, his Washington Ambassador did not appear at the White House functions where he had been a fixture in the Kennedy days. In fact, few ambassadors did, in a way that would do them the most good in the conduct of their jobs. Johnson began by entertaining them en masse. He seemed not to understand the response on one occasion, when he assembled all the Latin American envoys, both those accredited to the U.S. Government and those accredited to the oas, and asked them to tell him what was on their mind. There was an awkward hemming and hawing; as one who was there explained: "One thing a Latin diplomat won't do is talk to an American President in the presence of another Latin American diplomat—above all, another ambassador from his own country." But for the President, it was another argument for not lavishing upon diplomats more than a fraction of the solicitude he bestowed daily on Congressmen.

Similarly with the Soviets, Johnson filled the air with peace proposals for weeks, then turned to other things when nothing seemed to be coming of it, which set one influential European ambassador to wondering why the Johnson peace offensive "ran out of steam. In January, the President seemed to be serious about it. I can't imagine what put him off, but he does seem to have a rather short attention span." Another high-ranking diplomat who had not been able to engage the President in serious talks about anything, consoled himself after several encounters with the thought that maybe "he wasn't losing much by not knowing him well—he talks in such tremendous generalities, asks the most obvious questions; I wouldn't really know how to go about planting an idea."

What had put Johnson off, to borrow the ambassador's phrase, was that he was never really on in the conventionally accepted sense implied by the ambassador. He believed firmly in the great Vietnam peace campaign he launched in the beginning of 1966— for what it might produce. But he also believed quite firmly in it for appearances' sake if it did not produce anything; he could not see the point of pushing it endlessly, with undiminished interest and attention, in the absence of an encouraging response.

He believed in dispatching Attorney General Robert Kennedy for talks with Indonesia's President Sukarno in the early weeks, in search of a solution to the worsening Indonesia-Malaysia "confrontation." And if nothing much was to come of that, he also believed in earning an "E" for effort by having Kennedy make his report, on his return, to an open klieg-lit Cabinet meeting, rather than in the confidential confines of the President's office. He believed in sending Sargent Shriver off to the Middle East at the turn of the year as diplomatic trouble-shooter, and in ordering cabinet chiefs to barnstorm South Vietnam a few months later, for what good might come of it—and for appearances' sake. He believed, in short, in the appearance of motion, not so much as a

substitute for substance or meaningful action, but as an alternative to the appearance of inaction. He had always been obsessed
with trappings, with the sheer look of things, with putting on a
convincing show. (As one admiring American ambassador was to
say some months later, "I'd want to call on him on the way to a
new post even if he wasn't President—just for advice on how to
run my USIA operations. He's got all sorts of cute ideas.")

This is not to say that Johnson discounted content, or was dis-
interested in the meat of matters—though some were saying that,
too. But the new President, in this politically precarious period
when most matters of content and substance had been tempo-
rarily laid aside, felt more strongly than ever the need for
trappings. How else to project the impression of a can-do man,
when there is not a lot that he can profitably do? He was, accordingly, first baffled, then frustrated and resentful and often furious
at the reaction The Treatment sometimes seemed to evoke when
it was applied in the interests of diplomacy and world affairs.

"Khrushchev didn't think I was going to be a sap," Lyndon
Johnson was to protest, somewhat petulantly, to a visitor late in
the first year of his Presidency, and he was probably right. But
the significance of his saying it at all lay largely in the implication that he believed other people thought he *was* going to be—
and up to a point, he was right about that, too.

But if too many people had a tendency to expect the worst
from Lyndon Johnson in his handling of the world, it can likewise be said that at the beginning, Lyndon Johnson expected
more from the world—both the world at large, and the world
immediately around—and when he didn't get it, he seemed to
feel almost betrayed.

He had expected, out of innate energy and confidence and
exuberance and optimism and ego, that the world would be
more tractable, the Presidency more powerful, the influence of
the United States more decisive, the bureaucracy more immediately and faithfully responsive to his command, the press to be
in his pocket. He expected it, because, as he was to say somewhat
bitterly later in that first year, he fully believed he "had done
everything I could to avoid conflict, to avoid increasing tensions,
to avoid harassing." He had tried "to treat everybody the way I

would like to be treated." Over and over, he was to emphasize: "We must make allowances for the other fellow. A good way to treat him is just to assume that he wants to do for his own people what you want to do for yours." Again and again, he repeated a favorite refrain: "I try to be accommodating."

Congress, where he was a legend, was awed and responsive. The public seemed solidly behind him by all the pollsters' estimates in the beginning months. But foreign crises were exploding like Chinese firecrackers in all corners of the earth, and the movers and shakers of opinion at home and abroad—the White House press corps, the commentators, the foreign correspondents, the diplomats both foreign and domestic, the academicians—were not, in Lyndon Johnson's judgment, being accommodating.

As early as February, accordingly, Lyndon Johnson was beginning to dig in, defensively. Zanzibar and East Africa were making ugly headlines. De Gaulle was pushing "neutralism" for South Vietnam, in open defiance of U.S. designs; Johnson had protested in private and in vain against French recognition of Communist China. The Communists had shot down an errant U.S. aircraft over East Germany. There were Cyprus and Panama. In a February press conference, the President was making what seemed to be a strategic withdrawal from any appraisal of the world and the U.S. role in it, that he had been heard to voice before reaching the Presidency. In East Africa, he observed, "we can hardly hope to control events."

He had opened the conference with a prepared checklist of foreign troubles, and he had a moral to go with it: "This past week, the United States has demonstrated anew in at least eight different situations this nation's determination to insure peace and freedom in the widest possible area. Progress toward these ends is frequently slow and rarely dramatic, but it should be viewed in the perspective of history and not headlines."

A week later he went before a gathering of officials of the Internal Revenue Service, and chose this unlikely forum for a long impromptu discourse about foreign affairs; it was one of those rambling, off-the-cuff soliloquies of the sort which were to become anathema to his advisers, but which usually could be counted on to mirror with some fidelity whatever was uppermost in the President's mind.

"I have seen times when the skies were grayer," he declared. "We don't have on our hands this morning a missile crisis in Cuba. We don't have Laos (though he soon would have a renewed Pathet Lao offensive). We don't have the conference in Vienna that we faced the first few months of President Kennedy's Administration—the Bay of Pigs—all of those were major problems."

The things-could-be-much-worse ploy was to become a major bulwark of his defenses, in private as well as in public, and with that ploy, was beginning to come (mostly in private) the things-were-worse-under-Kennedy insinuation which was to do little to ease the tension between the White House "Texans" and the large army of hold-over Kennedy men. Another developing theme, which bore the unmistakable imprint of Dean Rusk, was that if the United States had troubles, they were "relatively speaking" less serious than those confronting the Communist world. The Russian-Chinese quarrel, the President said, is "something that must concern both of them."

Americans can also make mistakes, he patiently explained. Panamanians had no business invading the Canal Zone and shooting our soldiers, and the Communists had no business shooting down that aircraft—but American schoolchildren should not have incited the Panamanians by hoisting that forbidden flag, and the plane was off course.

As for South Vietnam, the President seemed to believe the less said, the better. He had not even mentioned the conflict, as such, in his State of the Union message a few weeks earlier—referring to it only obliquely in the context of civil rights (all races were serving side by side in the military advisory contingents in Vietnam) and in a broad allusion to the global threat of infiltration and guerrilla war. If Saigon seemed more than necessarily unstable to the assembled tax-collectors, the President had statistics of blinding irrelevance showing that in NATO nations alone in the past year, 10 out of 15 governments had changed hands, and that of the 113 nations in the world, 50 had had a change of government over the past three years. (Irrevelant statistics were to become a fixture in his foreign-policy presentation; he had his aides assemble endless data on telephone calls made, meetings held, hours spent in connection with a particular foreign crisis, as well as over-all figures on the amount of time he devoted personally to reading cables from ambassadors, studying foreign-policy position papers, and making decisions in the foreign field.)

Two other major themes were beginning to emerge, one drawn from an article of Johnson faith: "Regardless of what you hear and regardless of what some of the bellyachers say, we are a much beloved people throughout the world." He had traveled in many continents, and his plane had touched down in more than 30 countries, and "the wheels have never stopped, and the door has never opened, and I have never looked upon any faces that I didn't think would like to trade citizenship with me." It is not necessary to consider, for even a moment, the validity of this claim in order to gauge its impact abroad.

One note, however, reflected an easy-come, easy-go approach not normally associated with Johnson in his pre-Presidential days, but one which would emerge as a major campaign talking point in answer to the daring designs of Barry Goldwater for hurling U.S. weight around the world. "We cannot expect to mash a button," the President said, illustrating what he meant with a fine flourish of his thumb, "and have our wishes carried out all over the globe."

Also barely perceptible was the beginning of another Johnson trait which was to become increasingly a part of his defense under fire on all matters, but especially in foreign affairs, a field destined to draw down upon him the heaviest volleys of criticism in the months ahead. It was never enough to meet the challenge of dissenters on its merits; it was to become his unfortunate habit to intimate that the "bellyachers," knowingly or not, were playing disloyally into the hands of the enemy. "From time to time, you will hear alarmists and people who like to jump on their government, people who like to criticize, people who find it quite impossible to be affirmative and constructive," the President told the revenue men. "They will join with some of our opponents, and they will be almost as much of a problem as some of our other enemies."

All in all, it was a curious, dubious, scatter-shot defense from a man who was beginning to show how quickly public criticism can drive him to inordinate defensiveness. Later, as the Vietnamese involvement deepened, the assault on dissent was to grow more explicit: newsmen who wrote of the Administration's Vietnam strategy were to be accused of jeopardizing the lives of U.S. troops; Congressmen or commentators who counseled conciliation were to be very nearly consigned to the Communist camp. For this, he was to be assailed, in turn, for stifling debate; for denying, in fact, elemental Constitutional rights. The President, needless to say, never saw it that way. For him, it was not so much a question of legality or even morality as of utility and practicality. He would use arguments as he used institutions or individuals, for the sake of their instrumentality at any given time. Everything—the press, the Congress, the course of events abroad, the samplings of opinion at home, the inner tugs and hauls of the bureaucracies, the interplay of pressure groups—was there to be used, to be bent to his own purposes and priorities. It is for this reason that is next to impossible to examine his performance at any particular moment and extrapolate from it enduring policy unless one first understands the method behind it. It is for this reason that even a tentative recital of the Johnson record in foreign affairs requires initial comprehension of the complexity of the Johnson approach.

The Johnson Approach

Shortly after the 1964 election, Lyndon Johnson seemed preoccupied with his Great Society program in Congress and with
the civil-rights upheaval at home. He also seemed to be withdrawing from the problems of Europe and paralyzed by doubts
about what to do in Vietnam. One of his closest confidants was
asked whether the United States was not "disengaging" from the
world. His reply was couched in the circumlocutions common to
confidential advisers of Presidents, which can be taken to mean
nothing—or everything:

"The President approaches international affairs as an extension
of the game of national politics," he said. "There is no element
of isolation or withdrawal from the game of politics, whether
local, national, or international."

There it was, in capsule form—the essence of the Johnson approach to foreign policy. There, also, is as good a short answer as could be made, not just to the question of "disengagement" but to a broader question that had been troubling policy-makers and opinion-makers for a good many months before November 3: Just when would the new President, in earnest and in depth, begin putting his mind to the awesome agenda of foreign problems that had been piling up all through that long summer and fall while he had been out hunting down every last vote? For weeks before the voting, Johnson had abandoned the intimate Tuesday lunches with Rusk, McNamara, and McGeorge Bundy, which were his chosen forum (in contrast with the Kennedy "seminar system") for really serious consideration of international problems. While communications had by no means been broken with his top lieutenants, contact had been catch-as-catch-can; at a critical moment in the Cyprus affair, the President had to be called away from a Democratic fund-raising dinner; Congo crisis-managers recall tracking him down on some distant hustings more than once. Vietnam had been only the most conspicuous casualty of electoral distractions; it was over this stretch that the U.S. position on the MLF escaped Johnson control; the character of the U.S. attitude to the whole Third World altered significantly; the seeds of rebellion in the Dominican Republic were sown by lack of top-level U.S. attention to that historic trouble spot; the Congo slipped further towards rebellion; the United States dug itself deeper into its dilemma over U.N. financing. The momentum of an unattended bureaucracy was hauling the United States in directions Johnson was later to regret.

The election had been everything—and foreigners and foreign affairs were expected to do nothing except, where possible, advance the Johnson electoral cause. The Cabinet was conscripted to the crusade as never before; the Departments of State and Defense were mobilized to answer every Goldwater argument. Foreign visitors, whether Mexico's López Mateos, Canada's Lester Pearson, or NATO Secretary General Manlio Brosis were billed as feature attractions on the Johnson circuit. When the opposition hinted at the return of Soviet missiles to Cuba, reconnaissance flights were urgently stepped up to disprove the charges. Even

China's nuclear detonation on October 1 was turned into a political plus, of sorts. When the United States got solid intelligence
warning of the detonation three weeks earlier, the State Department took the unusual step of sharing these usually top-secret
gleanings in minute detail with the American public, in part for
the purpose of proving in advance that the Administration had
not been caught napping. When the explosion came, as predicted,
the President could boast that it was "no surprise to the United
States Government." In his private talkathons with newsmen,
Lyndon Johnson reasoned that a Chinese nuclear capability became a positive argument for his election: "We can't let Goldwater and Red China both get the bomb at the same time."

When asked if he planned an "intensive" campaign, Johnson
had replied in a rare understatement: "You know I do everything
intensively." He intended not just to defeat Goldwater but to
demolish Goldwaterism, and there were many among his foreign-
policy advisers who could only applaud; the specter of Goldwaterism, as it was understood abroad, was only aggravating the
impression, engendered by the Dallas violence, of a nation in the
throes of a social and political malaise. It seemed reasonable
enough, also, that Johnson should wish to make his victory as
crushing as possible; only the cruelest of accidents had elevated
him to candidacy, and it would have been out of character for
him not to wish to establish himself as a popular, national figure,
capable of commanding support from all areas and segments of
American society.

So there was a tendency to dismiss the electoral frenzy as a
passing phenomenon, peculiar to the circumstances. In the early
weeks of November, while a triumphant Johnson was down at
the ranch resting from his campaign labors, and Washington was
waiting for the next act of the Johnson drama, the policy- and
opinion-makers already had—or thought they had—the script
worked out. Exit Goldwater, it read, as the campaign hubbub
dies away; at center stage is Lyndon Johnson, his desk piled high
with the blueprints of a Great Society on one side, a catalogue of
world crises on the other. With the Great Society plans, the
master parliamentarian, with comfortable Congressional majorities, would have no problems. So he would be swiveled increas-

ingly toward blueprints for the world; there would be foreign travels and summit conferences; the foreign-policy making machinery would soon be humming because a freshly elected President, his power base secure, would naturally turn to the great, history-making international concerns, to his role as statesman and pre-eminent leader in a sorely troubled world.

It was all very logical and orthodox, and, in a certain sense, events would give it validity. Crises in the Atlantic Alliance, in Vietnam, in the Dominican Republic, in East-West relations— all these did turn Johnson toward the most intense concentration on international affairs. But not in the way the Washington script-writers had in mind. The interplay of foreign affairs and domestic politics that had been demonstrated in excessive degree in the political campaign was not, as it turned out, peculiar to the circumstances. The play of the one against the other; the addiction to instrumentalities; the balancing of forces and pressures for the accomplishment of multiple purposes, both domestic and foreign and all according to a firm set of priorities—this was peculiar to the man, as those of his principal counselors who had not already suspected it were quick to find out.

Methods and Mentors

Johnson arrived at the White House as a man uncomfortable in the presence of experts—out of his own vanity—and curiously untutored about the ways of bureaucracy. From his role as Congressional inquisitor, he knew how to make bureaucrats hurt, but he was less practiced in making bureaucracy work. He was eager —also out of vanity—to try things his way, but prudent enough not to rush irrevocably into situations he did not understand.

"There will be no Walloonias," said one knowledgeable Lyndonologist, as the Johnson Presidency began, in a reference to a Roosevelt proposal after World War II to carve a new state of Walloonia out of the Walloon areas of Belgium, Luxembourg, Alsace-Lorraine, and a portion of northern France—a proposal that raised sharp doubts in Sir Anthony Eden's mind about Roosevelt's grasp of fundamental geography.

Caution, curiously enough, is the single word that comes to

mind most quickly in any effort to define the Johnson approach to foreign policy. Any sensible politician runs scared, of course, but with Johnson it was more than that. He seemed, from all evidence, to see his own political position as chronically precarious; the permanence of his power under constant threat; his popularity susceptible to sudden erosion should he suffer a serious setback; the loyalty of his subordinates in need of regular reaffirmation. Some who knew him well attributed it to realistic awareness that his regionalism rendered him suspect; to realization that the election contest had been a monumental mismatch and hence no great test of his strength; to his acute dependence on men he inherited and kept for lack of any cadre of top-flight "Johnson men" with which to staff his government; to a recognition of a strange lack of charisma. It was probably a combination of all of this that gave rise within a few weeks after his immense Presidential victory to a long lecture to a select group of his most prominent foreign-policy advisers on the importance of prudence and on the awful ease by which his whole domestic and international political position could be collapsed by one breach anywhere along the front. As pieced together by those who heard it or heard reliably about it, it is perhaps worth setting down at this point; it embodies the essence of the Johnson philosophy of politics and bears heavily on his conduct of foreign relations in the first two years of his Presidency.

He had scored a sharp defeat for "screwballism," he told the group, and racked up a vote of confidence for "sanity." But he had no mandate for anything like Roosevelt's "one hundred days." Yet the liberals and other groups would be calling for just that; the columnists would be counting and keeping score. The Republicans and the entrenched elders on Capitol Hill would be watching for an issue on which they could deliver a stinging rebuff. And one defeat could break his stride, even wreck his program in the coming session of Congress. Perhaps the men around him (who were mostly foreign-policy experts) did not understand the pitfalls in large majorities, but the numbers are illusory. Indeed, party discipline breaks down when there is less need for every last vote.

The problem, as he saw it, was not the 1966 Congressional

elections. These would take care of themselves, with only slight losses in the House and Senate majorities if he had a successful session of Congress in 1965. Conversely, if Congress should find an excuse to turn on him in 1965—and there is always a built-in anti-Presidential vote ready to exert Congressional mastery over the Executive if once the potential for doing so is established by one significant Presidential defeat—there would be no hope of recouping in 1966 before the off-year election. So caution and prudence were called for. He must look "sane, sound, and solvent," and "all you fellows must be prudent about what you encourage me to go for."

For his part, he would be keeping a sharp eye on everything submitted to him, to be sure he was not sending anything provocative or controversial that would invite a defeat in Congress.

The President's concern was rooted in his reading of two precedents, which his oldest associates consider fundamental to his political concept of the totality of Presidential power. One was the "court-packing" proposal of Franklin Roosevelt in 1937. Johnson talked often of his determination to "avoid another 1937"; that was a time when Lyndon Johnson himself was coming of age politically, and the lesson he learned then was that opposition to the court-packing scheme was almost literally transferred into hostility to Roosevelt's foreign policy. He has the same burning concern about "another 1919"—the defeat of the League of Nations by the Senate—which he believed was equally lasting in its impact on Woodrow Wilson's command of Congress. By Johnson's reckoning, a President has a limited store of political capital, which must be carefully rationed in support of programs with reasonable promise of acceptance and against unforeseen contingencies. A poor hand, or one badly played, he always reasoned, could quickly get him in over his head and cost him all his chips.

Characteristically, the President had a story to illustrate his point. It was of a Texan who blew his entire year's paycheck on a bottle of whisky and a string of firecrackers, and then drank all the whisky and set off all the firecrackers on New Year's Eve. "I worked like hell to get to be President," he reportedly told the group, "and I don't want to set it all off at once."

The President's words of warning on this occasion concerned prospective legislation that might get him into trouble in Congress, but his concept of the interrelation between domestic and foreign affairs is a good deal more complicated than that. It begins with a firm conviction, as expressed by one long-time associate, that "the American people won't support any foreign policy unless their own needs are being met." That makes welfare programs at home a foundation for foreign policy. Lyndon Johnson would go further and offer the Great Society as an essential element of foreign policy, on the theory that a U.S. Government can deal effectively and from strength in the world only if it is seen to be dealing effectively with its own domestic ills. "Johnson always argued that the New Deal is what made Roosevelt a commanding figure around the world when the United States hardly had a foreign policy at all," one of the White House Texans once observed.

Johnson was reinforced in this view by his minister for foreign affairs, ironically enough; Dean Rusk talked long hours with him of the importance of aggressive U.S. efforts to deal with civil rights, with poverty, with the problems of the aged and the ill, with the great urban questions, and with other domestic issues as a fundamental prerequisite to a strong U.S. position in the world. Talking on this question, in December, 1963, just after Johnson came to power, Rusk listed civil rights in the United States as a "basic national commitment" and said that "until we meet these commitments, our voice is muted abroad. I would not suggest that there is not discrimination in many other countries. But more is expected of the United States. We are looked upon as a leader. They are watching us . . . and when we fail to meet our commitments, this has a major impact on other countries." When Johnson took to brooding about criticism that he was not spending enough time on foreign policy, Rusk even took the trouble to look up the work habits of FDR, and on more than one occasion took pains to reassure the President that the Johnson idol of the 1930's had not spent an inordinate amount of time on foreign-policy questions himself.

Johnson took special pleasure, by way of demonstrating the international impact of his domestic legislative achievements, in pointing out that some of his programs were the envy of foreign leaders—and at a time, he would say defensively, when he was being called a "buffoon" with insufficient sophistication to deal in the diplomatic realm. The Prime Ministers of Canada and Britain, he never tired of recounting to visitors, had asked for copies of his Medicare bill, and, he would add with an edge of sarcasm, "and I mean they are very enlightened, sophisticated, stylish people—I mean people with real class."

Other times, he would link foreign affairs to his legislative position in more practical terms: "I need domestic legislation much more than I need anything else," he would say. "The only foreign legislation I need is the appropriations bill. I can't have any foreign policy if I go broke or if the balance of payments is bad or if I have no army or if there are deep divisions in the Congress and the country."

At this point, the Johnson reasoning comes full circle and takes on deep significance in his approach to the major crises of his first two years. For example, the reasoning would begin with his assessment that it would be bad politics at home to cave in quickly to Panamanian rioters (even though he was prepared to be more than generous, by any previous standards, when the appearance of pressure was removed); that it would be unpopular to allow the U.S. position to collapse in Vietnam, even into a "neutralist" solution, because of the "appeasement" stigma this might carry with it; that even slight risk of "another Cuba" in the Dominican Republic would be political suicide; that a full cross-section of Congress was against the MLF; that disarmament proposals or recommendations for easing East-West trade barriers would stir the cold warriors of Congress at a period of maximum tension over Vietnam (but not, let it be noted, at other times); that foreign aid to countries whose citizens burn libraries or whose rulers denounce U.S. policy in Vietnam or elsewhere is political anathema.

A reply may be made, with great force, that a President ought to follow the unpopular, politically dangerous course for the sake of sound policy and good sense and in the long-range national interest. The case could be made, in short, that the test should be not what is popular, but what is the right foreign policy.

And the Johnson counterargument, continuing around the circle, would be that foreign policy and domestic policy are indivisible; that a foreign policy which wrecks his domestic political program or undercuts his power at home leaves him incapable of conducting any effective international policy. To the argument that a President is powerful enough to make a policy popular, he would answer that if in the effort, he makes himself unpopular, he becomes powerless. Johnson scorned the word "consensus" as the invention of pundits, but he did not scorn its meaning. For a nation's foreign policy to succeed, he has said privately on a number of occasions, it "must have a reasonable unanimity behind it." A close adviser, putting it somewhat differently, once declared that "the President simply doesn't believe out of all his experience that you can force a foreign-policy issue on the people."

All this is not to say that Johnson did not see valid arguments on the issue of national security, for the positions he took in Vietnam or Santo Domingo or Panama. It is simply to note that the positions he took also fit precisely into his grand concept of the domestic political realities underlying the conduct of foreign policy. No President, to be sure, could ever ignore the impact of foreign developments on his domestic political position, and few were ever unaware of the importance of their domestic political position on their standing and their country's influence abroad. So it might be argued that the Johnson approach is not unique, that his emphasis on the interplay of all political forces at home and abroad differed from his predecessors' only in matter of degree. But in practice, the degree of difference was so enormous, the intertwining of the two so nearly total, that it is impossible to extract a single element and extrapolate from it a reliable, enduring characterization of Johnson's foreign policy. There was a distinctive quality to the whole, a form and a flavor which people might call a policy because elements in it might correspond to a plan or a program or a doctrine that had been concocted in the conventional, traditional fashion by the foreign-policy-making process. The structure of government, after all, lends credence to distinctions between domestic and foreign programs, each with their own proponents and advocates.

But Lyndon Johnson does not deal in such conventional terms; he deals in the utility of things whose import, or permanence, or real purpose had always to be cast against his own intricate calculations, wholly known to no one of his counselors—calculations which could make a particular proposal an utterly valid bedrock of policy today and a positive pitfall tomorrow. It might depend on a recently received public-opinion poll, or the opposition of a key Senator whose support was more urgently needed for something of a higher priority. It might be an element germane to the merits of the matter, or merely useful as an argument—a timely cable from an ambassador, a newspaper report, the conclusions of a panel of private experts, an adverse recommendation from a pressure group, a Congressional committee hearing, the findings, however erroneous, brought back by a voyaging lawmaker, or merely one man's word, or one bureaucracy's stand against another's.

It usually came down not just to utility, but to multiple utility. Thus the sudden Johnson trip to Honolulu in early 1966, with a fair portion of his Cabinet in attendance, had as its primary purpose a congregation of Asian statesmen, together with the President, to emphasize the multinational involvement in Vietnam. (The proposal was first presented by McGeorge Bundy in September, 1965, before the President's gall bladder operation.) It was also intended to bring the President together with Saigon Government leaders, to establish a closer personal relationship between Johnson and his Vietnam military commander, General William Westmoreland, and to dramatize and advance U.S. efforts to promote economic, social, and political reform in South Vietnam as an offset to the seeming concentration on shot and shell. But its timing, when the President finally snapped up the proposal, was largely dictated by a desire to snatch attention away from the Senate Foreign Relations Committee hearings on Vietnam, in which Administration policy was coming under heavy attack. And to do this, the meeting had to be set up so quickly that there was no time to assemble the leaders of Australia, New

Zealand, the Philippines, Thailand, and Korea, which was a large part of the original intent.

When the President set up a committee of distinguished private citizens headed by former Deputy Secretary of Defense Roswell Gilpatric to study new arms-control measures and announced its creation on November 1, 1964, two days before the election, one of the most senior professional diplomats in the State Department privately wrote it off as an election gimmick. In its timing, it was. But its report was also one of the most careful, far-reaching, and thoughtful disarmament studies ever undertaken. While it served electioneering purposes, by calculation, it also had behind it the influence and encouragement of powerful Presidential counselors, also by calculation. Its findings, however, had still not been made public—or indeed made adequate use of—by early 1966. Why? "The President was all steamed up and then all of a sudden he seemed to lose interest," said one official in a position to know. "My feeling is he thought it simply wasn't the right time, in early 1965, that it didn't strike the right balance, to be pushing disarmament all that hard with the Russians when Vietnam was stirring cold war fever in Congress."

When the Dominican Republic intruded violently upon Johnson's preoccupation with Congress and Vietnam, he first moved frantically to get it damped down; and when criticism swirled around his military intervention, he felt compelled to counter-attack, to try to turn it, if possible, into an actual political plus. He knew, because he had argued the point in private with visitors, that it was no help to the peace-making efforts of the oas for him to introduce into the situation the complicating political issue of whether Communists were at the root of it, since this was not demonstrable beyond a doubt; yet he suddenly took to national television, on short notice, to proclaim that his fast action had, in fact, forestalled another Communist state in the Western Hemisphere.

As with events, so it was with individuals. Perhaps the most astonishing aspect of the Johnson personnel policy in the foreign field was that after more than two years, there were almost no Johnson men; rather there were Kennedy men and up-from-the-ranks career men, whose loyalty to the President had been put to prolonged and careful test. The key men were three—Rusk, Mc-Namara, and for two years, McGeorge Bundy. Others won the President's confidence only after prolonged probation; indeed, he treated the bureaucracies, collectively, as he might treat a foreign power, or a collection of foreign powers, with his staff as envoys playing them off against each other, balancing the forces at work —while simultaneously balancing these forces against that of the men of power on the Hill. While pursuing Kennedy policies to deal with what he considered to be Kennedy legacies, he used Kennedy men (just as with those problems he considered Eisenhower legacies, he was delighted to make use of the steady support of General Eisenhower). But he also leaned heavily on the professionals; maximum security, he seemed to believe, lay in a unanimous recommendation from "the country team."

And on the rare occasions when he made a distinctively Johnsonian appointment, extreme prudence, lengthy deliberation, and multiplicity of purpose were usually the guiding rules. Tom Mann was the first instance; other included his CIA Director, Admiral William Raborn, a favorite in Congress but with few credentials as an intelligence chief; Maxwell Taylor, a distinguished soldier who would give an air of efficient militancy to the job of Ambassador to South Vietnam for the sake of those who might question U.S. resolve, while also bespeaking prudence, for at the time he was appointed, Taylor did not favor an expansion of the war and neither, in mid-1964, did Lyndon Johnson.

But the most celebrated appointment of a "Johnson man" was the choice of Associate Justice Arthur Goldberg as Ambassador to the United Nations. Something quite out of the ordinary was indicated to fill the shoes of Adlai Stevenson, and the recruitment of a Supreme Court Justice, a brilliant negotiator, a man whose whole career was the very essence of the American dream, and a leading member of an important political minority group, was a masterstroke in itself. Almost certainly, however, there was even more to it than that. What Johnson—and Goldberg—may have had in mind is impossible to say, and it didn't stop people from saying that Goldberg would provide an interesting policy-making balance to the dogged, high-principled, moralistic, hard line of Dean Rusk (perhaps even a possible successor); that he was visible evidence of Johnson's yearning to find a negotiated solution in Vietnam; that he might emerge, if not as Secretary of State, conceivably as a Johnson running-mate in 1968 should Humphrey fall from grace; that he might also move into a position of political influence in New York, and that Lyndon Johnson might wish to have a beachhead in Robert Kennedy's power base. A lot of people were thereby to be kept on their toes. The Goldberg appointment, in sum, was authentic Johnson, and there were few who did not marvel at what they took to be its Machiavellian multiplicity of objective: entirely valid on its merits, every useful gain whether relevant or not to its main aim had been extracted skillfully, with the help of a showy send-off and regular manifestations of Johnson's special interest in "his man" at the U.N.

To serious students of government, Johnson was the master manager of "the processes," "the balancer of forces." To those who had known him longest it was all still politics. Just as he had manipulated the forces for and against him in the Senate, so, as President, he would cite the liberal promoters of peace in Congress as an irresistible pressure upon him, in argument with the war dogs in the Pentagon, and as quickly cite the Republican war dogs on the Hill and the pollsters' samplings of hard-line sentiment in the country as a force he simply had to reckon with, when answering the arguments of the advocates of negotiations and easy Vietnam settlement terms. It was never an easy game to follow, but after two years, the kaleidoscopic happenings had fallen into a certain mosaic in which it was possible to detect a distinctive, consistent design. Examined closely, it reveals, if nothing quite so grand as a Johnson Foreign Policy, at least a recognizable pattern of response and performance, a method of operation, a code of conduct for the international arena derived from domestic political experience and applied, with remarkably little adjustment, to relations with the world. Some of the fundamental strictures are perhaps worth setting forth at this point for whatever guide they may offer in following the critical developments in Lyndon Johnson's second year as President.

Lyndon Johnson's Common Law

Don't tread on me. Foreign officials, as well as his own advisers, came to learn that the least effective way to influence Johnson was to push him publicly—with rioting, or with rhetoric. Those who tried (Lester Pearson, J. W. Fulbright, Harold Wilson) provoked a rough response. Those who persisted fell from grace. Those who took cognizance of his political problems found him remarkably ready to take cognizance of theirs. Those who confined their critiques to private colloquy got a hearing—sometimes.

The prime time for decision-making is when everybody else has shown his hand. Critics called this dithering, or plain indecisiveness. But Johnson had a low opinion of the U.S. capability to order events, and scant interest in anything as unrewarding as preventive diplomacy, when there was no demonstrable need of action and no promise of recognition or reward. He didn't introduce the word "option" to the Washington vocabulary, but he recoiled from evangelists, resisted commitment, and prized those who made it their business to help him keep his options open.

Never lose, or at least never be seen losing. Authority, the President had always believed, derives from the art of persuasion, which in turn is most effective when reinforced by an aura of invincibility. The safest majority for him was always the largest majority, if only for the starkly practical reason that he knew how quickly in political life a majority can melt away. "One real slip and I'm done for," he said more than once, and with grim emphasis.

The proper time for public debate about a Presidential decision is after the decision has been made. He was roundly criticized for stifling criticism. But to a man of no intellectual bent, argument for argument's sake could be only an encumbrance to his aims. Lyndon Johnson saw it as the responsibility of a political leader to remove all encumbrances to his aims.

A free press was the one major mistake the Founding Fathers made. In theory it may be sound; in practice it is about as useful as an attack of hives. With Johnson, this was not just a sometime concern; it was a fixation. He and his closest associates made no bones about their concept of how a President's thinking ought to be conveyed to the public—by Presidential appearance on TV, without comment or interpretation or analysis. He relished favorable press comment, of course, and devoted endless hours to promoting more; but he was never satisfied.

Never slam doors, even to the opposition, as long as there is faint hope that some business can be done. The rule does not apply to enemies thought to be implacable—for example, the Communist Chinese. "Lyndon never had much time for nay votes," said an old-time Senate colleague. "But he always had time for aye votes, and for votes he thought he could switch."

We shall overwhelm. To Johnson, the notion comes naturally: The only way to do anything is at least several times larger than life. He did it with words. "The President always believes in saying things at least thirty times, on the theory that you may not have heard him, or understood him, or believed him, the first twenty-nine," an aide once explained. He did it with extravaganza, or with sheer force, or with dramatic effects, whether by a flying-circus peace offensive, or an extended tour of the White House living quarters, or a long harangue in the East Room, or a spur-of-the-moment visit, or the most effusive flattery—or the landing of 21,000 Marines in Santo Domingo. "When you move, you move with everything," Presidential aide Jack Valenti once said of this article of faith. "You remove all doubts."

Things you do may be irretrievable—but almost nothing you say is. True, the President is ever chary of binding public pledges —though he ignored them more than once; in private, he felt it is still less necessary to be scrupulously faithful to the precise facts. There is no harm in hyperbole, or even in a little dissembling, on behalf of a worthy cause; later will be time enough to straighten out the facts.

Almost anybody or anything can be moved if you can find the right levers; until you do find them, it is wiser not to try. "What do they need from us?" was almost the first question Johnson asked when confronted with an international issue or when readying himself for an encounter with a visiting foreign leader, and along with it came a related inquiry: "Where does the power lie?" It was Johnson's unfailing practice, when confronted with no clear opportunity for bringing power to bear or exerting influence, to step back and examine what could be done to reset the stage, to redress the power balance. That, essentially, was his approach in Panama; that was the point of his abrupt rebuff to Pakistan and India in the spring of 1965. It was a good part of the point of introducing air strikes against North Vietnam, as a means of piling more chips on his side of the table against the day when it might be possible to negotiate from greater strength.

Prestige is nice, but respect is more useful; respect derives, in the last analysis, from results. The President once put this precept rather more pungently to an august gathering of his most distinguished advisers when the question arose whether to honor an apparent U.S. commitment to a proposition which Congress seemed unlikely to accept. Face-saving, the President observed, was not his major purpose in life. "While you're trying to save your face," he declared, "you're losing your ass."

Doing something for nothing is a violation of every law of practical politics. With Johnson, barter was a way of life; he is faithful in the execution of his end of the bargain—and he expects others to be.

Surprise is a fundamental weapon. "When people know in advance what you are going to do, opposition has time to jell," is the way one Johnson devotee explained this law. This in itself helps explain that impression of impetuosity so out of keeping with the man of prudence. In fact, most of the time Johnson only *looked* impetuous.

Bill Moyers once discussed what he called the President's "studied impulsiveness" and "planned spontaneity."

"It's very important for the President to keep the element of surprise as a tactical weapon in the arsenal of moving his government forward," Moyers said. "If his moves are known in advance, if his options are identified prior to actual implementation, then his opponents . . . can move to choke off his options."

A career diplomat, who found some of the Johnson surprises (the flying peace offensive, or the sudden safari to Honolulu, for two examples) "alien to everything I had been taught to believe in thirty years about the proper conduct of diplomacy," was also willing to concede that it might just be effective. "The President is only impulsive about gimmicks, about things that relate to appearances," he declared. "The actual content of his actions is usually pretty carefully prepared."

Elementary rules, perhaps, but also infinitely complex in their application to international affairs, and most of them related, one way or another, in the opinion of many serious Lyndonologists, to that curious sense of insecurity. The emphasis on outsized, larger-than-life, eye-catching, headline-grabbing, transfixing activity; on invincibility, or perhaps intimidation; on supreme loyalty—all these were the mark of a man uncertain about his own capacity to command. Some observers laid it to hard realities: Johnson did not have, and probably never would have, charisma. He had always had to overwhelm, as well as maneuver artfully. "Kennedy could make a decision, or an appointment, or a speech and be convincing about it; it was enough for him that he was Kennedy and he was President," said one. "With Johnson, he seems to feel a necessity for circuses, sideshows, Roman candles, klieg lights, to get his point across." On one occasion Johnson argued for an hour with two close aides over inclusion, in a Vietnam speech, of an announcement that he was recalling two of his top men in Saigon for consultation; he wanted it in there for headline purposes and was only barely persuaded that a speech by the President of the United States was headline-making in its own right. (As it turned out, he made the announcement the next day to a swarm of Congressman at the White House, assembled for a Presidential lecture on the merits of U.S. policy in Vietnam, and wound up dominating the news pages two days running.)

But the effect, more often than not, of the accompanying pyrotechnics was to cast doubt on the real content of whatever he was saying or doing. Almost always there *was* real content; the aerial peace offensive was accompanied by a 37-day bombing "pause"; the big talk about bridge-building to Eastern Europe was backed up by imaginative disarmament proposals and bold initiatives to loosen East-West trade. Though Johnson embellished his foreign aid proposals more than once with meaningless figures—everything from Southeast Asian development to his emphasis on education, health, and famine relief had a habit of totaling up to a nice, round $1 billion—the programs were real.

Yet he contrived to make them sound, to the skeptical and

even to the dispassionate onlooker, somehow a little phony. And because they looked or sounded phony, they came under needless attack by the opinion-makers; this only served to aggravate their predisposition to distrust.

Some would argue that this was of no great consequence—that the world at large had been shouted at, and quarreled over, and bombarded by propaganda from the Communist camp and from the West in response for so long that shock treatment had become the only effective form of communication. Henry Kissinger had written, long before Lyndon Johnson reached the White House, of the degeneration of classic diplomacy into a "struggle to seize the symbols that move humanity." Lyndon Johnson, as one of his aides remarked after two years of the Johnson Presidency, was a "great symbol-seizer."

In time, the technique might prove uniquely applicable, for the decisions that confronted Lyndon Johnson increasingly were not of the sort that sold themselves; they were either expensive, or undramatic, or unrewarding, or inconclusive, or otherwise hard to justify. In 1964, they were inhibited by the pursuit of votes; in 1965, they were hedged in and encumbered by the over-riding, all-pervasive influence of a widening struggle in Vietnam. And while that problem would become his one great postelection preoccupation, the making of a Johnson policy for Vietnam was preceded by a brush with a much more mundane issue, which was nonetheless a significant preparation. It was to make him, to a far greater extent than he had been in his first year, the master of his own policy-making machinery.

MLF–Or, How He Does It

It is in the nature of big government that a good measure of mystique, a rich variety of motives, and evangelical zeal are almost essential to propel anything controversial or revolutionary through the bureaucratic bogs and on up to the bureaucratic peaks. For the same reason, a project once embedded in high policy is almost as difficult to dislodge. And nothing illustrates the point better than the famous case of the multilateral nuclear force (MLF), a U.S. proposal for a NATO flotilla of surface ships armed with Polaris missiles, whose atomic warheads would be under U.S. control. Employment and deployment of the missiles would be subject to close and continuing consultation among those NATO Alliance partners who wanted to participate and share the cost.

By April, 1964, when President Johnson first gave formal attention to it, MLF had acquired a life of its own, an almost automatic acceptance as something the United States had been pushing, off and on, for almost four years and would continue to push, largely for lack of an alternative way to knit closer collaboration among the allies with regard to nuclear defense. Or so Johnson had every right to assume. His review was routine. There would be heated disputes later about what he actually said at that April meeting. Some could have sworn he said, "We'll *go* on that one right after the election." Partisans of the proposal, including George Ball and NATO Ambassador Thomas Finletter, were soon to be accused of seizing upon a casual comment by the President as grounds for intensifying the MLF crusade. Opponents of the idea argued that the President merely said something like, "We'll *get* on to that one after the election." The President himself argued later that he had not meant to say much of anything; the truth probably is that he genuinely wasn't aware he had. There was no urgency then; his attention was turned elsewhere. But bureaucrats with a cause don't need much encouragement, and Johnson's once-over-lightly look at MLF in April was to embroil him in a knock-down, drag-out confrontation with his own principal advisers in December of that year, when a visit by British Prime Minister Harold Wilson finally forced him to put his mind to the problems of the Atlantic Alliance. When he did, he concluded after five days of stormy intramural debate that he did not wish to be committed in any way to the creation of MLF or any variation thereof.

It took some doing. Whatever the President said privately in April, more than enough had been said and done publicly by him and his subordinates in the interim to tie the United States more tightly than ever to the concept of a NATO nuclear fleet. Right after the April review, at a full-dress foreign-policy declaration at a meeting of Associated Press editors in New York on April 20, Johnson had declared, "We support the establishment of a multilateral nuclear force composed of those nations which wish to participate." On June 12, after Johnson had met with West German Chancellor Erhard, a White House communiqué reported the two men had "agreed that the proposed multilateral force would make a significant addition to [the] military and political strength [of NATO] and that efforts should be continued to ready an agreement for signature by the end of the year."

As late as October 20, 1964, the MLF proposal was still sailing serenely on, still propelled by unequivocal pronouncements from high policy-makers. On that date, Dean Rusk, no MLF zealot, made a brief speech on a significant occasion: an MLF "pilot ship," mixed-manned by crews of eight NATO nations, was visiting Washington. Named the "U.S.S. Claude V. Ricketts" after a U.S. Admiral who had been one of the staunchest supporters of the concept, the ship had been the personal brainchild of John F. Kennedy and had toured the Mediterranean to demonstrate that mixed nationalities could man a ship of war. Said Rusk: "Mixed-manning and ownership of weapons will not automatically assure growth of the North Atlantic partnership, but they will mark a major step forward and can help to build a framework for continuing progress. This mixed-manned ship . . . is not only tangible evidence of our earnest intent to proceed toward MLF . . . [it] is living proof that NATO ships can be effectively manned by differing nationalities."

This was the heart of the MLF idea, which began with the assumptions that many Europeans did want a larger role in their nuclear defenses, that the wrong way to do it was for each NATO member to build its own independent nuclear deterrent, and that the only way for the nonnuclear nations to achieve a larger sense of participation would be through joint ownership and mixed-manning of an MLF. This was also a main point of criticism —that mixed-manning simply wouldn't work. But there was Rusk stoutly insisting that it would, and that the United States intended to see that it did.

Yet, less than two months later, Johnson was saying he could not see how he was committed. The MLF was all but dead. All U.S. commitment to any particular formula for reorganizing NATO's nuclear defenses had been erased. The next move had been put squarely up to Europe.

How this bit of artful dodging was done—and why—is worth recounting in some detail, not just for its impact on Alliance policy, but for what it tells of Lyndon Johnson and of the workings of policy-making machinery when after the election, he finally began to fasten his grip more securely on the controls. It was a classic exercise in the adroit use of White House staff as a diviner of Presidential inclinations, a protector of Presidential interests, a widener of Presidential choices, and a gadfly in the governmental processes when the President was confronted with a spirited, consecrated, nearly united bureaucracy. It was illustrative on another count because while it suggested a striking Presidential independence from the clear consensus of his counselors, it was independence of a negative, defensive sort. Johnson rarely took positive action in defiance of a majority of his advisers. But he often refused to follow majority counsel which seemed to be propelling him along a perilous course. It was usually his instinct in such cases to justify inaction by broadening the consensus to bring the weight of Congress or his own reading of public opinion into the scales—by withdrawing, in short, from the treacherous quagmires of diplomacy to the familiar footing of domestic politics. And withdrawal, more often than not, was accompanied by a covering barrage against his counselors, so that in the end, it scarcely seemed to be a withdrawal at all.

In the course of the protracted conferences in preparation for the Wilson visit, Johnson assailed the men around him, questioning their competence as well as their counsel. It was at one of these sessions that Johnson ticked off each man in turn. Ball was upbraided for the "disgraceful" caliber of ambassadorial candidates served up by the State Department. Dean Acheson, sitting in as private consultant, was needled "as the man who got us into war in Korea" and had to "get Eisenhower to get us out of it." McNamara was derided for his easy assurances that the MLF could be sold to Congress; commended, sarcastically, for his command of Senate politics, and reminded that if MLF was to be sold to Congress, the job would have to be done by the President himself. Acheson, according to reports, finally broke the mounting tension by declaring: "Mr. President, you don't pay these men enough to talk to them that way—even with the federal pay raise."

Rough as some of the sessions apparently were, they were also instructive. Few who were there or heard about it would thereafter make any quick assumptions about what would be palatable and what would not, when presented to Lyndon Johnson. Few would come unprepared to present their case in minute and, if possible, irrefutable detail. And few would presume to speak for the President without being quite certain where he stood. It was a memorable object lesson in Johnson decision-making, a major development in the President's move towards mastery of the "processes," a significant turn in the U.S. approach to Alliance policy. But it becomes more meaningful if one first examines what the President was making a decision about.

The Nuclear Armada

It all began, you might say, with the Sputniks and the subsequent stationing of batteries of Soviet atomic missiles in western Russia, zeroed in on Western Europe. This immediate Russian Communist threat, against the background of a dazzling display of technical prowess, looked more menacing than ever to a Europe which had to rely on the will and intent of Washington for about 98 per cent of its nuclear-defense capacity. The British could lay claim to independent nuclear status, but ban-the-bomb pressure was strong. The French could talk about their embryonic *force de frappe*, but nobody was much impressed. Accordingly, there was growing pressure from West German military circles (and some German politicians as well) and from the top level at SHAPE for stationing American medium-range missiles on the Continent. They were to be operated under the "two-key system" —in which Europeans man and operate the weapons, while the warheads remain in U.S. custody. The theory was that this arrangement would somehow involve the United States in a firmer commitment to permit use of the warheads in Europe's defense.

But prevailing U.S. opinion during the Eisenhower and Kennedy years had been cool to the idea of equipping the Germans with such weapons, even under the "permissive-link" prohibitions on use without American consent. On the other hand, most U.S. policy-makers had believed through the years, something probably ought to be done to give the West Germans a greater role in their own nuclear defenses. It had been an article of faith in postwar U.S. policy that the best insurance against a revival of German militarism was to accord the Federal Republic a respectable, equal role in Alliance affairs. One argument was that second-class status would only drive the Germans to more intense nationalism. Another was that U.S. failure to respond in some fashion would put intolerable pressure not only on the Germans but perhaps other Western Europeans to arm themselves with atomic weapons, thus advancing proliferation of independent national nuclear deterrents in Europe and elsewhere, and raising the odds on the chance of nuclear war.

There was nothing to be done about the U.S. monopoly short of a U.S. initiative to do the "proliferating" by granting some part of its final authority over the use of its warheads or simply to deal out nuclear weapons to its allies; Congress would not have countenanced this move, even if any of this country's nuclear-age Presidents had been inclined to it.

Thus, back in the waning days of the Eisenhower Administration in 1960, the idea of at least a token NATO nuclear force had been conceived. The plan was that the United States would contribute a few submarines with Polaris missiles, Great Britain might commit some part of its present or projected nuclear force, and the way would be open for French participation as well. As the idea evolved under the Kennedy Administration, mixed-manning became the crucial element—the idea of submarines was abandoned for technical reasons—and a planning group of eight nations, including the United States, Britain, West Germany, Italy, Belgium, the Netherlands, Turkey, and Greece, got down to a considerable degree of detailed agreement on a 25-ship force, each ship to be armed with eight missiles. The vessels would resemble merchant ships, cruise close to the coast of Europe, keep constantly on the move to elude enemy submarines, and take as their principal targets those batteries of Soviet medium-range ballistic missiles in western Russia which were covered by longer range U.S. missiles (over which Europe had no influence).

With this plan, Europe would actually be participating in the operation and ownership of a nuclear force. Even though the warheads would still be U.S.–controlled, this would presumably put the United States under even greater obligation to honor its NATO commitments to forestall a Soviet nuclear attack. In the process, West Germany would receive a "vaccination" of sorts; a modicum of influence in Western nuclear defenses, the theory went, would immunize the Germans against rampant revival of militarism. Agreement with this analysis was far from unanimous; some thought the immunizer would act as an appetizer, and others argued that the risk of militarist revival was so slight that nothing needed to be done. It was never an easy matter to bring up, even in a Western community pledged to forgive if not forget.

American policy-makers also had a "British" argument for MLF; if the British could be persuaded to surrender all or part of their nuclear force to a NATO arrangement, Germany's nonnuclear status would be less "second class," and if the French would do the same (presumably post–De Gaulle), the result would be not only to foreclose an independent German nuclear capability but ultimately to envelop the independent British and French forces as well. This would reduce the total number of Western deterrents to two—one American and the other a collective European or NATO affair. By this line of logic, MLF became not just a piece of armament, but an exercise in disarmament. Atlantic deproliferation, in turn, might act to discourage other potential nuclear powers—Japan, for example, or India, Egypt, or Israel.

As a practical matter, the MLF was deficient on every count, including the test of military efficiency; in its early stage, its nuclear "sharing" would be illusory, for it would be a long time before Europe was sufficiently cohesive to operate a collective nuclear force, and a long time before the United States would be ready to surrender any significant part of its monopoly of control over warheads. There was no assurance that the French would ever come in; the British blew hot and cold. The whole idea invited ridicule. It became known in some European circles as the "multilateral farce."

But the face remained that it also partially served all the purposes for which it was designed; besides, it was something to discuss at a time when there was agitation for some solution and no alternative. There was even a bit of hope among some U.S. officials that if it was discussed long enough and in sufficient

depth, those Europeans who hankered for a greater voice in nuclear affairs might discover how costly and complicated it all was,
and stop hankering. So the idea lived on, and it should have
surprised nobody that after Johnson so much as hinted an interest in April, that the dedicated advocates of MLF should have
sprung into action. Though Johnson apparently was unaware of
it, Kennedy had soured on the proposal in 1963; now, with Johnson apparently "signed on," the MLF advocates began grinding
out speeches, confidently citing the President's April endorsement.
A special MLF task force was established in the State Department,
headed by Gerard C. Smith, who was given the title of Special
Adviser to the Secretary of State. A former counsel of the Department, Smith was an early MLF adherent. Meantime, Finletter and
others were giving it a hard sell in Europe and ruffling the
tempers of opponents, who were stirred to register complaints.
These complaints were finding their way to Washington and to
the White House, often by courtesy of touring Congressmen
eager to seize upon some evidence of maladroit U.S. diplomacy.

Trouble was building up on other fronts.

Britain's new Labour Government had found it convenient,
while still campaigning for election, to talk as if it wanted to un-
load all the United Kingdom's atom weaponry (in order to ap-
pease the Labour Party's ban-the-bomb left wing); to do this, it
had been assumed the British would need a receptacle—and
therefore be obliged to cooperate with the United States in estab-
lishing some sort of NATO nuclear force. But after his election (by
a minuscule majority), Wilson had to take into account Tory
sentiment for retaining British nuclear capability, and a widespread British reluctance to let the Germans anywhere near
atomic weapons. Furthermore, there was the cost—something that
restrained European enthusiasm all along the line. So Wilson had
cooked up an alternative named the ANF, for Allied (or sometimes
Atlantic) Nuclear Force, an open-ended grab bag into which
almost anything could have been put, including British V
bombers, U.S. Polaris subs, and even an MLF component, though
the British were not enthusiastic about this last point.

When MLF was just a bright idea, the French were content to
scorn it. Now it began to appear that MLF or something like it

might actually materialize and De Gaulle felt disposed to turn actively against it in November, 1964, and to threaten dire reprisals against NATO unless the MLF was dropped. The commotion this stirred up as the subject leapt back into the headlines was beginning to unhinge Ludwig Erhard's caretaker coalition government in Bonn. Erhard's Christian Democratic Party was sorely split on the issue, and there were signs it would just as soon defer a choice on MLF—with all its implications of a choice between the wrath of Washington and the wrath of De Gaulle— until after elections, then less than a year away.

Finally, the Russians were beginning to hurl dark threats as MLF seemingly moved closer to realization, arguing that giving the Germans even a tiny finger on a NATO nuclear trigger would gravely endanger the peace, intensify the tensions of cold war, and wreck chances for a nonproliferation treaty.

These, briefly, were some of the forces at work, and while most of Johnson's senior policy advisers thought they by and large amounted to conclusive arguments against MLF, all the points were to figure in the five days of intensive debate that preceded Harold Wilson's trip to Washington on December 8.

The Sinking of the Unsinkable MLF

If Harold Wilson had not come to Washington, it is hard to say when Lyndon Johnson would have gotten around to grappling with the thorny issue of MLF. As it was, he was still wrangling with his aides and counselors when the British Prime Minister and his entourage walked briskly past the windows of the President's oval office on their way to the Cabinet room. There they sat for more than an hour while Johnson fumed and fidgeted, heard out final arguments, and finally wound up rejecting the draft "position paper" prepared for him by a working party that included Vice President Humphrey, Rusk, McNamara, Ball, McGeorge Bundy, and the U.S. Ambassador to Britain, David Bruce. This would have committed the United States to some form of ANF plus MLF, depending on what the British could work out. The President's decision was to rule against any firm U.S. commitment to any formula for overhauling the NATO nuclear arrangements. But a case can be made that this step backward was also a necessary prelude to any step forward toward a more promising American role in Alliance affairs. Only ultimate results would tell, and the pace of constructive change in the Atlantic Alliance in the absence of urgent, demonstrable need is always slow. But some strong hints of how and under what circumstances Lyndon Johnson would move in the future can be seen in a capsule account, assembled from conversations with a number of officials involved, of his first deep plunge into the NATO nuclear issue. And the strongest hint may lie in the first question he asked at a Saturday morning meeting, assembled at White House request after what the State Department had expected would be a reasonably routine briefing session the previous day. Plainly, Johnson hadn't been satisfied. His first questions went to the heart of the matter: what happens, he wanted to know, if nothing is done to rearrange NATO's nuclear set-up, if the Germans are given no larger share in influence and responsibility over nuclear decisions? Would Germany be driven by frustration into trying to develop its own national deterrent?

On that score, he apparently got not one answer from his advisers but a bewildering variety of projections. The line-up, by all accounts, had Ball, McNamara, Acheson, and Bruce by and large on the side of MLF, ANF, or a variation. This group more or less agreed that doing nothing would lead the Germans to seek U.S. medium-range missiles under the "two-key" system as a starter. German insistence on a separate German deterrent would follow within a decade or less, they argued, if for no other reason than because the existence of separate French and British deterrents would make German's second-class status increasingly indefensible for any aspirant to German political leadership. Bundy was skeptical that this could come about that soon.

But on this score, if on little else, Johnson was on the side of the "theologians." He maintained a constant position throughout the exchanges over the next four days that doing absolutely nothing was too dangerous, that the Germans would be bound to react—perhaps violently, that they would want their own nuclear weapons in much less than a decade. He would do so, the President is said to have declared, were he in the Germans' shoes.

But the discussion had not proceeded much further before Johnson asked the question that turned the tide against a firm line with Wilson on MLF or any close variant. The question was really a series of related questions, beginning with exploration of the intensity of support for MLF in Europe. When opinion was divided and inconclusive on this score, the President popped the pivotal question: How to sell a skeptical Senate on a controversial proposition when even the potential European partners have, at best, two minds about it?

"I don't want to be a Woodrow Wilson, right on a principle, and fighting for a principle, and unable to achieve it," the President reportedly declared, reverting to his League of Nations analogy. At this point, the outer limits of the ultimate decision had been set, and the debate was to bounce back and forth endlessly between these boundaries, fixed unconsciously or not by the President from the start. He would slam no doors on the Germans; but neither was he buying the optimistic estimates of his advisers about the prospects in Congress, because on this subject, at least, he was moving in familiar territory.

He and Humphrey had been taking soundings on Capitol Hill, and Johnson would continue to do so during the course of the discussions. And the more the President talked to his old colleagues, the more he became convinced that the prospects were bleak, and the more he was able to assert his command over the discussions. At one point, when one of the pro–MLF faction confidently claimed the backing of Senator Fulbright, Johnson was in a position to bring him up short; he had talked to Fulbright "ten minutes ago," he snapped, and Fulbright had told him he was against it. Humphrey played a key role in developing the Congressional argument. One after another, Johnson ticked off the names of Senators unfavorably disposed: Mansfield, Anderson, Russell, Jackson, "the whole spectrum." His advisers insisted that because there had been no recent go-ahead from the President, no real effort had been made to win over Congress, but Johnson was not impressed. "I can't move, if I don't have the troops," he complained.

With that question resolved, at least in his own mind, the President hacked away at the problem that remained: How to handle Wilson, and the Germans, without involving the U.S. in a commitment to MLF or ANF or some variation of the two? According to those familiar with the course of the debate, Johnson, having pretty well decided that opposition from Congress was too strong (it came both from liberals who disliked the idea of giving Germans even a pinch of nuclear power, fearing this would blight disarmament proposals, and from conservatives who wanted to cling to the American nuclear monopoly), seemed almost to be trying to convince himself that it really didn't matter because nobody in Europe felt strongly about MLF or ANF anyway. He had conceded early in the discussion the danger of a German "inferiority complex" and the importance of giving the Federal Republic at least the "symbols" of equality. But he grabbed at every evidence offered that perhaps this need not be done right away, that there was really no U.S. commitment to do so, that the British would resist it, or that the United States could not readily strong-arm the shaky Wilson Government.

At the outset, the responses from most of the men around him were quick and confident—the Germans were pictured as eager, the British as at least susceptible to reason, and Italians ready to follow along. The President, in short, was assured that he could carry the day if he applied a little leverage. Since it was becoming increasingly apparent that Johnson did not want to apply leverage because he did not want to add MLF or ANF or anything similar to his legislative workload for 1965, this merely set up for the President the question of what would happen if his advisers were right, and Wilson caved in. Wouldn't he then be faced with selling Congress a proposition that Congress didn't want?

So it went, around and around, until, at one point, it occurred to Johnson to ask what his predecessor had felt about all this. The answer came from McGeorge Bundy, whose influence as guardian of options and protector of the President was perhaps never more effectively displayed than in the episode of the MLF. Bundy had sensed trouble building earlier in the year. With the MLF partisans in full cry, the President's position uncertain, and the Wilson visit coming up, Bundy had called in Richard Neustadt, a political scientist, a former White House staffer under Harry Truman and consultant to John Kennedy, and an authority on the exercise of Presidential power as well as NATO affairs, for an independent appraisal of the MLF–ANF issue, in Europe as well as Washington. Bundy, while no MLF "theologian," had nothing particular against the MLF personally. He simply didn't want President Johnson married to it in the sort of shotgun ceremony that he thought the State Department partisans were trying to stage. He did not think the West Germans wanted it nearly as badly as the State Department contended (and he had assembled some evidence of his own to reinforce his argument). He doubted Harold Wilson was really keen about any new arrangements (and he also had collected some evidence on this point). He thought the President ought to have a better reading than he was getting of the possible repercussions in Europe, because this would have an important bearing on the prospects for Senate approval; a treaty rammed down Europe's throat would be that much harder to sell to skeptical Senators. Beyond that, he saw it as his obligation to warn the President of possible pitfalls, and he believed the MLF advocates were giving Johnson a rosier picture of the prospects for the MLF adoption in Europe than the facts merited. So he had set out to give the President more running room, and he was ready, when Johnson inquired about Kennedy's view, with a memorandum which Bundy himself had prepared for Kennedy in mid-1963. He was also ready to state what the late President's reaction to it had been. According to one official, the gist of the Bundy memorandum was that nobody in Europe was ready to move on MLF, and the gist of Kennedy's response was, "If the Europeans don't want it, then the hell with it." "If the European don't want it" now became a Johnson refrain—in fact, Johnson's life raft—even though the circumstances in mid-1963, when Macmillan was beset by the Profumo scandal, and the Government in Bonn was in mid-transition from Adenauer to Erhard, and Italy had no government at all, were hardly comparable.

It was not the only life raft the President was thrown. The back-and-forth continued through the long weekend, and at a Sunday evening session. Johnson had in hand a cable just in from Ambassador George C. McGhee in Bonn, reporting that there were indeed new signs of reluctance on the part of the West German

Government to push ahead with MLF. Exactly what prompted McGhee to chime into the debate at this critical juncture is not clear, but it is at least interesting, if not conclusively relevant, that some time between the Saturday and Sunday sessions the White House staff also made available to the President a memorandum which similarly suggested that the divided CDU in West Germany was eager to duck a showdown on MLF. Those who were in favor of not pushing the President were not leaving things entirely to chance. Besides the year-old Bundy-to-Kennedy memorandum, the President also had, by Sunday evening, a fresh Bundy appraisal, raising anew some doubts about the military utility of MLF, questioning the wisdom of pressing the Wilson Government with its slim House of Commons majority, and raising other questions about the feasibility of "doing MLF." Bundy had observed the formalities; he notified Secretary Rusk of his intent to present this "lawyer's brief," but Rusk, who was otherwise preoccupied with meetings in New York in connection with the United Nations, had not been sitting in on the earlier discussions with the President, and his number two man, George Ball, who had been sitting in for him, had not been alerted to it. Ball was reportedly taken aback when the President suddenly began reading from this second Bundy brief, even though by the rules of the game, it was quite in keeping with the White House staff concept of President-protection.

By this point, Lyndon Johnson had apparently made up his mind that MLF or ANF or whatever was not sufficiently in demand by anybody to justify a battle in Congress—even though Ball, McNamara, and Bruce were still doggedly arguing that the United States had no alternative but to be in favor of something of the sort. At one awkward moment, the argument was pressed that the U.S. was indeed committed and that to back away would be to surrender the initiative to De Gaulle. But Johnson was just as dogged in his insistence that he could not see how *he* was committed, and since that was obviously the way he wanted to see it, nobody felt emboldened to read the fairly recent record back to him. There was even some disposition, despite the Erhard communiqué and the New York speech (not to mention four years of U.S. Government commitment), to concede that maybe underlings had overdone the MLF crusade. Such is the way with Presidential commitments. Johnson clung tenaciously to a vague, tangential, 10-year-old Eisenhower letter to Diem to reinforce his case for escalation of the U.S. effort in Vietnam, but he was quite prepared to ignore his personal commitments to MLF when it did not fit his current purpose.

It is difficult to pinpoint the moment when the ultimate solution began to take shape. But it was Rusk, reportedly, who first staked out the most promising area of compromise by suggesting that the whole question be tossed back to Europe; no deadlines would be imposed for the British and the Germans and any other interested parties to work something out, and the United States would commit itself to no specific formulation, but it would be understood that the United States expected the British Government to meet any reasonable, minimum German demands, including, if the Germans were adamant, some mixed-manned elements in a NATO nuclear force. Johnson saw pitfalls even in this highly conditional compromise. However, there was the outside chance the British and Germans might agree to something, a situation that would then have to be presented to a hostile Congress; or they might agree to something after much anguish, freely expressed, and with loud cries about U.S. "pressure" to assuage their own domestic public opinion, a situation that would make Senate ratification all the harder. Or they might not agree and blame *that* on the United States.

So this, too, was ruled out by the President, and while Harold Wilson waited in the Cabinet room on Tuesday morning, Lyndon Johnson made his ultimate decision: He would take a hard line generally with Wilson from the outset (and, from some British accounts, he did indeed lead off with a barrage of criticism against British economic policies and the trouble they were causing the United States, which not only had its own balance-of-payments problems but was being called upon to help the British with theirs). But once having seized the offensive, the President would sit back and permit Wilson to present his ANF plan formally. The United States would offer comments, the question would be batted back and forth, Britain would be encouraged to try it out on Bonn, and the United States would give careful consideration to anything the two European principals might work out. Meanwhile, MLF would lie in limbo, available for use in whatever new formula might emerge, but no longer the centerpiece of U.S. nuclear policy for NATO.

The Aftermath

On Wednesday, December 8, 1964, the White House made public a communiqué on the talks between President Johnson and Prime Minister Wilson which came a good deal closer than such documents usually do to describing the full product of their diplomatic exchange. It did so, because the facts in the case were bland, and noncommittal enough to fit the format of a public communiqué. The two leaders, it said, "recognized the importance of strengthening the unity of the Atlantic Alliance and its strategic nuclear defense. They had discussed existing proposals for this purpose and an outline of some new proposals presented by the British Government. They agreed that the objective in this field is to cooperate in finding the arrangements which best meet the legitimate interests of all members of the Alliance, while maintaining existing safeguards on the use of nuclear weapons, and preventing their further proliferation. A number of elements of this problem were considered during this initial exchange of views as a preliminary to further discussions among interested members of the Alliance."

And that's roughly the way it was. The British were to talk to the Germans; the United States would talk with both; if anything came of those conversations, other interested parties would be brought into the act. Wilson pronounced the encounter "completely successful." He had been obliged to yield nothing visible and nothing invisible that was in any way final. Hailing a "total identity of view," he noted pointedly, in passing, that there had been "no theology"—an obvious reference to those irrepressible MLF crusaders—and projected an Anglo-American relationship that gave promise of being "closer than ever in the years ahead."

At the State Department, it was still possible for the embattled men advocating the MLF to put up a bold front. Their formula for NATO's nuclear reorganization, so long espoused by American officials and American Presidents, was not dead, newsmen were advised. Rather, "what is emerging is a broader view, an expanding concept, bigger than anything we have talked about." A high official insisted that the idea of mixed-manned surface ships remained a significant part of this larger package, indeed "an indispensable element which we are in no sense abandoning." The Johnson performance, as viewed from the inside of the U.S. Government by those who dealt with him and would have to continue to deal with him, was reflected in the comment of one weary member of this group: "He is a very impressive man."

Another intimate adviser was to look back upon the episode and describe it as a "prime example of an elemental aspect of the President—his capacity for balancing the forces, for bringing together all the elements of the decision-making process, in Congress, as well as within his own administration, and in the interested power centers of Europe as well."

President Johnson, however, was left with a lingering disquiet, a sense that however well the Wilson encounter may have turned out, something was wrong in a system which had allowed him to lose, if even for a short time, his control of that branch of the governmental system which was his by right to command. By way of foreclosing further free-wheeling—on the NATO question, at least—he moved quickly to nail down the new line. His principal national-security advisers were assembled to agree on a memorandum setting forth in no uncertain terms Johnson's outer limits for future presentation of U.S. policy, at whatever level of government, on the crucial defense issues in the Atlantic Alliance. Among the basic principles clearly enunciated were these: no new nuclear arrangements for NATO would be approved that were not agreeable to both Britain and Germany, and not at least discussed in advance with France; nothing in any U.S. proposal for promoting greater Alliance cohesion was to be represented or interpreted as an effort to arrest Europe's own efforts at economic or political integration. (In other words, the U.S. did not intend to drive De Gaulle into isolation at the expense of the Common Market or related projects for strengthening political integration of The Six.) "Pressure tactics" were to cease. The United States would not foster "special arrangements" with any of its allies, or impose arbitrary "deadlines" for acceptance of any U.S. proposals; the door was to be kept open always for De Gaulle.

Not content with simply laying down the law discreetly within the government, Johnson thereupon leaked the whole memorandum to *The New York Times,* apparently on the theory that its publication would make it somehow more meaningful and irreversible abroad as well as at home.

Soon thereafter, the MLF apparatus within the State Department was, if not completely broken up, at least scattered and driven underground. The special advisory job of Gerard Smith was abolished. Silence was the word on MLF, and there was joy and relief among those who either actively opposed it or, more often the case, considered it simply an unwelcome irritant.

But it wasn't that simple then or more than a year later when the whole subject came up again in a December, 1965, meeting between Lyndon Johnson and Ludwig Erhard. By that time, the original MLF formula was indeed dead. But the basic problem that gave rise to it was still alive, and the prospect was that something at least faintly related to the original MLF might still materialize. For early in 1965, it became obvious that if the Europeans did not like MLF, they liked still less the impression they had received that the United States had quietly withdrawn from the whole problem. Indeed, the European response was nearly ludicrous; a Europe that had been griping loudly about American dominance and interference was suddenly confronted with a United States that looked and sounded genuinely uninterested in doing much of anything to solve Alliance problems until her European allies took some collective initiative on their part. There were anxious European whisperings about an isolationist revival in U.S. policy. Many who had been peevish at Washington for acting like an overbearing parent were beginning to think the dreadful thought that maybe Washington really didn't care.

As the London *Economist* put it, in January, 1965, "President Johnson, Mr. Wilson and Herr Erhard cannot afford just to stand by and blame one another for collective failure . . . the responsibility lies first with President Johnson." The *Economist* deplored the past "stupefying few weeks . . . in which American policy has remained entirely passive." But it also noted a "curious effect on some of the allies. Those who so lately felt themselves grievously bullied now protest that it is impossible to get anything decided if the leader will not lead."

There were exaggerated reports of Lyndon Johnson's wrath at the State Department "theologians." The National Security Council memorandum, which *The New York Times* had obligingly paraphrased in such official-sounding terms, became, in the European imagination, a doctrine of disengagement from Europe. As word of Europe's anxiety filtered back to Washington, even some of those officials who had welcomed the change of course in Alliance policy began to fear that Lyndon Johnson, in his haste to get his own hands firmly on the controls, had swung the helm too hard. On January 16, 1965, when the question of the MLF, and future Alliance policy, was raised at a ranch-house news conference, Johnson was armed with an answer carefully drafted by the State Department. It professed the "greatest of interest" in the outcome of discussions between the British and the Germans as a follow-up to the Wilson visit to Washington, and while the President's prepared response did not endorse MLF as such, it did say that the United States deems it "highly important to develop arrangements within the Alliance that will provide an opportunity for the nonnuclear members to participate in their own nuclear defense while avoiding the spread of national nuclear systems. I strongly hope in these talks there will be progress that will allow us to move on to fruitful multilateral discussions."

That comment, by itself, was sufficiently opaque but when a reporter asked specifically whether "we are still strongly in favor of a mixed-manned nuclear fleet," the President answered: "Yes, I said that just now."

By any literal reading, this would seem to have recommitted Johnson to MLF and reversed the result of the Wilson talks. But a more accurate reading of where the matter then rested could be found in a cable dispatched simultaneously by Rusk, with White House approval, to all U.S. ambassadors in Europe. It began by noting apparent misinterpretation in Europe of the U.S. position, to the effect that the United States was less interested in the nuclear problem and had scuttled the MLF completely. The U.S. envoys were told, in effect, that the National Security Council memorandum was by no means intended to halt all U.S. pressure on Europe to reach a meeting of minds on the reorganization of NATO's nuclear defenses. The United States fully supports this objective, the cable said, and its support centers on the ANF proposal, which, it was pointedly stated, could well envelop the MLF in its original form as an integral component of a larger joint set-up. The United States, it went on, still sees the same advantages in some sort of NATO nuclear force —the nonproliferation argument, the opportunity for more effective participation by Europeans in their own nuclear defense, and the increased cohesion this would give the Alliance. But the United States wants the widest possible consensus, and at least an opening for the French, if not actual French participation, the message said. The heads of mission were told that U.S. interest and continuing support for this approach should be stressed —a directive which put the "activists" back into business again but with a more precise sales pitch and under a tighter rein.

The end result of it all, then, was to strike a balance that was to prevail throughout 1965 and on into 1966. As it turned out, the British-German talks made little conclusive headway before they were overtaken by West German preoccupation with its September election and with the subsequent reshuffling of the Erhard Government. The next important move was not to come until Chancellor Erhard met with Lyndon Johnson in December, 1965. But in the meantime, the MLF was precisely where Johnson wanted it to be, and where it should have been all along—in the middle of the table, as one proposal among many, to be accepted or rejected without prejudice to the U.S. position or injury to U.S. prestige. The American seal of approval had been removed, subject to replacement any time the West Germans saw fit to state plainly their support for it, or for the ANF, or for some variant. The ball was in Europe's court. This didn't make the Europeans feel comfortable, and neither did it free President Johnson from criticism for lack of leadership.

But the effect, if curious, was also healthy. In the fall of 1965, the West Germans finally faced up to the nuclear issue; a parade of officials made pilgrimages to Washington, testing the mood

and talking up the need for a solution to the NATO nuclear question which would give West Germany some form of active participation in an Alliance nuclear force. From Bonn came a
succession of rumors and trial balloons, all seeming to reflect a
profound desire for something in the nature of ANF or MLF.
Foreign Minister Schroeder and Defense Minister Von Hassel,
the leaders of the pro–MLF faction in the CDU, were publicly declaring the government's insistence on what came to be known
as a "hardware" solution, meaning some formula that would give
the Germans some voice in the operation of actual weapons
systems.

Meantime, the United States had not been entirely idle. As a
stopgap during the waiting period, Secretary McNamara had
advanced to NATO the idea of a compact "directorate" of key
countries to discuss Alliance nuclear problems; this was enough
to keep the question under consideration during the waiting
period and provide a mechanism for more meaningful action
once enough NATO members were ready to act. It was also innoc-
uous enough not to give De Gaulle much to shoot at.

The climax finally came quietly, in a closely held exchange of
views between Chancellor Erhard and President Johnson at the
White House in December. Little was made known of their private conversation, and public attention was directed off into
outer space by a U.S. offer to collaborate with the Germans and
other interested Europeans in a space-satellite probe of Jupiter.
Meantime, the United States was coming forward with proposals
dealing more directly with the nuclear question, including a
highly significant, if somewhat undramatic plan to permit the
NATO allies to participate actively in the real nuts-and-bolts of
nuclear defense planning, the long-range procurement decisions,
which as much as anything else would determine the effectiveness
of Alliance defenses over the long haul. But Chancellor Erhard
also made a strong case, in private, for the ANF–MLF approach.
President Johnson, for his part, reiterated U.S. readiness to pursue the matter, but with one proviso: by this time, Johnson had
come to conclude that no new nuclear-strike force should be
created, as the original MLF proposal envisaged. Any new weapons system would create complications for the U.S. effort to

promote disarmament and wider *détente* by pushing for a non-proliferation agreement with the Soviet Union. But the United States remained committed to a variation, at least, of the ANF formula, and open-minded about some application of the mixed-meaning feature to existing national forces if the West Germans were adamant. Early in 1966, a special committee of NATO nations, largely composed of those who had expressed original interest in the MLF, began work on recommendations to be presented to the McNamara "directorate."

By this time, the MLF, as originally constituted, could legally and logically be pronounced dead—but not in vain. Its spirit lingered on and would influence whatever arrangements might ultimately emerge. And its demise as a pet U.S. project had admirably served the Johnson judo principle.

It had elicited a European, or at least a West German, initiative as an antidote or alternative to the precise designs of De Gaulle, however they might unfold. Lyndon Johnson could no longer be the wrecker of the Alliance. Just conceivably, he might become the architect of a grand redesigning of outdated relationships. At the very least, he had reset the stage to his advantage. All of his options were safely back in hand.

EIGHT

Vietnam–The Orphan War

From the day the French were driven out, Vietnam was an orphan, and the war that would be waged over it was destined to be always an orphan war.

U.S. involvement would grow mightily, yet insidiously, in slow stages, with each step hard to fault. Essential, immediate needs would be looked after. But nobody, not least the American Government, ever seemed quite capable of looking ahead to the long haul, of planning in practical terms for a future that was feasible. For a half-dozen deceptive years after the French defeat in 1954, there was no war at all. When it flared up again in 1960, the 14 nations which had assumed responsibility for the remnants of the French Indonesian empire in the 1954 Geneva Accords were thoroughly incapable of discharging their responsibilities collectively. It was probably inevitable that the United States, under Eisenhower, should have taken Vietnam as its own unilateral charge with a 1954 promise to help the South Vietnamese help themselves. Under the Truman Doctrine, the United States had assumed a role in the maintenance of freedom all around the globe, and there was no reason to believe in 1954, or indeed in 1960, that discharging this obligation in Vietnam would entail involvement in what would amount, by 1966, to an Asian land war.

In 1960, it was still possible for the State Department to speak in terms of "something close to an economic miracle" in South Vietnam under Ngo Dinh Diem, and for Senator Mansfield to report that "by any measure, Vietnam has made great progress . . . in the improvement of internal security, in the creation of the forms and institutions of popular responsible government where before few existed, and in the advancement of the people of Vietnam." Yet that was just about the time when there were the first signs of stepped-up guerrilla activity, though the numbers, estimated at 3,000 Vietcong, were small. On September 10, 1960, the Third Congress of the Communist Party of North Vietnam called for the liberation of South Vietnam from "the rule of the U.S. imperialists and their henchmen" in Saigon. In December, the National Front for Liberation of South Vietnam, the political arm of the guerrilla insurgency, was formed.

Still, Eisenhower left Vietnam on the Kennedy Administration doorstep without so much as an explanatory note. In January, when the outgoing President was running down the checklist of international legacies to his successor, including such familiar points of crisis as Berlin, Cuba, and Laos, he apparently did not think Vietnam worth mentioning—to Kennedy's subsequent astonishment. "This is the worst one yet," he exclaimed after reading a detailed intelligence report on Vietnam a month after taking office. "You know," he said in disbelief to White House adviser Walt W. Rostow, "Ike never briefed me about Vietnam."

History will doubtless be a long time fixing the precise point at which the United States first stepped irretrievably into the deep and costly U.S. military intervention that was still widening in early 1966. The point here is not one of history; probably there will be blame enough to spread liberally over at least three Presidential administrations. Lyndon Johnson traced his escalation of the U.S. war effort to Eisenhower's 1954 letter to Diem promising U.S. support to "assist the government of Vietnam in developing and maintaining a strong viable state, capable of resisting attempted subversion, or aggression through military means" and basing the U.S. efforts on "performance" by the Saigon Government "in undertaking needed reforms." (Republicans, in turn, prefer a genealogy which begins with the 1950 Truman Administration pledges of "economic and military equipment to the Associated States of Indochina and to France in order to assist them in restoring stability and permitting these states to pursue their peaceful and democratic development.")

But even loyal members of the Kennedy Administration will concede that the character of the U.S. effort was altered fundamentally, perhaps irrevocably, in late 1961 and early 1962, when President Kennedy greatly expanded the American military-assistance effort, both in numbers (from an assistance group of about 500 men to nearly 10,000 by the end of 1962) and in the nature of the mission. It was then that U.S. troops began edging into combat under instructions to shoot when shot at; it was then that U.S. pilots began conducting air operations in South Vietnam, with Vietnamese airmen along very largely for appearances' sake. As with most Vietnam decisions, this was a compromise to meet an urgent need; while it included heavy emphasis on political-, economic-, and social-reform programs and a heavy content of counterinsurgency technique, it still fell short of total commitment to a long-range program for Vietnam's future, as most Vietnam decision-making would continue to do. Kennedy had dispatched Rostow and Maxwell Taylor in October, 1961, for an on-the-spot inspection. Their recommendations came close to being a blueprint for what was to come under Lyndon Johnson. Taylor foresaw the need for a heavy infusion of U.S. combat troops for limited combat activities. Rostow argued hard for contingency planning of air strikes and other activities in North Vietnam as reprisal for any substantial increase in Hanoi's intervention in the South. But Kennedy shied away from combat involvement, and Rostow's controversial "Plan 6" was filed away. Even so, the U.S. military entanglement deepened. The standard military-assistance group, common to all U.S. arms-aid programs, was replaced by a United States Military Assistance Command (MAC–V) in early 1962. Hanoi was quick to denounce it as a "military base" in violation of the Geneva Accords and as a "direct threat" to North Vietnam's security. The number of American military personnel had grown beyond 25,000 by the end of 1963. As their casualities grew apace, the cloak of "advisory" status began to wear thin; people were beginning to speak increasingly of the U.S. military involvement as a "war."

There was, however, an aura of optimism about the outcome of it all—an aura which seemed to depend, as much as anything, upon the durability, proven over the comforting stretch of nine years, of the regime of Ngo Dinh Diem. On October 2, 1963, McNamara and Taylor (then Chairman of the Joint Chiefs of Staff) returned from an inspection trip and announced after a meeting at the White House that "the major part of the U.S. military task can be completed by the end of 1965, although there may be a continuing requirement for a limited number of U.S. training personnel." A White House announcement the same day said the two men had "reported [to Kennedy] that by the end of [1963] the U.S. program for training the Vietnamese should have progressed to the point where 1,000 U.S. military personnel assigned to Vietnam can be withdrawn."

Though McNamara would have to bear the brunt of this misreading of the future, its real roots ran deep into Pentagon politics, and, in a sense, into the strange bureaucratic bifurcation which had been confounding the U.S. effort in Vietnam throughout the Kennedy years (and would continue through the early Johnson years). Knowledgeable officials insist that neither Kennedy nor McNamara felt quite so confident about Vietnam then as he sounded. But the top military commander in Saigon, General Paul D. Harkins, had become a controversial figure, there was talk of replacing him, and under the principle of mutual protectiveness that animates Pentagon politics, this was added incentive for putting the conduct of the military aspects of the struggle in Vietnam in the best possible light.

The real problem, however, lay in the lack of definition in key branches of the U.S. Government concerning what the Vietnam struggle was all about. The military, naturally, saw it as a war —something to be won or lost. And they wanted to win it and get out before it widened into a conflict that might drag them into open combat on the Asian mainland. Most high-ranking army men had taken a solemn vow after Korea of "never again"— or, at least, never again without unlimited air support. A case could be made that as a war, Vietnam was going almost as well as McNamara and Taylor said it was a few months before Kennedy's death and the beginning of the Johnson Presidency.

But a sizable group of government opinion-makers, including some influential people in the State Department—which would have to live with the problem of Vietnam after the "war had been won"—saw it in far more complicated terms. They could envisage a technical knockout of the Vietcong, or at least a reduction of the insurgency to the level of a "police problem," as some put it. But they could also see before them growing political trouble, an alarming wave of Buddhist unrest, powerful opposition to the repressions of the Diem regime, and an appalling lack of will in Saigon to engage in the sort of political, economic, and social reform which would make South Vietnam a stable, or even governable, national entity after the suppression of the worst part of the insurgency had removed the political pretext for martial law and authoritarian rule. In short, they could foresee the whole structure collapsing and South Vietnam once again becoming prey to Communist subversion and infiltration almost the minute the "war" had been "won" and U.S. forces had gone home. And some were fearful that collapse could come long before the war was won.

It was this analysis which led to U.S. pressure on Diem, in the autumn of 1963, to mend his repressive ways. "I don't think the war can be won unless the people support the effort," Kennedy said in a television interview on September 3, "and in my opinion, in the last two months, the government has gotten out of touch with the people." At the same time, he added pointedly: "In the final analysis, it is their war. We can help them, we can give them equipment, we can send our men out there as advisers but they have to win it." The pressure backfired when Diem and his powerful brother Nhu resisted reform, when U.S. economic aid was quietly closed off to intensify the pressure for it, and when a group of senior South Vietnamese generals finally overthrew his government on November 2.

There was logic in the argument of the anti-Diem faction. But his downfall also demonstrated a certain logic in the contention of most U.S. military men—that the promotion of political reform at the risk of political upheaval in the midst of a war would be bound to hamper conduct of the war. It did. A succession of military coups and a ceaseless struggle for power in Saigon not only sapped the war effort but encouraged Hanoi in its conviction that stepped-up help to the Vietcong might well bring quick victory for the Communist side. This was the fundamental dilemma of Vietnam confronting the Kennedy Administration, and it was passed on to Johnson, in large part because many of the top men who had counseled Kennedy would continue to counsel Johnson. How Kennedy might have moved to resolve the conflict is impossible to say, but almost certainly there would have been significant changes in policy. According to the account of Arthur Schlesinger, Jr., in *A Thousand Days,* Kennedy "no doubt . . . realized that Vietnam was his great failure in foreign policy, and that he had never really given it his full attention." So it was still an orphan when it was passed along to Johnson, and the options open to a new President, whose every move was examined microscopically for the slightest sign of slackening resolve or intention to alter course, were not the same options that would have been open to Kennedy. Further U.S. disengagement—perhaps through early negotiations with Hanoi—might have been possible for Kennedy. He might have made an effort to disconnect the dominoes by de-emphasizing the potential impact on other neighboring Asians of a losing U.S. effort to shore up a nation apparently incapable of helping to save itself. This was known as the "good doctor, sick patient" theory and it had strong adherents in the policy-making machinery. Or Kennedy might has seen U.S. prestige inextricably engaged and moved to bring U.S. power to bear more forcefully in 1964. Instead, transition made the timing out of joint. While Hanoi followed its own inexorable momentum, U.S. momentum was abruptly interrupted by the sanctification of "continuity," by the special electoral pressures on Johnson beyond those that an established President would have faced, by the bizarre foreign-policy issue that was to dominate the Johnson-Goldwater campaign. For another long year, Vietnam was fated to be an orphan war.

The Holding Operation

With Vietnam, for most of 1964, Lyndon Johnson was in the awkward role of contortionist; he was propping up the tottery Saigon Government—or governments—with one hand, jabbing threateningly with the other in an effort to deter Hanoi, all the while faced around toward the American electorate, shouting reassurances. The result was a confusing cacophony of hawklike cries and dovelike coos. In a warm letter of encouragement to General Duong Van Minh, the military chieftain then in command in Saigon, Johnson, on December 31, 1963, pledged "on behalf of the American Government and people a renewed partnership with your government and people in your brave struggle for freedom." He said: "The United States will continue to furnish you and your people with the fullest measure of support in this bitter fight," and he promised "Big Minh" that the United States would have no part of any scheme to "neutralize" South Vietnam. Not even obliquely was there mention of what South Vietnam might do to help its own cause, by political or other reform.

In a February, 1964, address at the University of California, Johnson did stress that the conflict in South Vietnam was "first and foremost a contest to be won by the government and the people of that country for themselves." But in that same speech, he first introduced the threat of wider war, though in a curiously circumlocutory way. "Those engaged in external direction and supply would do well to be reminded and to remember that this type of aggression is a deeply dangerous game," he declared. This was vivid language, sure to catch the eye of newspapermen as they hurried through the advance text; but just in case it didn't, the then White House Press Secretary, Pierre Salinger, made his way around the crowded press plane to alert newsmen to the phrase and elaborate upon it with background guidance. This should be interpreted, he advised, as a clear warning that the United States might feel compelled to expand the war to North Vietnam or even China in order to fulfill its commitments to South Vietnam. This unattributable interpretation was dutifully disseminated, and it immediately kicked up reaction from those opposed to deeper involvement in the Vietnamese war. The "signal," of course, had been intended for Hanoi; but the flaw in the semaphore system of diplomacy was always that when the signaling is done publicly, everybody can listen in. The domestic backlash was such that Dean Rusk was obliged to summon a news conference for the purpose of playing down any speculation that the United States might "go North." From the White House came the curious news that the President himself could not imagine how such an extreme interpretation of his words could have gotten around.

So it went through the spring and early summer of 1964. One moment, McNamara was in Saigon, cavorting with the local government leaders like a politician running for office, and Dean Rusk was saying that if the Vietnam Government "could continue now, as we think it will, to finish up its pacification program, there is a country that can plan an important, strong active role among the free nations of Southeast Asia." As for thought of negotiations, Rusk, in a joint news conference with the President in April, said flatly: "There is no known question, at least no question that I know about, on which negotiations would appear to be successful." The next moment, both men were warning darkly that continued intervention by Hanoi could bring "the initiation of military actions . . . against North Vietnam" and a widening war.

Ironically, it was left to Senator Fulbright to state the harsh realities in terms which were remarkably prophetic, though not entirely consistent with the opposition role he was increasingly to take later on. On one point, he agreed with Rusk. "The hard fact of the matter," he said in March, "is that our bargaining position is at present a weak one; and until the equation of advantage between the two sides has been substantially altered in our favor, there can be little prospect of a negotiated settlement."

His remedy, however, placed him a full year ahead of official, acknowledged Johnson Administration thinking. "It seems clear," Fulbright declared, "that only two realistic options are open to us in Vietnam in the immediate future: the expansion of the conflict in one way or another; or a renewed effort to bolster the capacity of the South Vietnamese to prosecute the war successfully on its present scale." The Johnson Administration remained anchored to unsuccessful execution of option number two for a year; when it finally elected option number one almost a year later, it found itself increasingly at odds with Senate Foreign Relations Committee Chairman Fulbright.

But there were those in the State Department who shared the Fulbright sense of urgency. The Kennedy braintrust on the policy-planning side of the war was an energetic triumvirate consisting of Under Secretary of State Averell Harriman, Assistant Secretary Hilsman, and a young White House staffer, Michael Forrestal, who later moved over to State. In the aftermath of Diem's downfall, the political shambles in Saigon and the deteriorating situation in the countryside encouraged them in the belief that quick efforts were indeed necessary to turn the tide. The efforts would have combined an improved counterinsurgency program with larger emphasis on the social, political, and economic aspects of the struggle to serve as an antidote to the revolutionary rallying cry of the Vietcong—and more U.S. troops would be needed. One proposal would have brought as many as 100,000 American Special Forces rapidly onto the scene, not to take formal battle stations but to concentrate on more sophisticated counterguerrilla activities. The triumvirate was speaking of a bureaucratic overhaul with one politically oriented civilian "czar" in charge, and they even had a candidate—William Sullivan, later to become U.S. Ambassador to Laos—in mind.

But McNamara, whose voice was always influential, had trouble enough holding the U.S. military in line; mustering a big new U.S. force for Vietnam would have opened up heated arguments; in early 1964, the Defense Secretary was still of the view that the war could be won the way it was being waged. And, more important than anything else, Lyndon Johnson not only did not want controversial new initiatives; he did not really have time for careful consideration of the Vietnam war at all. "The word was to keep the tough decisions away from the White House," one of the State Department proponents of urgent action said at the time, "and this would have taken a major effort by the President." So the triumvirate was broken up. Hilsman was the first to go. Harriman was switched from the top political job at State to a roving ambassadorship and not restored to grace until early 1966. Forrestal resigned. The center of gravity in Vietnam policy-making shifted to those who, for one reason or another, could think of little else at the time than to stand pat. The military had its own built-in paralysis against expanding the war. Dean Rusk was doggedly against losing it, firm in his determination that Hanoi "must leave its neighbors alone," convinced that Vietnam was a major test of U.S. will and the effectiveness of Communist wars of liberation—with implications for the validity of U.S. commitments and for national prestige around the globe. But he was not for pushing new courses of action at a time when the President was in an unreceptive frame of mind; at the White House, Mac Bundy apparently shared this view. It is difficult to detect the degree of Johnson influence in any of this. But the absence of decision-making, as Dean Rusk was to say in quite another context (in defense of U.S. intervention in the Dominican Republic), can amount to a decision in itself. And the decision was more of the same, and not much more, in Vietnam.

There was less and less safety, however, in standing completely pat. First there was the Laotian flare-up, which the President was able to damp down more or less surreptitiously. Then in August, there came a quixotic attack by North Vietnamese torpedo boats on the "U.S.S. Maddox," a destroyer operating in the Gulf of Tonkin, and the President felt compelled to invoke the Lyndon Law "Don't tread on me." In the process, he also demonstrated vividly his capacity for extracting from almost anything—even an apparently adverse development—a political gain. At the first torpedo-boat assault, the United States merely protested to Hanoi and warned of reprisals if it happened again. For reasons still puzzling to most onlookers, the North Vietnamese response was a second attack two days later against the "Maddox" and the "C. Turner Joy." To most of the President's advisers, it seemed a direct affront that could not be allowed to go unanswered lest grave miscalculations of U.S. resolve develop among the Communist war-managers in Hanoi and Peking.

Politically, there were limits as to just how prudent Lyndon Johnson could afford to be. He wished to appear more prudent than Goldwater. But he did not wish to appear to be a pushover. So there was little argument about launching retaliatory air strikes against the torpedo-boat facilities on a one-shot, tit-for-tat basis, and only brief debate over the details. (Rusk wanted one target removed from the list because civilians might be endangered, and Johnson agreed; but in the case of a second target which the Secretary of State thought was too close to the Chinese frontier but which the Pentagon considered militarily vital, he sided with McNamara and against Rusk, by his own account.)

The Tonkin incident was a brief flare-up, but it lasted just long enough to provide an opportunity for Johnson to arm himself with an overwhelming mandate from Congress to do just about anything he felt was necessary in Vietnam. On August 5, the day after the second torpedo-boat raid and the retaliatory American air strikes, the President sent a message to Congress stating that the shooting itself would have made a Congressional resolution essential "in any event" but that there was an additional argument because of the fact that the United States faced three months of political campaigning. "Hostile nations must understand that in such a period the United States will continue to protect its national interests, and that in these matters there is no division among us."

Congress had no real choice, even though nobody could make much sense out of the torpedo attacks and what they might portend. Two days later, by a unanimous vote in the House and with only two Senators dissenting, Congress wrote Lyndon Johnson a blank check for Vietnam, authorizing the President "to take all necessary measures to repel any armed attack against the forces of the United States and to prevent further aggression." Johnson did not find a need to draw on this account for six months, but he was still drawing on it, to the increasing chagrin of his Congressional critics, in 1966, when U.S. forces were deeply committed to warfare in Vietnam, debate over the war was intensifying, and many lawmakers were asking who gave the President authority for such drastic measures. You did, the President was pleased to be able to reply.

It was not, strictly speaking, a completely convincing answer, as even Administration officials would concede. On paper, it looked convincing, and with the public at large, it doubtless served Johnson's purposes well. But Congressional acts have "legislative histories" which must also be taken into account in weighing their real intent, and the legislative history of the Tonkin resolution is interesting, for an effort was made by Senator Gaylord Nelson to amend it precisely for the purpose of preventing its use as justification for a major change in the U.S. mission in South Vietnam. Nelson would have put Congress on record against "extension of the present conflict" and in favor of a continuing advisory military role. He was talked out of pushing the amendment by reassurances he received from Fulbright, who as Chairman of the Foreign Relations Committee was responsible for interpreting what the Administration had in mind. And he gave it as his opinion that the Nelson amendment was "an accurate reflection of what I believe is the President's policy," and, therefore, superfluous.

"I am concerned about the Congress appearing to tell the Executive Branch and the public that we would endorse a complete change in our mission," Nelson declared, and Fulbright responded: "I do not interpret the joint resolution in that way at all. It strikes me, as I understand it, that the joint resolution is quite consistent with our existing mission and our understanding of what we have been doing in South Vietnam for the last ten years."

In early 1966, Fulbright was publicly blaming himself for a "mistake" in not accepting Nelson's amendment. But by that time, of course, the U.S. mission in South Vietnam has already undergone fundamental change—at least in the way it was being carried out. And Johnson had been in a position all along the way to argue that, on the face of it, he had acted well within the law. Meantime, the Tonkin resolution had served a useful purpose in the pre-election period, even though at that point Johnson distinctly did not wish to widen the conflict. Further North Vietnamese attacks might still have forced his hand—forced him to take the very same sort of aggressive, dangerous steps he was accusing Goldwater of advocating. Had that happened, he would have at least had advance Congressional approval for whatever steps he had to take.

What developed was a deadly race against time; increasingly the question agonizing the war-planners in Washington and Saigon was whether South Vietnam could be kept from crumbling without a much more vigorous U.S. effort before November 3. If this developing challenge was evident to the President in mid-1964, however, there was little evidence of his concern. Indeed, the line offered publicly, and privately, in response to Republican arguments that the Communists should be denied a safe sanctuary in North Vietnam from which to subvert the South, was that the insurrection in the South was largely a home-grown affair. Maxwell Taylor made the argument privately, just before embarking for Saigon as Ambassador; bombing the North or otherwise moving to choke off infiltration, he contended, would still leave an indigenous, hostile force of 60,000 or so insurgents capable of foraging off the countryside, capturing needed arms and ammunition, and carrying on the war.

The State Department's Director of Intelligence, Thomas Hughes, speaking in Panama on June 8, declared that "by far the greater part of the Vietcong forces in South Vietnam are South Vietnamese, the preponderance of Vietcong weapons come not from Communist countries but from capture, purchase, and local manufacture." In other words, there was no real need to expand the war beyond the South, leaving aside the question of risk.

"We Are Not Going North"

Any political campaign would have had a distracting impact on the conduct of the U.S. effort in Vietnam—or any other place. But the 1964 Johnson-Goldwater contest was not just any campaign, and its impact was therefore a good deal more serious. The trouble started, some would argue, back in October, 1963, while John F. Kennedy was still President, and it started because

Barry Goldwater never did seem to know what he was trying to say. What he said in Hartford, Conn., in the course of his campaign for the Republican nomination, was that NATO "commanders" ought to have authority to use tactical nuclear weapons without explicit authority from the President. Almost as soon as he said it, he and his advisers started saying that he didn't really mean it. Every awkward effort he made to explain just what he did mean only served to strengthen the impression of a man hellbent for total victory over Communism at whatever risk of nuclear war.

It was a hopeless issue for a political campaign, because the essence of it—the actual arrangements for the delegation of authority to fire nuclear weapons—was, of necessity, a state secret. It was a hopeless issue for Goldwater, moreover, because it cast him not just against the Democrats but against the world of governmental officialdom. This strategy made it a matter of his word and judgment against that of responsible civilian and military figures who were obliged to uphold the existing arrangements while also free to beg off, on security grounds, from meaningful discussion of the issue.

But Goldwater seemed incapable of letting the matter drop. Because as an Air Force Reserve officer he was also constrained by security, he could not really attack the existing system in detailed, understandable terms, all he could do was sound increasingly, alarmingly, and even irrationally aggressive.

For Lyndon Johnson, this situation was like an exposed jugular, and the instinct to go for it was irresistible. Add to this Johnson's country-style campaigning, and the result could only be to sow seeds of confusion in the Communist power centers of the world. Country-style campaigners apply a quaint, rustic, zesty simplicity to complex questions (as witness Harry Truman's 1948 appraisal of Stalin: "I like old Joe; he's just a prisoner of the Politburo"). In the closed societies of the Communist world, however, words are weighed carefully for export, and the assumption, too often, may be that foreign statesmen weigh their words with equal care. No one can say what impact the Johnson campaign theme in 1964 had upon Communist readings of U.S.

intent. But many of the same diplomats who, in 1965 and 1966, were to upbraid critics of Vietnam policy in Congress and in the press for the confusion this might be causing in Hanoi or Peking, were equally disquieted in 1964 over the possible impact of the message Lyndon Johnson was ever more strongly transmitting from the American hustings.

What he was saying, emphatically and repeatedly, was that he did not intend to lead the United States into a wider war in Vietnam. And while he was sometimes careful to qualify his pledge with such phrases as "at this time" or "if possible," just a few random samples of Johnson oratory in October of 1964 make his message unmistakable: it was not his commitment to Vietnam, it was Dwight Eisenhower's; while he intended to honor it, he also intended to avoid a deeper U.S. involvement in the fighting.

"There are those that say I ought to go north and drop bombs, to try to wipe out the supply lines, and they think that would escalate the war." he said in a speech on September 25. "But we don't want to get involved in a nation with seven hundred million people and get tied down in a land war in Asia."

What was his answer? Certainly not to "go south," to "get out and come home . . . [because] we don't like to break our treaties and we don't like to walk off and leave people who are searching for freedom," he explained in the same speech. "We're hoping that some way, somehow, these people that are invading them and trying to envelop them and trying to take their freedom from them will some day decide that it's not worth the price, and they will leave their neighbors alone, and we can have peace in the world. But we are not about to start another war, and we're not going to run away from where we are."

The image of Goldwater as the Democrats had gleefully helped paint it, and as the American public was rapidly coming to accept it, the image of the reckless international adventurer who would impose U.S. will and U.S. might upon the world at the risk of holocaust—this was always Johnson's backdrop. A good many of his close advisers who knew what he was saying in closed-door discussion of foreign policy considered a largely impromptu campaign speech in Manchester, N.H., on September 28, as perhaps the best public expression of his real beliefs. The adversities that had crowded in upon him in his first year in office were tempering his view of the U.S. role in the world. He began, as he usually began, with a brisk rundown of U.S. military potential, ticking off the billions that had been spent and would be spent for weaponry, cataloging the bombers and ballistic missiles. But once having offered assurance that the United States had power enough to protect itself, he dwelt at far greater length on the limitations of that power to order world events to American liking. He spoke of the "illusion that the United States can demand resolution of all the world's problems and mash a button and get the job done." He said his country had "willingly accepted the responsibilities of world leadership, and when our own vital interests are challenged we act. But we are not the sole captain of the ship."

Another illusion he was pleased to attribute to his Republican opponent was that "force, or the threat of force can solve all problems." A third illusion was that "we could, if only we tried hard enough, put an end to all difficulty and danger and then retire from the world." In a moving passage, he declared that "the sound of gunfire in Asia echoes in the homes of Manchester. The speeches of a leader in Moscow or Peking helps shape the life of a subway rider in New York. An angry cry for freedom in Africa requires an understanding act in Washington. And as long as this nation endures we are going to be engaged in the affairs of the world. I welcome this involvement. I believe the American people welcome it. It may bring danger but it brings an added dimension to the prospects of freedom. In this world, as in life itself, there is really no escape from problems. You can't run away from them. [There is] no escape from peril."

But again he repeated: "We are not going north and we are not going south." Again he declared, "I didn't get you into Vietnam. You have been in Vietnam ten years. President Eisenhower wrote President Diem a letter in 1954 when the French pulled out of Vietnam, and he said, 'We want to help you to help your people keep from going Communist, and we will furnish you advice, we will furnish you assistance, and we will furnish you equipment if you will furnish the men, and if you want to fight for your freedom we will try to help you.'"

And in Manchester, as at other way stations along the campaign trail, he repeated the familiar refrain on escalation: "As far as I am concerned, I want to be very cautious and careful, and use it only as a last resort, when I start dropping bombs around that are likely to involve American boys in a war in Asia with seven hundred million Chinese. So just for the moment, I have not thought that we were ready for American boys to do the fighting for Asian boys."

Later in the month, in Akron, Ohio, it was the same thing. "Sometimes our folks get a little impatient," the President declared. "Sometimes they rattle their rockets some, and they bluff about their bombs. But we are not about to send American boys nine or ten thousand miles away from home to do what Asian boys ought to be doing for themselves." Over and over, and on three occasions alone in that one speech, the President evoked his favorite prophet, Isaiah. "There is only one road to peace," he said, "and that is to work at it patiently, deliberately, wisely, step by step, year by year, never to become reckless, never to become weary of the journey and irritated with folks who may not agree with you the first time you talk to them."

The top Vietnam planners of the U.S. Government had met in Honolulu in June, stirring speculation of a substantial step-up of the U.S. effort, and Johnson, in private conversations, was emphatic in his denials that any such plans had been brought to him. All the possibilities, he said that time, were under constant review—including "neutralization," or air strikes above the 17th parallel, or a wide range of intermediate and undercover harassing operations against Communist infiltration. But the President spoke feelingly in private as well as in public of the dangers of wider war, of the possibility of provoking a massive Chinese intervention.

"We know there are two hundred million in the Chinese Army," he told a visitor that fall. "If one little general in shirt sleeves can take Saigon," he continued, in a reference to the most recent military coup against the South Vietnamese government, "think about two hundred million Chinese coming down those trails." And he added, shaking his head emphatically: "No, sir! I don't want to fight them."

Meanwhile, there were clear signs of growing anxiety, if not at the highest official level, at least at the lower working levels of the government; the experts could read the signs in the increased political shambles in Saigon, in the increased rate of infiltration, in a tide of war that was running unmistakably against the South Vietnamese. "It is going to be close," said one of the State Department's most reliable authorities as the U.S. election day approached.

By September, a new and, to some, more compelling argument for not moving quickly to expand the U.S. effort was beginning to take precedence above all others; this was the argument that the government in Saigon, roiled by continuous fighting and struggling for power among the generals, could not stand up under the strain of a systematic expansion of the war to North Vietnam and the risk it would bring of a wave of terrorism and subversion by the Communists in reprisal, or even, conceivably, of North Vietnamese air strikes to the south. Over and over, the President was repeating, in private as well as in public, his assurances that the United States would not "pull out and go home." But he shared the view of a number of his advisers, including, at this stage, Maxwell Taylor, that a political structure as rickety as the one in Saigon was in no shape to carry the war to the north.

So it went, almost, but not quite, up to election day. Then, two days before the voting, Vietcong forces launched a surprise attack on the U.S. air base in Bien Hoa killing five Americans, wounding 76, and destroying six B-57 bombers. The symbolism of this assault could hardly have been lost on American policy-makers. The B-57's were American symbols. They had been moved into South Vietnam, and based at Bien Hoa shortly after the Gulf of Tonkin flare-up, and they were quite deliberately intended to serve notice upon Hanoi that the United States had readily at hand the capacity to deliver a crushing air attack on the North.

The planes were there at the instigation of Secretary McNamara (with the concurrence of Rusk, but without any extended discussion with Johnson) for the specific purpose of impressing Hanoi with U.S. air power. It was another signal, another token of U.S. resolve, or at least it was so intended by McNamara and Rusk, and they had no end of encouragement from the Air Force, which welcomed the opportunity to draw attention to the potential in U.S. air power. Paradoxically, it was State Department officials, not Pentagon men, who raised most vigorously the question of whether the planes could be adequately guarded. The question was the subject of an animated discussion at a staff conference presided over by Rusk; anxiety was voiced that the Vietcong would accept the challenge and try to destroy the giant bombers. According to one account, Rusk put in a call to McNamara and was instantly reassured. The attitude of the military, as conveyed later to the State Department men, was that base security was something for the military to worry about.

So the transfer of the planes did not become an item of dispute between State and Defense and therefore did not become an item for Presidential decision.

But the military, as it turned out, did not have the base-security problem in hand. Despite repeated nagging by State Department experts, some of whom had predicted with astonishing accuracy (based on hard intelligence) that Bien Hoa must be considered a high-priority Vietcong target, the B-57's, which had arrived in August, were still not adequately dug in by the end of October. They were demolished by the Vietcong mortars. The symbol had been buried. From the U.S. Embassy in Saigon came an urgent recommendation by Ambassador Taylor for reprisals in the form of air attacks on the North similar to the post-Tonkin attacks. Not to act after Bien Hoa, it was argued, would undo whatever useful purpose might have been served by the Tonkin retaliation against the torpedo boats. U.S. resolve would be more than ever in doubt.

Shortly after the Bien Hoa incident, Maxwell Taylor was to express frank puzzlement, in private conversations, at Johnson's failure to do anything in response to Bien Hoa. But some members of his embassy staff were to concede later that their recommendations for reprisals of the Tonkin tit-for-tat variety were forwarded to Washington with very little expectation that anything would be done about them two days before a national election. The election was too close at hand, and the arguments in favor of temporizing came from diplomats as well as politicos. An upheaval in Moscow had brought new, unknown leadership. Even before, there were those in the State Department, including Ambassador Llewellyn Thompson, who had been arguing that "going north" would run a real risk of forcing the Soviets back into tighter allegiance with Communist China at a time when it seemed to serve U.S. interests not to do anything that might heal the breach in the Communist world. Since nobody knew what had brought the downfall of Khrushchev and to what extent it had been influenced by internal Soviet concern over the Sino-Soviet split, there was all the more reason not to drive the new crowd in the Kremlin back in the direction of the more militant Peking line.

Beyond this, there was awareness in the State Department and elsewhere that almost anything drastic that was done during the summer and fall of 1964 would have been suspect in its motivations, however difficult it was to determine precisely the degree of sophistication with which Hanoi or Peking or Moscow would read American action in an election year. Johnson, according to his associates, felt strongly that any major move in Vietnam, should it become necessary, would only have maximum impact once the election was passed, and that no move as serious as a deliberate expansion of the Vietnam war should be made unless it had the best possible opportunity to achieve maximum effect. "The other side would not have believed in any response we made during the election campaign," said one man in close touch with the President's thinking at the time. "He felt he had to get Goldwaterism defeated soundly in order to make it an American response, instead of a political response." Apparently that was the reading of the White House staff, for the decision was made not to present Bien Hoa to the President as a yes-or-no, make-or-break proposition. "At Bien Hoa, we were dealing with a man who could give only a fraction of his time and attention. I am not sorry I recommended against a response and in favor of treating it as an isolated incident. If I had it to do over again, I would do it the same way." Yet neither the official who said this nor a good many others would deny that the failure of the United States to respond to the Bien Hoa provocation, coming on the heels of a conciliatory Vietnam line in the campaign, in which Lyndon Johnson plainly made manifest his profound disinclination to widen the war, must certainly have encouraged Hanoi and Peking in the belief that Tonkin had been a special case, and that U.S. installations could be attacked with impunity. Nobody said it quite that baldly, though Dean Rusk was to tell *The New York Times* later that "perhaps the Communist world misunderstood our Presidential campaign."

Future events strongly suggest that the Communists indeed had misunderstood. And if a measure of misunderstanding is inherent in the free play of politics in an open society, a measure of consistency is no less vitally essential to the conduct of a continuing confrontation with the Communists.

No one can conclusively demonstrate what would have been the result if the United States had responded at the time of Bien Hoa; perhaps the Communists still would have gone on misreading the United States and extending their Vietnam effort. They might have done so under misapprehension that this would not ultimately bring a much tougher U.S. response or in confidence that in any event the odds would always be in favor of Asian manpower against American firepower, however large this trouble might become.

But it cannot be excluded, if there was any logic in Tonkin, and, indeed, any logic in the subsequent American escalation of its involvement in the war in 1965, that the Communists at that stage might have decided to settle for what would have been half a loaf under any agreement that could conceivably have been arranged; at that stage, the Vietcong bargaining position was strong because the Vietcong military position was strong. It is also possible that Hanoi, if not Peking, would have concluded that the prudent course lay in keeping the conflict relatively small, even in the absence of a negotiated settlement. A little more than a year later, when the war had gotten a lot bigger on both sides, this sort of *de facto* stabilization of the struggle, without formal accord, was at least an alternate U.S. objective. A strong, unmistakable response at Bien Hoa might therefore have stabilized the struggle, if not settled it, at a far lower and less costly level of U.S. involvement. It was just about at this time that

Hanoi was beginning the process of pushing large numbers of troops and quantities of matériel down the roads and trails into South Vietnam in what was to become a major effort to deliver a knockout blow against the South Vietnamese forces. Only access to the inner secrets of the Hanoi Government and a far clearer view of the tugging and hauling that was going on between the hard-liners and the soft-liners in the North and in Peking will ever settle this point; and hindsight makes it easier to argue that Bien Hoa was a mistake. But in the context of what was to come later—a similar sneak attack on an American billet in Saigon and, finally, the crucial Vietcong assault on the American installation at Pleiku—a strong case can be made, retrospectively, that American inaction at Bien Hoa encouraged Communist miscalculation of U.S. intent, and indeed, convinced the Communists that they could step up infiltration and engage in acts of terrorism aimed deliberately at Americans in South Vietnam with impunity. Had the United States responded at Bien Hoa, the result might simply have been to advance, by three or four months, the process by which the United States massively built up its fighting force in Vietnam—only the timing, rather than the course of the struggle, might have been affected. But it can equally be argued that a stronger American reaction to Bien Hoa would have been sufficiently convincing to give the Communists serious pause, and thus perhaps have hastened the day when both sides would have been ready—simultaneously—to reduce the level of hostilities or even to negotiate.

The Bypath to Peace

On August 6, 1964, just two days after the Gulf of Tonkin torpedo-boat attack and the retaliatory U.S. air strikes against North Vietnam, United Nations Secretary General U Thant came to Washington to meet privately with President Johnson and then with other U.S. officials. He went away with the feeling that the United States would be "receptive" to an attempt on his part to promote diplomatic contact, if not outright negotiations, between the U.S. and Hanoi. There were "no assurances" offered by the United States, everybody seems to agree. But Thant felt, either from something Johnson said to him alone or from declarations by other officials, that he had a go-ahead. So he tried. And the consequences of his effort were to provoke dark headlines, deep confusion, sharp controversy—but precious little peace—more than a year later, when a magazine article posthumously quoted Adlai Stevenson as saying that the U.S. Government, and particularly Defense Secretary McNamara, had opposed U Thant's "patient efforts," and that the U.N. Secretary General was "furious."

"HANOI OFFER IN '64 TO DISCUSS PEACE REJECTED BY U.S.," said headline in *The New York Times* on November 16, 1965, over a report on the magazine article by commentator Eric Sevareid and a State Department statement in response to it. "STATE DEPARTMENT FINALLY ADMITS U.S. REJECTED HANOI TALKS," said the *New York Herald Tribune*, which carried an "angry denial" by McNamara that he had been responsible for blocking U Thant's efforts.

The implication plainly remained, however, that the Pentagon had torpedoed peace talks and that the United States had bungled its way by a well-marked exit to Vietnam peace in its blind rush to escalate the Vietnamese war. The atmosphere was not improved by the fact that in November, 1965, the United States had indeed become bogged down in a large Asian war over Vietnam, or by State Department talk of the "sensitive antenna" of Dean Rusk, which allegedly would have told him if Hanoi had really been serious.

But the real significance of the U Thant peace probe does not hinge on assessing the intentions of Hanoi at the time, or, perhaps, at any time over the long stretch from the beginning of the Johnson Presidency until well toward the end of 1965. For the fact of the matter is that over that stretch, neither McNamara nor any individual U.S. official can fairly be held accountable for the failure of a host of efforts to generate negotiations for peace. The dominant factor working against negotiations was a collective attitude of mind, traces of which could be found running through the spectrum of U.S. opinion and including the appraisals of Senator Fulbright and Adlai Stevenson as well as those of Robert McNamara and Dean Rusk.

Public attention was caught by every reported Communist "peace feeler," by every hint that Hanoi might wish to negotiate. But the attention of policy-makers centered on coldly practical questions: what sort of settlement could conceivably be negotiated, given the existing balance of forces in South Vietnam, even assuming a willingness on the part of the Communists to talk? And what would be the most propitious time? When those questions were answered, the answers were remarkably uniform in their downgrading of prospects for constructive bargaining. In March, 1964, Senator Fulbright thought the war was going so badly that an equitable settlement safeguarding U.S. interests was probably impossible. In mid-campaign, the war was going even worse. And the tragedy of the electoral timetable was that it allowed the military and political situation in South Vietnam to deteriorate still further. It is against this background that the single most celebrated "peace initiative" prior to the fateful U.S. plunge into deep involvement in Vietnam in the spring of 1965 must be cast. What emerges is a tangled tale of casual exchanges, curiously lackadaisical follow-ups, and outright contradictions, all of which are richly revealing of the mood of Lyndon Johnson and his principal advisers at the time the United States was moving almost inexorably toward a wider Vietnam war.

Three astonishing aspects of the affair stand out in bold relief:

One: According to at least five officials in a position to know with considerable certainty, President Johnson never again heard of the U Thant initiative in any serious, formal way from that day in August when it apparently received some vague, generalized endorsement from him until the following February, when his attention was drawn to the subject with considerable force by a press-conference comment by U Thant in New York. Deploring the lack of progress towards negotiation and implying that the United States had perhaps not been as zealous in its quest for peace as it might have been, Thant went so far as to assert that "the great American people, if they only knew the true facts and the background to the developments in South Vietnam, will agree with me that further bloodshed is unnecessary."

The suggestion that the U.S. Government wasn't leveling with the U.S. public produced a minor explosion in the White House

—and an intemperate response. "The United States has received no proposal from U Thant," was Press Secretary Reedy's cold retort; when that was quickly proved misleading, to say the least, the adjective "meaningful" was added to the word "response." But the damage had been done; another crack had been needlessly opened up in the Johnson Administration's already suspect credibility. By this time, the United States had already launched the early-February air strikes against North Vietnam, and the wisdom of this course was under serious question. The impression that the President had kicked off a wider war without checking out the option of a negotiated settlement had set in.

In fact, that option had been checked out by Dean Rusk and by others and their negative conclusions taken into account in the calculations of the President. But the fact also seems to have been that the hit-or-miss diplomacy conducted by the U.S. Government and U Thant that followed the August meeting in the President's office never engaged the attention of the President. It was largely handled by Adlai Stevenson and Dean Rusk.

Two: However promising Adlai Stevenson may have thought the U Thant initiative was when he looked back on it, he did not put great value on its prospects at the time. According to one of his closest advisers at the U.N. mission and to officials at the other end of the pipeline in the State Department, Stevenson was fully aware that nothing very profitable was possible in the way of negotiations at least until after the election; he had, after all, run for the Presidency twice himself and had some feel for the demands of a Presidential campaign. He could assess the practicality of launching diplomatic initiatives in an atmosphere charged with partisan politics. His initial reporting to Rusk and others of U Thant's own progress reports was by phone or in conversations in Washington. "We never even got a written memorandum from Adlai," a State Department official declared when the ruckus over the U Thant peace overtures flared up in November, 1965.

Three: So informal and casual were the exchanges between U Thant and Stevenson at the United Nations that the Secretary General's own versions, offered at different times to a variety of U.S. officials (and to the author), differ widely. One critical exchange with Stevenson has been variously established by Thant as having taken place either in November of 1964 or in January of 1965. U Thant was a busy man in a big job. He had a burning desire to stop the Vietnam bloodshed, and it might be unreasonable to expect him to recall the fine points of the urgent diplomatic effort he was conducting. But the difficulty in reconstructing the episode in terms that all the affected parties can agree upon does offer some insight into the character of the undertaking; it was deadly serious, but there also seems to have been a widespread feeling from the beginning—at least on the U.S. side—that hopes for it were doomed.

Indeed, it was born in an atmosphere of skepticism. In the August White House sessions, U Thant brought up the idea of a private exploration of the prospect of direct talks between the United States and Hanoi and suggested Burma, Cambodia, or perhaps Pakistan as possible go-betweens (although he conceded he had already sounded out his own country, Burma, which had declined to act as an intermediary). He was told at one point by McGeorge Bundy that the United States had already sent a "signal" to Peking by courtesy of another Asian neutral nation and had encountered stony silence. But Thant was given to believe the United States had no objection to his probe, and accordingly, in the middle of August, he contacted a high Russian official and had him relay a proposal to Hanoi that the North Vietnamese enter into direct diplomatic contact with the United States. There was no presumption that these contacts would be real negotiations. In the first week of September, Thant got an "affirmative reply" to his request—a reply which was later to assume the dignity and dimension of a "peace feeler" from Hanoi, even though there was nothing in it that necessarily presupposed a disposition to make peace. Thant's idea was to stage the contact in Rangoon, and he obtained Burmese permission for that; he had in mind a simple contact between the American Ambassador and the North Vietnamese Consul General, both resident there, thinking that would attract no attention. Thant was against the dispatch of a big-name U.S. diplomat; he was apparently conscious of the need for extreme secrecy.

At this point, the reconstruction of events becomes complex; it entails considering alternate versions, including alternate versions from the same man. U Thant has insisted that he told Stevenson in early September about Ho Chi Minh's willingness to talk, presumably right after he got the word from Hanoi. But Washington officials argue that as far as they can tell, Stevenson wasn't informed until late November. Some of the late U.N. Ambassador's close associates believe he may indeed have gotten the word from U Thant in September, or at least at some point before the election, and decided not to pass it along until after the voting on the theory that it wouldn't get a fair response while the campaign was on. That is the account of one man extremely close to Stevenson. What also seems possible is that the whole thing was kept on a thoroughly informal, noncommittal basis for as long as possible, so as not to risk having it killed off in the unfavorable election climate. Thant, for example, insists he got an answer of some sort from the United States in October, raising questions about the prospective place for negotiations, the participants, and other details. Then, by one U Thant version, in late November he was told that the United States wasn't interested, largely because of fear that the secrecy would be broken and that this would shatter the already shaky governmental structure in Saigon. U Thant remembers chiding Stevenson on this point, asking "What government—Minh, Khanh, Suu, Tri?" Thant also recalls a U.S. insistence that South Vietnam would have to be allowed to sit in, and his reply that this would ruin the prospects because there would be demands for the Vietcong as well.

Twice in December, Thant sounded out the United States again with no success. Around this time, Thant was hospitalized with an ulcer. In January, he apparently attempted to revive the Rangoon scheme and float some other suggestions as well, including a proposal for an open conference in Geneva of the U.S., Russia, mainland China, Britain, France, and the two Vietnams. But this latter idea floundered, he claimed, when the Russians, French, and British insisted on knowing the U.S. response before giving their own, and he was unable to get any U.S. answer until the middle of January, when largely procedural aspects were again apparently discussed. At that time, everybody seems to agree that the U.S. attitude was indeed negative; the government in

Saigon was in shambles. It also seems to be agreed all around that at the end of January, U Thant was told by Stevenson that the United States was "negative" on negotiations on the two familiar counts—that Saigon would have to sit in, and that even then, the South Vietnamese political structure probably couldn't stand up under the strain. U Thant passed this word along to Ho Chi Minh, and he has indicated his belief that it probably reached the Hanoi Government about February 5, 1965.

On February 7, the Vietcong launched three attacks against U.S. and Vietnamese military installations, the most important of which was an American compound at Pleiku, where seven American soldiers were killed and 109 wounded. The next day, the United States struck back at the North with bombing attacks in what was to mark the beginning of regular air warfare against North Vietnam and the beginnings of a major escalation of the U.S. combat effort in the war.

There was almost certainly no connection between the U.S. rejection of negotiations relayed to Hanoi at the end of January (even assuming the rejection did in fact reach Hanoi on February 5) and the Pleiku assaults (which would have required more advance planning and preparation than that). However, it also seems probable that the distinctly negative U.S. attitude towards negotiations must have been known to Hanoi long before February. The U.S. Government seemed to have difficulty in bringing itself to say "no" with finality or in convincing terms. Thant insists that he found it regularly impossible during December and January to get from Stevenson anything more than vague indications that the "matter was under consideration" or that he "had no word yet." On one occasion in January, Stevenson apparently told Thant that the U.S. reluctance to open up contacts with the North was based on its own unrewarding soundings of Hanoi. But when Thant tried to pry out of Stevenson a hint of what channel the United States was using, Stevenson could only guess that "it might be the Canadians." The tireless Thant took the trouble to check with Canadian Prime Minister Lester Pearson, who denied he was the U.S. intermediary. Even in February, U Thant was still trying to get a more final reply from Stevenson. In late February, he complained to Rusk that he still didn't know with absolute certainty where the United States stood. He finally got a formal flat refusal on February 27, according to a subsequent announcement from U.N. headquarters.

By that time, U.S. air strikes against North Vietnam had become a regular affair.

Still, one should not form the impression of an Administration deaf to the one great opportunity for a peaceful settlement of Vietnam late in 1964 and in 1965. The Administration did have channels of its own—channels rated more reliable for serious soundings than the United Nations, where rumor is rife and secrecy a sometime thing. Leaving aside the volunteer peace promotion of well-intentioned amateurs (and of some volunteer travelers to Hanoi who were not, by U.S. lights, all that well intentioned), the United States had direct as well as indirect lines to Hanoi whose dependability rested on their undetectability. How good these contracts were and how accurate the readings of the results must therefore be taken on faith. On this point, controversy will center for as long as the Vietnam war lasts. There were serious students outside the government, as well as inside, who minutely examined the long-distance dialogue between Hanoi and Washington and seriously challenged the prevailing interpretations in Washington of Hanoi's "signaling," some who saw chinks of interest in negotiations where others saw only a stone wall. One who persevered along this course was columnist Joseph Kraft, whose carefully developed contacts among Vietnamese and others in Paris, Algiers, and elsewhere gave him reason to believe that Hanoi, at various stages along the way, was seriously interested in a settlement, both before and after the beginning of U.S. air strikes in the North. He also saw a genuine possibility of doing business separately with the Vietcong, or with the National Liberation Front, the insurrection's political arm. By mid-1965, this approach was getting increasingly serious consideration in official Washington; by early 1966, it had become a subject for public debate.

But the key question in this or any other approach to the prospect of negotiation was always the same: just what sort of settlement did the United States have in mind? By 1966, this too was beginning to be a subject for serious public debate. But any

examination of how the United States got into the Vietnam war
in such a big way has to begin with acceptance of the fact that
this question wasn't being debated much by the men from whom
Johnson could logically have sought counsel in the last months of
1964 and the first few weeks in 1965.

For at that point, the United States was bent on expunging
South Vietnam of any lingering Communist threat. The infiltrators from the North were to be driven out, or obliged, under
settlement terms, to withdraw. Vietnam was to be delivered "free
and clear" of Communism. Hanoi, in Dean Rusk's litany, was
to be required to "leave her neighbors alone."

Since Hanoi, at about that time, held sway over more than
half of her southern neighbor and could see the Saigon Government crumbling before her very eyes, it is scarcely surprising
that the "signals" from Hanoi should not have encouraged optimism about the sort of settlement the United States had in mind.
Nor was it surprising that the United States should have had
little interest in negotiating, for it could see the same things in
South Vietnam that Hanoi could see.

As a practical matter, then, U Thant was tuned in on the
wrong frequency. The right frequency—and as good a measure as
any of official U.S. thinking at the time—is perhaps best indicated
by a conversation in December, 1964, between Under Secretary
Ball and French President De Gaulle. Ball was a dogged and
consistent "devil's advocate" about almost everything the United
States did in Vietnam from mid-1964 on. But he was a loyal
Administration man. (It was a familiar Johnson stratagem to send
known dissenters to argue on behalf of his policies.) Ball's December presentation to De Gaulle can therefore be taken as an
accurate reflection of the attitude which was to project the United
States into a widening conflict in South Vietnam in the first
months of 1965. And the Gaullist line came close to approximat-
ing the line of that still small body of those who cautioned against
deeper involvement in Vietnam—including, ironically, George
Ball.

Somewhat paraphrased, Ball's opening presentation went like
this:

The United States and France, judging from earlier discussions, have the same objective—an independent, viable South Vietnam. Their differences are over how to achieve it. The United States and France likewise appeared to agree that the insurrection was largely being directed by Hanoi. Under the circumstances, the United States saw only two alternatives: either build up a strong and stable government in Saigon to which the public would rally, and thereby create a capability in the South to resist the insurrection and bring it under control; or exert enough military pressure on North Vietnam to discourage the promotion of insurrection in the South by the North.

The United States *had decided that if it could not achieve the former alternative within a "reasonable" time, it would be forced to try the latter,* even while realizing the serious risk of involving the Communist Chinese actively in the struggle.

The United States does not want to do that, but it was important that Hanoi realize that the United States would do that. As for negotiations, there was an argument for trying to reach a diplomatic solution and some justice in the judgment that Peking is a powerful factor in the picture. Nevertheless, the United States felt that such an effort at that time would so undermine the morale of the government in Saigon that it might well collapse, leaving the way open to a quick capture of South Vietnam. Past experience, moreover, did not argue for an agreement with either North Vietnam or Communist China, since neither of them had shown much inclination to honor the agreements they had already signed. As for internationalizing the crisis in Vietnam, the United States thought this would be of little use until the insurrection had been brought under control.

Perhaps most important, the United States believed that no arrangements with the Communists had ever worked out unless the countervailing forces created some sort of equilibrium—as in Austria or Finland. In South Vietnam, the balance of power did not furnish the United States with a reasonable basis for bargaining.

The United States believed that China was roughly in the same situation as Russia in 1917, primitive, aggressive, militant, obliged to expand at the expense of its neighbors, and committed so firmly to this that it was unlikely to make any worthwhile deal or live up to it.

De Gaulle's answer, also paraphrased, began with a declaration of fundamental difference:

He did not accept the U.S. reading of China. As France saw it, China was the paper dragon [although he did not put it quite that way]. China had enormous internal problems and none of the intellectual, military, and agricultural resources that Russia had. The Chinese, at least for the next few years, were in no shape to embark on aggression. The negotiations the French had in mind would bring together the key powers and perhaps some major Asian nations at the bargaining table under circumstances which would make it impossible for the North Vietnamese to go on killing South Vietnamese without offending world opinion.

He was sympathetic with the U.S. problem, which, he noted, the French had labored under for a long time, and hoped that the U.S. estimate of the outlook was correct. But he felt called upon to state his view that it was wrong, that the United States could not win, that deeper U.S. involvement in military operations would only increase public hostility to the United States, and that eventually the hostility would be reflected in Saigon, which would not wish to be dominated by a major power, even a major power trying to be helpful. The United States should try to sound out Peking.

Ball interjected that this would not be understood at all in South Vietnam. As for a cease-fire, he said, Ho Chi Minh would simply disown terrorist activity, which takes place largely at night, and continue it in the face of negotiations or an internationalization of the effort to bring peace. Instead of the rebellion losing momentum in a *détente*, it would gain, because the Saigon Government would be obliged to honor a cease-fire.

At this point, De Gaulle bluntly disassociated France from any escalation the United States might embark upon, saying that France had found Asia a "rotten" place to fight in. "You cannot win it," De Gaulle said, winding up with a gracious offer of good offices any time the United States came looking for a middleman.

"Military pressure" on North Vietnam, "collapse" of the government in South Vietnam should diplomatic solutions be so much as discussed, a lack of "equilibrium" in the balance of forces—these were the essential, underlying factors in the Johnson Administration's Vietnam thinking at the turn of the year. And they pointed directly toward urgent measures to tilt the balance of forces the other way. The path to peace was not open, because neither Lyndon Johnson nor the key men around him—McNamara, Rusk, McGeorge Bundy—could see it leading anywhere. Johnson saw the situation, characteristically, in terms of an analogy to domestic politics. "I don't have to negotiate with Goldwater," he declared in one meeting with his aides, by way of demonstrating why, in his view, the Communists could think of no good reason for wanting to negotiate anything but surrender with an enemy which seemed in the process of suffering disastrous defeat.

The Highway to War

Pleiku was the trigger. Or so it seemed, when the Vietcong attacked American installations at that central highlands provincial capital in South Vietnam on February 7, 1965. Retaliatory U.S. aerial bombardment in North Vietnam was followed three days later by a similar Vietcong assault on an American billet in the coastal city of Qui Nhon, which brought further air retaliation and finally systematic air strikes to the north, the landing of the first contingents of U.S. combat troops, on March 6, for "perimeter defense" of American bases; and, ultimately, full-fledged combat, freely conceded as such, with U.S. soldiers pouring ashore.

But Pleiku was the trigger only in a technical sense. For if there was arguable diplomatic, political, and military logic in Lyndon Johnson's decision to escalate the U.S. effort in South Vietnam to build a stronger bargaining position—if not win total victory— there was also a high degree of political craftsmanship, no end of stage-management, and a good measure of legerdemain. As one of the very few high officials who opposed it at almost every step was to say later: "It was almost imperceptible, the way we got in. There was no one move that you could call decisive, or irreversible, not even very many actions that you could argue against in isolation. Yet when you put it all together, there we were in a war on the Asian mainland, with nobody really putting up much of a squawk while we were doing it."

To the President's admirers, his handling of Vietnam in the early months of 1965 was more than just skillful—it was a triumph of international and domestic politics. For if one accepts the need to right the "equilibrium," then it cannot be denied that Lyndon Johnson moved to do so with a bare minimum of dissent at home and less foreign opposition than might have been expected. And he did it, at least for a good many months, without giving the Communist Chinese or the Russians provocation in such intolerable degree that they felt obliged to move in any drastic way to the defense of Hanoi.

He did it, in brief, by making it all look like a logical sequence of almost unavoidable steps, starting with a simple, one-shot retaliation for Pleiku. It would not, of course, be fair to say that Johnson knew all along how far he planned to escalate; his moves had been carefully "calibrated," to use the term much favored by the war-game players among the policy-planners, to meet the real or anticipated moves of the enemy. But there was a master plan, and large parts of it dated back to before election day. Urgent consideration of what to do about Vietnam had begun among the President's advisers well before the November vote.

By one account, that of *Newsweek* White House correspondent Charles Roberts, Johnson himself had actually made up his mind to initiate air strikes against North Vietnam in October. Roberts, in his book *L.B.J.'s Inner Circle,* states flatly that "the President . . . told me in May, 1965, that he had made the decision to bomb four months before Pleiku . . . at the height of the Presidential election campaign." It seems more likely, however, that the decision made then by the President was more of a personal conclusion that something would have to be done to turn the tide of battle in Vietnam than a considered decision which he communicated to his aides—for some of his closest advisers hotly deny that any such "decision" was conveyed to them. In May, 1965, Johnson had Vietnam and the Dominican Republic on his hands and was under heavy attack for his quick and seemingly impulsive resort to force as a cure-all for international problems. Had he really planned the bomb raids north of the 17th parallel as early as the previous October, he would be exonerated of the charge of impulsiveness but guilty of gross deceit. For his public campaign promises in October not to "go north" were matched in private by far more fervent expressions of his hopes and intents not to widen the war. There is little reason to doubt his sincerity; indeed, in November, aides found it difficult even to draw his attention to serious consideration of the Vietnam war. In December, Vietnam was once again subjected to full-scale, high-level review, and the air was full of speculation that drastic new moves were afoot. But once again, the President led the chorus of denials, in private as well as in public.

Deadly serious contingency planning was going forward, nevertheless. The arguments, however, were not running all one way, and the President took pains to hear out the advocates of restraint. He studied reports that the Tonkin retaliation had done less to boost sagging South Vietnamese morale than many had expected. There were also projections suggesting that the most effective bombing of the North would not seriously cripple the insurrection, barring substantial improvement in the capability of the South Vietnamese to prosecute the war. There were warnings of adverse world reaction, of the danger of escalation, of the risk of a clash with the Chinese. Maxwell Taylor was still on a cautious tack, arguing that any new moves against North Vietnam would be to invite disaster unless the political and military base in the South could be made more secure. Among the Washington sages, the betting in November and on into December was still running against major U.S. escalation of its effort in the war. The military argument was still going in circles; the army still didn't want to take on that orphan war without air power, and widespread use of air power to pound communications lines in the North was still thought liable to provoke reprisals which the Saigon Government would be unable to withstand.

Then, abruptly, the argument turned around; in December, the shambles in Saigon began to reach such a critical condition that officials feared total collapse might well be imminent. The generals were undercutting one another and quarreling with Ambassador Taylor as well. Suddenly, it began to be said that doing nothing was coming to be more dangerous than doing something —almost anything—to keep the Saigon Government from going down the drain. This became the principal argument for expanding the war to the North, taking precedence over the arguments that air strikes would inhibit infiltration, or at least introduce a new element on the U.S. side of the scales in any future bargaining. It is impossible to pinpoint the moment of decision, but a conversation with a high State Department official the week before the Pleiku attack made it clear that the Johnson Administration had, by the first week of February, made up its mind to expand the war; the rest of the problem was timing, and method, and appearances. "We could hang on there for ten years," said this official, four days before Pleiku. "But as a practical matter, patience is wearing thin, in Congress, in the Administration, in the country, and a decision to change the rules of the game, one way or another, seems probable before very long."

"Almost all the cable traffic between here and Saigon is on going north," this official added. One fear was that U.S. "credibility" vis-à-vis the Communists was deteriorating, he said; Russian Premier Kosygin was en route to North Vietnam, a move which most American experts interpreted as a sure sign that the Russians did not think the Americans were prepared to escalate the war. "They think Hanoi is going to win," said one Kremlinologist at the time, "and they want to be part of the action now that they think there is almost no risk of getting into a confrontation with us."

The President's problem, however, was how to make any new moves, such as air strikes to the north, more acceptable at home or abroad. He could not readily argue that he needed to correct the "equilibrium" without inviting the question of why it had been allowed to get so badly out of balance. He could not suddenly announce plans to send in ground troops, though many officials were arguing privately that ground troops, in the tens of thousands, would be the logical consequence of any considered U.S. effort to carry the air war north. Indeed, in late 1964, the President had a prediction from one high official that as many as

300,000 U.S. troops would wind up in Vietnam once the process of escalation got under way in earnest. He could not declare war; Congress would have wondered why, all of a sudden. But he could seize on the next available pretext to *begin* the process of enlarging the U.S. effort by striking North, and in following this course of action, he would not be as much at the mercy of events as one might suppose. There had been a second "Bien Hoa" of sorts on Christmas Eve, when a Saigon hotel used to quarter American officers had been blown up by terrorists, killing or wounding 45 Americans. (Such was the political chaos in Saigon at the time, however, that it was not clear for two days whether this was part of the Saigon intramural scuffling or of the struggle against the Vietcong.) Hanoi Radio, however, had been regularly calling for terrorist attacks on American installations. Moreover, U.S. intelligence had shown itself astonishingly well tuned in to the Vietcong and the top management of the insurrection in Hanoi. More than once, intercepted instructions had proved the capability to anticipate Vietcong attacks. About the first of February, information reaching Washington convinced experts at the State Department that an assault on Pleiku, or a comparable target, was imminent. The experts felt sufficiently confident to forewarn a group of Washington officials, headed by McGeorge Bundy, which was headed for Saigon and to caution them to "have your contingency plans with you," as one responsible official put it.

So the Administration was hardly unprepared to move, and it was well armed with follow-up moves and a rich array of arguments in support of them. On February 27, the State Department made public a "White Paper," with 71 pages of facts and figures detailing expanded infiltration and seeking to document the hand of Hanoi in control of the insurrection in the South. Weeks in preparation, it had been planned for just such a "contingency" —to make the case for expanded military action against North Vietnam. Meantime, Llewellyn Thompson, a special adviser to Rusk on Soviet affairs and a veteran diplomat, was taking pains to reassure Soviet Ambassador Dobrynin in private talks that the U.S. escalation would be restrained, fitting to the military needs, and not intended to plunge Asia into world war; in Warsaw, limited U.S. objectives were also spelled out by Ambassador John

M. Cabot to his Chinese Communist counterpart. Lawmakers were briefed unendingly; newsmen were summoned for backgrounders. Almost imperceptibly, the United States switched from reprisal raids to systematic bombing of the North without ever quite admitting publicly that this was established policy. As one White House staff man said of Johnson at the time: "He doesn't really believe in policies or decisions—he believes in happenings."

In the course of this happening, the whole Administration argument had been turned around and headed in a direction that would later prove dangerous for the President. During the election campaign, the case had regularly been made that the most important content of the insurgency was home-grown and self-supporting; now the argument became that there really wouldn't be much difficulty cleaning up the South if the infiltrators from the North would just go home. From this came the conclusion that the proper aim of the expanded war effort must be to "win" —to pummel Hanoi into "leaving its neighbor alone." This argument was to grow in force as U.S. involvement grew, and would, by the end of 1965, create a growing problem for Lyndon Johnson. It was no problem, of course, as long as it was accepted that the insurrection could be crushed. And increasingly, U.S. public opinion was to veer toward the view that with an investment of so much blood and treasure, the insurrection *must* be crushed.

But even in late 1964 and early 1965, Johnson was hearing warnings that this might not be the outcome of an escalated U.S. effort at all. Some advisers, such as George Ball and Llewellyn Thompson, thought it less than realistic to expect the Communists, with their powerful hold on so much of the South, to accept either defeat or a settlement which obliged them to surrender these gains. Hanoi, it was argued with considerable clairvoyance, would up its ante to attempt to match a U.S. escalation, and Communist China, in turn, would be hard put to stand by if Hanoi did not prove up to the job. Johnson had every reason to be more than aware of this danger from the start. Indeed, visitors found him deeply concerned about "being pushed by the bomb boys" and determined to limit the escalation. He talked more of targets he had scratched from the Pentagon list because of their proximity to Hanoi or Peking than he talked of crushing the insurrection or of total victory. His concept, from the start, seemed to be that of a beleaguered Senate Majority Leader seeking to improve the balance of force, in pursuit of a better bargain through negotiations, rather than of turning the rout of the Vietnamese into a victory against the Vietcong.

He seemed convinced that Hanoi wouldn't negotiate while winning, but he still put emphasis on negotiation and compromise. "There's a small percentage that want to bomb Hanoi and there's a small percentage that want to get out," he told visitors, not long after Pleiku. "But I'm the ringleader of a political settlement." He talked with feeling of his hopes to avoid committing U.S. ground forces in large numbers and in one conversation discounted the possibility of providing absolute protection for U.S. air bases on the grounds that this might take 100,000 troops; by 1966, he was to have more than twice that number in Vietnam.

But in late February, 1965, he sounded as if he believed the balance could be improved with a minimum of added American leverage. His discussion of the first two retaliatory attacks, following Pleiku and Qui Nhon, was almost offhand. To one visitor, he lampooned the "crisis" tones of the television broadcasters, the long faces, and the grim talk of big, black limousines assembled for weighty policy-making.

"They woke us up in the middle of the night, and we woke them up in the middle of the night. Then they did it again, and we did it again," was the way he described it. If he suspected he was on the front edge of a major plunge into a fair-sized ground war in Asia, he hid his concern masterfully, dismissing all the excitement as the sort of thing that happens periodically.

Many officials close to the President insist this mood was to last only briefly. But it is also widely agreed that it was not until March of 1965 that Lyndon Johnson really began to give Vietnam intense and continuous attention. "That was when he really got into it and made it his own problem as only Johnson can do, once he gets engaged," said one man close to him during this tense period.

But by that time, it can also be argued, the force of events, the momentum of contingency plans, and the lack of acceptable alternatives were already propelling the United States toward a steadily widening war.

Inevitably, the demands of base security to protect the growing American investment in air power impelled the Administration to furnish more men for perimeter defense; the South Vietnamese, it was argued, should more properly be employed in hunting and killing Vietcong. So it was that on March 6, two reinforced U.S. Marine battalions, numbering approximately 3,500 men, were sent ashore on what was officially announced as "limited duty." These were the first combat units organized as such, and both Rusk and McNamara were quick to reassure the nation that the role of these American combat units would be limited strictly to defensive operations. Said Rusk: the Marines' mission "is to provide local, close-in security. It is not their mission to engage in pacification operations." McNamara was equally categorical: he said the U.S. combat forces were "to patrol within narrow limits" of the fast-growing U.S. airbase at Da Nang "and thus they should not tangle with the Vietcong."

But "tangle" they did, and as their numbers grew and their combat role increased throughout the spring of 1965, the State Department took the initiative in a public-relations campaign designed to prepare American citizens for the certain prospect of increased casualties. In Saigon, military officials briefed newsmen on what was delicately described as the "combat-support" role which had been quietly assigned to the newly arriving U.S. forces; the word was passed out that U.S. troops were indeed available for combat duty in emergencies, when help was called for by South Vietnamese forces in trouble. By early June, with 50,000 troops now in Vietnam and with the Vietcong's annual "monsoon offensive" getting underway on a larger scale than Washington's war-managers had anticipated, it seemed likely to the public-opinion managers that this "emergency clause" was likely to be invoked more and more frequently—as indeed it was. In June, a State Department spokesman made a valiant effort to spell out the terms of U.S. combat involvement in order to cushion the shock of its discovery by Congress and the country. But the headlines this effort elicited in turn produced another of those White House explosions, and the clarifying statement that ensued from the White House opened up another crack in the Administration's credibility. Yes, the White House said, there was carefully limited authority for the use of U.S. troops in combat, but there was nothing new in it—it had been there from the beginning. The White House reaction was characteristic; it was Johnson's constant endeavor to concede the least possible change in basic U.S. policy for Vietnam, partly by way of keeping it as consistent as possible with the terms of that 1954 Eisenhower proffer of assistance to Diem. But in this case, the struggle for consistency only served to introduce new inconsistencies. For if the orders had been the same all along, how was one to explain the categorical assurances by Rusk and McNamara in March that the incoming Marines were not supposed to "engage in pacification operations" or "tangle with the Vietcong"? The explanation offered at the time by a senior State Department official was, by his own admission, a little lame. The military commanders in Saigon, he said, had not expected that U.S. troops would be needed as quickly, or in as large numbers, for emergency "combat support." So there seemed to be no particular point in broadcasting it at the start. This might have stirred needless anxiety at home and given needless provocation to Hanoi or Peking or Moscow, especially if things had worked for the best, and it had turned out that U.S. troops hadn't really been needed for combat duty in large numbers at all. There is reason to believe that this was the genuine hope of the military planners in Saigon and Washington; their argument for the introduction of combat forces in growing numbers began with the case that U.S. air bases ought properly to be guarded by U.S. forces, freeing South Vietnamese guards for combat; then it was argued in Washington councils that the U.S. combat mission would only be temporary, while the South Vietnamese built up their own combat forces through a stepped-up recruitment drive. Only gradually did it become inescapable that the enemy was responding with increased escalation on its side, and that the South Vietnamese weren't going to be able to handle a war that was rapidly moving out of the guerrilla class, with its squad-sized units or perhaps platoons, into the battalion or regimental league.

There were, unquestionably, persuasive arguments at every step of the way for not acknowledging any larger U.S. involvement or commitment than was necessary—in hopes that the worst wouldn't happen. For every acknowledgment, every warlike pose, only encouraged a comparable response from the other side. It was, therefore, probably a sound strategy for a war of semaphore —a contest in which "signals" and the appearance of things and the general attitude struck can matter as much as, or more than, the respective casualty rates. It was also a strategy peculiarly suited for Lyndon Johnson, with his profound preference for saying no more and doing no more than is absolutely necessary at any given time, in hopes that somehow the more unpleasant things won't have to be done at all. But if this is a sensible approach to politics, it also is a good deal better suited for the cozy confines of the Senate cloakroom than for application to a complex, many-faceted international crisis under merciless global observation. For it was, at heart, not an easy strategy to grasp, if one accepts that Johnson's main purpose from the start was to pursue settlement by improving his bargaining position. The aim, in short, then becomes quicker peace through fiercer war—an unappealing proposition to sell.

Indeed, the Administration was quickly and increasingly caught up in a cross-fire of criticism, from those who wanted more war, faster, and total victory; from those who wanted peace and never mind the terms; from those who found the basic tactic certain to boomerang into an ever larger war. Yet, the escalation remained, for most of 1965, very nearly a political masterpiece. Only Senators Morse and Gruening consistently fought the President's policy up until the big outbreak of opposition in early 1966, and even at that stage, only a score or so of Senators, out of a hundred, could be counted consistently and openly opposed to the President's aims. It was fully a year after Pleiku before opinion polls began to detect signs of public disaffection with the U.S. course, and it was a confusing disaffection, compounded of antiwar sentiment and of advocacy of more war, quickly, to end it all. Meantime, over that year, more than 200,000 U.S. troops had been dispatched to Vietnam; the "never again" syndrome had been demolished in slow, insidious stages.

As for the enemy, whatever the Chinese might ultimately do,

by early 1966 they had not done anything nearly as drastic as many feared they would in the course of this steady build-up of U.S. power on the Asian mainland.

Critics argued—and will doubtless continue to argue—that somewhere along the line the hand had been misplayed, that somehow the mix of increased military pressure and increased diplomatic efforts for settlement had not been right. Even when Johnson altered the mix in his celebrated April 7, 1965, address at Johns Hopkins, by offering to engage in "unconditional discussions" in search of a settlement and by throwing in proffers of nearly boundless bounty for Southeast Asian reconstruction and economic development (including bounty for North Vietnam), there were many who continued to argue that it was too little too late. Only a much longer perspective will tell. Only time would test the highly flexible, somewhat cumbersome, often awkward, and even more often inscrutable Johnson policy for Vietnam. But from early 1965 onward, there was, at least, a distinctively Johnson policy—however much Vietnam might remain an orphan war, adopted but unwanted.

NINE

Interlude-
Reflections of a
Statesman

"Kennedy had stolen Adlai's intellectual thunder," a close associate observed in a conversation at United Nations headquarters in mid-December, 1963. "With Lyndon, the Governor has had more contact by telephone and in person in the first three weeks than he had with Kennedy in three years."

Some 15 months later, a weary, seemingly dispirited Adlai Stevenson was to say in the course of a long talk at his office in New York on March 14, 1965: "I wish I had more influence on him, more time. I get inquiries from the President, but only intermittently, and not as much as I would like.

That Adlai Stevenson and Lyndon Johnson could ever have been close confidants or intimate collaborators was not conceiv-

able. It is hard to think of two men more contrasting. The sophisticated Stevenson could never quite understand the full limits of the Johnson power hunger, the compulsive, all-pervasive emphasis on the politics of things. Johnson, for his part, could never understand the Stevenson diffidence, or appreciate the Stevenson intellect; and his mockery and mimicry of the man who had twice run for President, and twice lost, was known to most of Washington. But at the beginning, the two men could find community of interest. Johnson wanted the chief of all the eggheads to be visibly, actively laboring in his cause. Adlai Stevenson hungered for a larger hand in foreign-policy making. He had, after all, been somewhat less than close to John F. Kennedy. He had deeply wanted to be Secretary of State. But whatever prospect there might have been for this, it evaporated in the hurly-burly of the Democratic convention in Los Angeles in 1960 when Stevenson made what the Kennedys considered an insufficient effort to disavow a brief, abortive, and abrasive rising of the liberal left on his behalf, and then declined to heal the breach by placing Kennedy's name in nomination. So the man who had twice led his party and had been its most eloquent voice in the lean Eisenhower years, found himself little more than a symbol, a hostage to the irreconcilable eggheads, an envoy to that special wonderland of the United Nations were nothing is entirely real. Stevenson suffered through the Bay of Pigs and became the victim, however inadvertently, of clumsy dissembling by Washington. He suffered again in the second Cuban crisis when his confidential counsel offered to the President was publicly classified as Munich-style appeasement while others with better credentials in the Kennedy camp escaped attention for their advocacy of even more pacific remedies.

Kennedy, moreover, was an intellectual in good standing. And because he was also President, the politically inclined eggheads quite naturally rallied to him. For them, Stevenson remained a much beloved and heroic figure, but a hero of another day. Politics had passed him by, and in the harsh nature of the process, the party's left wing had less need for him.

But Lyndon Johnson did need him. So it was that at the outset, Adlai Stevenson was ardently sought after by the man in the

White House for the first time in a long time. He had a sense of participation.

It was not all a matter of personal gratification by any means. Stevenson had genuine admiration for Lyndon Johnson's political skill, his energy, his instinct for command. As a patriot, Mr. Stevenson would, in any event, have seen the urgent need to rally around. For all these reasons, Adlai Stevenson was a loyal, enthusiastic booster for Lyndon Johnson in the beginning days. Ultimately, the basic incompatibilities would set in; ideological differences, the disparity in their roles, fundamental conflicts of purpose would all work to erode the relationship. And while this very process might reasonably be expected to color Adlai Stevenson's mood, his judgments of Lyndon Johnson, as set forth in two long conversations, one in the early days, and one in the first months of 1965, are no less revealing on that account, for the erosion in this relationship rather closely paralleled the erosion in Lyndon Johnson's relations with the egghead community at large. The very nature of the United Nations makes it a uniquely valid vantage point; while only a short air-shuttle hop away from Washington, it is also its own world, as remote in some ways as a foreign capital, with diverse interests and a detachment which give it a perspective all its own.

In an interview on December 18, 1963, Stevenson described the events of the first few weeks of the Johnson Administration, as they appeared from his U.N. vantage point. What follows is a paraphrase of Stevenson's remarks from extensive notes taken at the time. There is no claim to recapturing the Ambassador's precise words except where notes showed literal quotations. The conversation jumped from one topic to another, and the Ambassador's remarks have been somewhat reorganized in chronological order.

At the first meeting of the Cabinet after Kennedy's death, Stevenson had made a long talk, drawing on his special position as a sort of elder statesman of the party. He had spoken feelingly of his past experiences and knowledge of the new President. The next day Johnson was "obviously grateful." Stevenson had his first meeting alone with President Johnson the day after Kennedy's assassination. The new President was "worried tremendously" about foreign affairs. "He realized it was the area he knew the least about." Stevenson told him that one decision was urgent; a U.S. position had to be formulated for the United Nations on the question of banning the use of outer space for all but peaceful purposes. This was Saturday, and the U.S. policy statement was due the following Monday. Any change in the U.S. position at the United Nations would be quickly perceived. Stevenson was gratified by the President's reply: "Write your own statement, don't even bother checking it with me. But you might want to look up my 1958 speech on the subject." It turned out to be almost identical, although in broader terms, with the United States line in 1963. (Smiling, Stevenson interjected that Johnson knew quite a lot about outer space. He "had muscled Senator Symington" out of that particular specialty in the Senate, and Symington had resented it, but Lyndon knew it was an area of great public interest.)

He had told Johnson at this meeting that the President must make a declaration soon to reassure people of his foreign-policy views; that there would be many who would worry about the image of a parochial politician, about the threat of neo-isolationism, about a "certain illiberality" that might affect some areas, such as Africa. Johnson asked what he should do, and Stevenson had urged him to address the United Nations. The President immediately agreed to do so. Stevenson had much to do with preparation of the speech, and it had gone off well. "Everybody turned out for the reception afterwards, even the Cambodians." The French Ambassador to the United Nations was positively effusive about the effect on his "colleagues," the French African states. It had been a forceful declaration of U.S. devotion to the United Nations.

The President had complained that the response to his speech by the General Assembly had been chilly. Stevenson had told him that applause was against the rules during the course of a speech and that the breaks for applause for Johnson were without precedent. On hearing this, the President was visibly reassured.

The President had mingled surefootedly with the delegates and managed to remember the names of a number he had met in his Vice Presidential travels. He made a big hit by striking

just the right note with U.N. General Assembly President Carlos Sosa-Rodríguez, who had been shaken down by Secret Service men on arrival at a luncheon Stevenson had given for President Johnson. These things happen, the President had explained, adding that only a few days earlier, his own daughter had been forbidden to enter the White House one night by a guard, despite her best efforts to prove that she was the President's daughter.

Stevenson's great concern at that time had been with the problem of how to maintain U.S. momentum in the push for a *détente* with the Soviet Union. He wanted the new President to make it as clear as possible, as quickly as possible, that he was prepared to carry on in the spirit of the previous Administration, to move forward from the nuclear-test ban that had been signed in 1963. At the United Nations, the Russians were being more amiable than ever; Stevenson and Russian Ambassador Nikolai Fedorenko were on a joking, first-name basis, in sharp contrast to his chilly relationship with Fedorenko's predecessor, Valerian Zorin. He had long since given up predicting on the Russians, who blow hot and cold, but it was pretty clear that they were "zigging—or zagging, if you will—toward *détente* for their own purposes, and we should exploit this for our purposes." He had given Lyndon Johnson a written elaboration of his earlier quick verbal briefing on this subject, urging him to try to sustain momentum.

"I told him to grab this dove of peace and shake its tail feathers out," he said.

He was afraid that Johnson would become so quickly absorbed with his first Congress and then with his re-election that there would be little time for foreign-policy making. But he also had full confidence that the President, with his sure political instincts, would not be deterred by concern that American public opinion might resist a too rapid *rapprochement* with the Communists. Kennedy had worried about this until he took that swing through the Northwest not many weeks before his death and discovered that the test-ban treaty was more popular with the people than it had appeared to be with Congress. "Johnson knows this. He is astute enough to realize that the public is often far ahead of Congress on these things, that the opponents are long on volume but short in numbers."

Stevenson was soon to write an eloquent introduction, lavish in its praise of the new President, to a collection of Lyndon Johnson's public speeches which was hastily assembled in book form under the title *A Time for Action.* He wrote of Lyndon Johnson's "extraordinary managerial skill and political pragmatism . . . his vitality, his courage, his intelligence." Lyndon Johnson, he said, "is a master of the art of the possible in politics. . . . He is a leader—a mature political leader—who knows that the role of a leader is to lead; to fall back if necessary, but always to lead and lead boldly, unafraid of the spears and arrows aimed at anyone who gets out in front in our political life. . . . I suspect he would rather be judged by what he does than what he says. For Lyndon Johnson is first and foremost a man of action . . .

"Lyndon Johnson knows the perils, the challenges, and the opportunities that confront us in this restless and perilous world of the 60's. As the President's representative he has seen Europe, Asia, and Africa at first hand. . . . He has walked among the mighty and the meek, and talked to them in their palaces and villages. He knows, and is forever reminding us, that in too much of our planet, human degradation is still the rule and human dignity only a dream. And he knows that in this nuclear age there is no rational alternative to peace.

"His style, people will say, will be different from John Kennedy's. Of course it will. But the drive, the convictions, the principles and programs that were a part of the New Frontier will never be lost so long as Lyndon Johnson is President. . . . Knowing his energy, his determination, and his goals, I also know that he will always be ahead of us, leading the way, pressing, persuading and pulling us forward to those goals that he has long cherished . . ."

This public paean, taken together with what Mr. Stevenson was saying more privately, provides a rough measure of his state of mind in the early days of the Johnson Administration. Quite evidently, he felt himself to be solidly ensconced in the high councils, to a degree he had never been before.

About a year and a half later, in March 1965, Adlai Stevenson once again discussed the Johnson role in foreign affairs in somewhat greater depth. He was under extra pressure; there had been an urgent call from the White House that morning conveying the President's request that Mr. Stevenson lend a hand in the drafting of a civil-rights speech to Congress that night. But for upward of an hour, Stevenson quietly gave voice to some of the frustrations, as well as the rewards, of 15 months as President Johnson's envoy to the United Nations. The summons from the White House suggested that Stevenson might still be enjoying the same sense of intimacy with the President that he had so plainly been relishing in the beginning of Lyndon Johnson's Presidency. But it quickly became clear that this was not the case. He had a harried manner, betraying not only the pressure of that day's White House assignment, but of the hectic pace of U.N. business. He seemed not so much beaten as battered.

Above all, he was wistful. There were unmistakable indications of a state of mind which was to reveal itself poignantly in an interview he had with Eric Sevareid just two nights before he died of a heart attack on a street in London on July 14, 1965. He obviously felt cut off from the center of things. He was, by his own admission, not in the best position to discuss accurately the inner workings of the Johnson foreign-policy making machinery. (In the later conversation with Sevareid, Stevenson revealed considerable unawareness of who was doing what to whom in Washington; he had a mistaken view of Secretary McNamara's role in allegedly blocking U.S. agreement to a proposal for Washington-Hanoi peace talks relayed by U.N. Secretary General U Thant in the fall of 1964 and further mediation efforts in early 1965, and a somewhat clouded concept of the role in all this of Secretary Rusk as well.) But he had ample basis for judging the Johnson performance in considerable detail, and this conversation, too, is perhaps worth setting down in its entirety, almost as it transpired, as a thumbnail appraisal of one competent observer who was careful to qualify all that he said with the preface that he was more remote from the peak of power and policy-making by March, 1965, than he would have preferred to be.

He had known Johnson since 1935, in Washington, when Stevenson was with the AAA and Lyndon was working for Richard

Kleberg, a Texas Congressman. "And, of course, I have seen him on and off in the political picture, and finally, naturally, I do have a special position, having run for President twice."

In all the time that Johnson had been Vice President, Steven-son had talked to him about foreign policy only twice. Once was on the way to the funeral of the former U.N. Secretary General Dag Hammarskjöld. Johnson apparently thought it "a little infra dig" for him to be there at all. He was impatient with all the "candle-holding processions and did not seem to have much feel for the occasion or the implications of it for the United Nations."

Stevenson had also talked to Johnson once about Vietnam. "He was a Diem man, but he kept his counsel." For that matter, Stevenson could not remember when Vice President Johnson had done much talking at all in National Security Council meetings.

Everybody had believed at the beginning that Johnson would have a breather in foreign affairs, but the breathing spell lasted "only twenty minutes." There were riots in Panama, and Johnson did not handle that one the way Stevenson would have wanted. He took too long. Stevenson was trying to work out something through the Costa Ricans in the United Nations, but Johnson did not take his advice. He was too concerned with popular reac-tion in the United States.

The appointment of Tom Mann as the top figure in Latin American affairs in the State Department also caused a certain dismay.

He did not know whether Johnson was a new convert or an old convert to the United Nations. He just could not say. But certainly the President was interested. For a time, Stevenson received queries, memos, and requests from Lyndon to drop around for more talks about foreign policy. But that is hard to do from New York. For a while, he tried to be in Washington more, and Johnson gave him an office in the White House. "But the bicker sessions never really came off." Johnson always professed a great desire to sit around with Stevenson and chat about foreign policy any time the Governor wanted to drop by. But on the few occasions that he did, the results were mixed. "Johnson can listen. But he has this obsession about talking." In a way, the President cannot be blamed on this account. He has doubtless heard much of it all before.

"He keeps saying that the Air Force comes in every morning and says, 'Bomb, bomb, bomb.' And then they come in again in the afternoon and they say, 'Bomb, bomb, bomb.' And then the State Department comes in and says, 'Not now, or not there, or too much, or not at all.' "

The President's touch in Vietnam was admirable. Johnson had worked out a measured response in the careful selection of targets and seemed to be trying "to strike an awfully difficult balance between not losing South Vietnam and not doing things that would close off better relations with the Russians—the one great hope for moving towards peace."

Stevenson was deeply concerned that everything that was done to step up pressure in Vietnam also pushed the Russians into the appearance of closer allegiance to the Communist Chinese and, therefore, soured relations with us.

Johnson was fully aware that his place in history would be established not by a tax bill or even by a civil-rights bill, but by what he does in the world. "He talks about this all the time." After the State of the Union Message in January, 1965, Stevenson had had another long talk with Johnson, and had told the President that he had saddled Congress with the greatest load in history, and that it was time to run his attention to the rest of the world, to foreign affairs. "I said he should spend eighty per cent of his time on foreign affairs, and he agreed completely and said that is exactly what he intended to do, but that the Congressional program was important and that he would have to find time to do both, both time and energy." Right now [March, 1965, when the civil-rights disturbances in Selma, Ala., were at their worst], "civil rights is everything."

Stevenson believed the President was sincere in his desire to spend more time on foreign affairs. But in practice, he was probably reversing the ratio, giving only 20 per cent of his time to real consideration of the problems of the world. And the result of this was that Johnson seemed always to be "forced into foreign policy, always reacting, always responding."

Johnson's preoccupation with "consensus" was troublesome.

The President "has not yet learned that you cannot always have a consensus on foreign affairs, that you sometimes have to do the bold, unpopular thing in order to lead." He wished he had the President's ear more often. But it's difficult being in New York, and also difficult with the chain of command. This is so, "despite my own particular political position and the fact that I have no special aspirations or whatever so that I can talk candidly to him, and I always have."

He does occasionally ask advice such as, " 'Should we send arms to Jordan, and if we do, should we send arms to Israel as a counterbalance?' "

Mr. Johnson had questioned him closely on whether the United Nations could play a role in Southeast Asia. The President seemed to be "needled or pushed" toward this line of inquiry, not so much by genuine interest in the U.N.'s potential as by the endless prodding of Senator Wayne Morse to turn South Vietnam over, lock, stock, and barrel, to the United Nations for a solution. Stevenson had sent the President a long memorandum explaining the prospects and limitations of the United Nation's role in South Vietnam. Johnson had thereupon asked Adlai to talk to Morse. But he had "begged off that one."

He thought the President fully understood that the United Nations cannot take on quarrels between the big powers and that its best role in Vietnam would be, in Stevenson's phrase, that of "compliance inspectors." He had explained to the President the usefulness of the United Nations in exploring attitudes on such questions as "How much does North Vietnam want to avoid being a vassal state of China?" or "What would the Chinese accept in the way of a Vietnamese settlement?" He conceded that there were other diplomatic "tracks," not necessarily running through the United Nations, such as the British, and the Russians, and the French. But without going into detail about the controversial peace promotion by U.N. Secretary General U Thant in late 1964 and early 1965, he lamented that the United Nations was not being used the way it could be in this respect.

The President was very sensitive to the impression he would create from the very outset, in the world at large. He was not unaware that his experience was limited to "those good-will tours." But he still had "no real comprehension, or at least was acquiring it slowly, of American relations abroad, of the alliance commitments, of the complexity of it all."

"Johnson *reacts*, not just to crises, but to political pressures, especially from Capitol Hill."

The President was to be commended for his ability to pick and choose the bits and pieces of advice that are given to him. "Frankly, I have been astounded at the way he has sometimes rejected even the majority advice around him. This is not easy to do." Stevenson had the feeling that Johnson had perhaps a more moderate influence on the judgment of his senior advisers, and "often he has acted on his own." One reason for this was that Johnson seeks not just a consensus among his advisers in the Executive Branch, and still less a collection of yes-men around him, but a consensus embracing all this and the powers in Congress as well. As a result of this, however, Johnson often winds up not following *precisely* the advice of any of the men around him, certainly not in the sense that Eisenhower took his lead on foreign policy from John Foster Dulles. Nor is he *precisely* following the advice of his old friends on Capitol Hill. Instead, he is acting on an intricately balanced amalgamation of all of this counsel combined. And the further result of this is to make the President all the more doubtful and questioning, not about the decisions to be made, but about decisions already made.

"It obviously unsettles" the President when, in his effort to reconcile the varying advice from downtown, as well as Capitol Hill, he is obliged to take action of which none of the men around him wholly approves. "This causes him constantly to question decisions he has already taken."

There was no self-pity, no bitterness in the tone, no specific violent point of disagreement, not even any very serious charges that he was prepared to lodge, for the record, against his chief —though complaints he had, and would have in larger measure before his death. In March, his criticism had more to do with manner and method and technical competence in the complexities of foreign affairs, and it was balanced by undisguised admiration for a political master from a man who had been something of a practicing politician—though something less than a master, as he would be the first to admit—in his own day. By July, however, the Stevenson ledger would show, according to auditing by those who saw him just before he died, a fresh entry on the debit side against the foreign-policy performance of Lyndon Johnson. For in the interim, there has been a revolution in the Dominican Republic, and Johnson had intervened with American troops.

The Dominican Republic– "Just Like the Alamo"

Partly it may have been because the world, with a kind of grim impudence, was not working to Lyndon Johnson's clock even before the Dominican Republic erupted in revolt in April, 1965. Widening warfare in Vietnam was preoccupation enough, when all he wanted was to shepherd his Great Society through Congress, and to deal as best he could with his own country's seething racial unrest. Partly the key to Johnson's conduct in the days just after the Dominican upheaval may lie in the Texas hills, and in the insights of a historian of the American West, Walter Prescott Webb, who offers the thesis that the very absence of rich history and long tradition in that region encourages a talent for "taking something small and blowing it up to giant size . . . They write

of cowboys as if they were noble knights and the cowmen, kings."
There were few noble knights in the grisly business that broke
out in Santo Domingo on April 24. It was a tragedy with no coherent plot. It had to be played a step at a time, and by ear, and
with only the faintest prospect of ultimate success. The essence
of it all was anarchy, and if there was a case to be made for the
application of American power, it rested on justifiable ignorance,
sheer uncertainty, plain prudence, and stark necessity. For power
in the Dominican Republic in those dark days, as McGeorge
Bundy put it, was "in the streets."

But to Lyndon Johnson, it was "just like the Alamo." As he
later described the moment of decision, he had told the National
Security Council: "It would be hard for me to live in this Hemisphere if I sent in the Marines, and I couldn't live in this country
if I didn't." And with a wave of his arm, he went on: "Hell, it's
just like if you were down at that gate, and you were surrounded,
and you damn well needed somebody. Well, by God, I'm going to
go—and I thank the Lord that I've got men who want to go with
me, from McNamara right on down to the littlest private who's
carrying a gun."

So it went, in a geyser of public and private explanations and
justifications for days after the first, fateful decision had been
made. Events had impelled the President to act against every instinct—without his trusty consensus firmly in hand. The irony
is that he probably had it with him all the time. But his flailing
around in search of it, his irrelevant rationalizations and often
inaccurate reconstruction of events, conspired to turn an essentially unmanageable and, in some ways, unavoidable crisis in a
fundamentally unstable and crisis-prone Caribbean nation into
a crisis of confidence in the President himself. It turned an effort,
born, curiously enough, of caution, and largely designed to fill
what seemed to be an ominous vacuum, into an unreasoned, reckless, impulsive piece of jingoism. It produced, in short, what was
probably the lowest ebb in Lyndon Johnson's standing as a world
statesman in all of the first two years or more of his Presidency.

In Washington, there was genuine alarm, not so much about
the merits of the Dominican case, but about the ability of the
Johnson Administration to conduct sensible, coherent policy.

Partly it was a matter of atmosphere; Marines seemed to be landing everywhere at once; by mid-May, there were 100,000 American fighting men engaged in two widely separated "wars."

Partly it was the appearance of the government; there were not enough crisis-managers, from the President on down, to go around. "One more outbreak, and we would be out of business," said one State Department official at the time, as Latin American hands were being hauled off regular jobs to help man a special round-the-clock crisis headquarters (known as the flap-house), and top-echelon men were being dispatched around Latin America to explain what the United States was up to—or to the Dominican Republic to try to sort things out.

But in large part, it was the appearance of the President himself. "Now I am the most denounced man in the world," he declared, in a speech to the Building Trades Council on May 3, which must be marked down as one of his least fortunate public appearances. It began with a dazzling rundown of the economic gains the Johnson Administration had brought the workingman but wound up in an impromptu, folksy, flag-waving, rambling defense of his Dominican policy.

"What is important," the President declared, "is that we know, and that they know, and that everybody knows, that we don't propose to sit here in our rocking chair with our hands folded and let the Communists set up any government in the Western Hemisphere." And again: "If they are going to put American lives in danger, where American citizens go, that flag [he swung around to point at a flag behind the podium] goes with them to protect them." He had a story about Huey Long, who had once been subjected to prolonged attack in the Senate for venturing into another state (Arkansas) and helping elect the first woman to sit in the U.S. Senate. Long's defense struck the President as appropriate to the Dominican circumstances. After the denunciations ceased, Long had walked over to the then Majority Leader, Joe Robertson, and said: "I wasn't in Arkansas to dictate to any human being. All I went to Arkansas for was to pull those big, pot-bellied politicians off this poor little woman's neck."

Even the President's recital of the events leading up to his decision to land Marines was, to say the least, hyperbolic. He said he had received a telegram from the U.S. Ambassador to Santo Domingo, W. Tapley Bennett, "that said 'you must land troops immediately or blood will run in the streets, American blood will run in the streets.' That is the unanimous decision of every man on the American team." What Bennett actually said must be examined in greater depth, but the portions of that celebrated "critic" cable that are pertinent at this point read as follows: "The country team is unanimous that the time has come to land the Marines. American lives are in danger . . . *if Washington wishes they* [the Marines] *can be landed for the purpose of protecting evacuation of American citizens* [author's italics]. I recommend immediate landings."

The President's Building Trades speech sounded like new doctrine. Johnson seemed to be declaring that U.S. troops would land anywhere, anytime that a local conflict brought danger to American civilians in the area. The liberals were aghast. The opinion-makers were hard at it again, retouching the impression of an impetuous, sophisticated, hot-tempered President, quick to resort to force, hostile to all revolutionary forces that carried a taint of Communist influence. The influence of Tom Mann was seen in every move. The second thoughts then setting in at home and abroad made those first impressions of a year earlier pallid by comparison. And like the first impressions, the second thoughts were to have a lasting impact on the judgment of men of influence abroad and at home even though they were founded, to a considerable degree unsoundly, on appearances.

What were the Dominican realities? The answer must be carefully couched for it is not the purpose here to untangle all the unknowns and unknowables of that affair, or to pass judgment upon the validity of widely varying judgments of the Dominican events. The revolt was one thing as seen from, say, Caracas, and quite another as seen from Brazil. It looked different from the vantage point of downtown Santo Domingo than it did from the American Embassy, just outside the rebel zone. An ambassador from a Latin nation with a delicately balanced, progressive, constitutional coalition government (Venezuela, for instance) could see the revolt as a constitutionalist revolution to be encouraged; to have seen it otherwise would have endangered political cohesion at home. A military regime, as in Brazil, could see it as a test of Latin resistance to Communism and applaud, at least in private, the U.S. decision to intervene.

But the performance of Lyndon Johnson must be examined from the vantage point of the White House, and the view from there was something else again. It might not have been the clearest view; indeed it was exceedingly murky at critical moments. But it was the only view that Lyndon Johnson had, and it was perhaps best summarized by John Bartlow Martin, Kennedy's Ambassador to the Dominican Republic, who was called back as a Johnson trouble-shooter and dispatched to the scene of the conflict in its earliest days. He returned with the fixed impression that it had been total, uncontrollable chaos, almost from the start. In a conversation, he ticked off the rival groups, including the left-wing but non-Communist instigators of the uprising, any number of quarreling military factions, and at least three pro-Communist parties—"All of them in it for their own motives." His recollections, like the events themselves, came in something of a jumble:

"In a matter of minutes, and certainly in hours, rebels were passing out weapons, forcing gas stations to fill bottles to make Molotov cocktails. The carnage began. It became a social war—kill, kill, kill; just senseless killing. A blood bath was building up. The spraying of machine guns, haphazardly. The slaughter went on and on.

"In the process, the military became completely committed to the mess they were in. All ideas were swept away. Political parties were swept away. All doors were closed—except the Communist door. They were the disciplined ones—and they were with the revolution. This was more important than the names and card files of Communist agents. Everything had been swept away, the whole political party structure, everything was drowned in this blood bath."

This, almost all observers agree, is a not too overwrought approximation of what the Dominican Republic had been reduced to only a few days after the uprising on April 24. The debate was to rage on what Johnson should or should not have done to help bring the Dominican Republic back to "normalcy." But before examining Johnson's actions, it is first necessary to consider why anarchy set in so fast, and what, in the Dominican Republic, is normalcy.

The "Showcase"

"Normalcy in the Dominican Republic," said one old diplomatic hand on the island, "is a government in the palace and a coup a week." Less cynically, normalcy in the Dominican Republic is not really "republican"—nor is the country even a nation. Juan Bosch, the poet-philosopher-politician, concluded in a history of his country that it had been cursed by fate since its discovery by Christopher Columbus. Colonization by Spain; invasion by Haiti (which occupies the other half of the ancient Island of Hispaniola); an earlier occupation by the U.S. Marines; and, finally, the cruel, 30-odd years of Rafael Trujillo's tyranny, ending with his assassination in 1961—none of this was calculated to prepare Dominicans for nationhood. For most of the lifetime of all of its present-day inhabitants, it had been part private estate, part penal colony under Trujillo's ruthless, rapacious rule. Few of its citizens could remember having cast a vote. Most of its intellectuals had fled. Authority was vested in a corrupt military. A Hemisphere was ashamed. So the United States set out, under the Kennedy Administration, to make what had been a caricature of all that ails Latin America into a showcase of democracy and reform and economic development. U.S. foreign aid and U.S. specialists poured in to coach the police force on the use of tear gas instead of tanks, to show farmers how to farm, bankers how to bank, teachers how to teach. After a precarious period of provisional government, honest-to-goodness elections were set up for December, 1962; the oas pitched in as referee; the Americans printed gaily colored ballots for the benefit of that two-thirds of the population which could not read or write. The people elected Juan Bosch President, and he lasted all of seven months before the military threw him out.

The showcase had been smashed, and now the Dominican Republic was to be made an object lesson of another sort. The Kennedy Administration did not recognize the new military junta; foreign-aid programs were ripped up by the roots. At this point, fate intervened to make the punishment still more severe. Having made its point, the Kennedy Administration was preparing to ease back into a working relationship with the Dominican Government in hopes of influencing it back towards constitutional ways. But the assassination of Kennedy and the trials of transition in the United States delayed the decision to resume relations for a good many weeks. Calamity followed calamity; world sugar prices plunged well below the 9-cents-a-pound Dominican production costs, bloated by padded payrolls. Devaluation threatened, and the United States was urgently asked for help. But Tom Mann did not see the Dominican Republic as a potential showcase, and the U.S. response was, in the view of many authorities on the spot, unnecessarily stiff. As monetary devaluation threatened the economy, and declining sugar revenues drained foreign-exchange holdings, the Dominican Government, now headed by a civilian, Donald Reid Cabral (but still largely in the hands of the military), was obliged to subscribe to the stern dictates of the International Monetary Fund in exchange for financial relief. Reid Cabral, who, in retrospect, came to look more and more appealing to American policy-makers as the April insurrection raged on, was in many ways as able a head of government as the Dominican Republic could possibly expect, and he moved forcefully. With an almost reckless disregard for traditional Dominican sensitivities, he cut deeply into sugar payrolls, cancelled Christmas bonuses for workers. Having alienated the workers, and thereby the political left, he turned on the military and the political right by cashiering corrupt officers and trying to trim superfluous defense spending, the major source of private income for the military men. So it should not have been surprising, when the lid blew off on April 24, that Donny Reid discovered he did not have a friend in court.

But that accounts only for Reid's inability to put down what began as a badly timed, premature, and not very well-organized coup by officers partisan to Bosch; at that very time, there were probably two, and quite possibly three, other separate military coups in various stages of preparation against Reid. But it does not really explain the tireless intriguing, the raw intensity of feelings on both sides, the ferocity of the fighting, the mindless bloodshed, and the suddenness with which all authority broke down. It does not explain the comments of shaken U.S. officials who went to the island and talked to the leading figures on both sides and came back muttering about the "lies, the plain nastiness, the double-dealing, and, above all, the blind, unreasoning hate."

It was not just a question of temperament, or the usual Latin volatility. The Dominican man on the street is probably no less likable than other Latins. But Dominicans probably have suffered more and seen far less of anything resembling normal life, and by a quirk, or perhaps several quirks, of fate they had found no outlet for the pent-up emotions of the Trujillo years. They were uniquely ready to explode. By the chill analyses of some authorities who had spent a long time on the scene, they might even have been said to be overdue for the blood bath that John Bartlow Martin talked about. The thought is not so shocking to the Latin mind; in the first days of the rebellion, when news reached Bosch and his attractive, intelligent Cuban wife, in San Juan, Puerto Rico, that aircraft of the military junta were strafing the city of Santo Domingo, she responded, according to Tad Szulc in his book *Dominican Diary*, "It is all for the best. Let them learn that democracy has its price in blood." A number of American officials would argue along much the same lines; in the natural order of things, they contend, the downfall of Trujillo might have been expected to touch off a bloody uprising, with vengeance duly visited upon the *trujillistas*. But the family of the slain dictator hung on for a while longer, the military maintained a tight grip, the lid stayed on. It was kept tightly on, again, when Juan Bosch was overthrown, and one U.S. diplomat serving in Santo Domingo at that time recalls that "a lot of the young, revolutionary-minded people of the left were always a little ashamed that they did not rise up then."

The Dominican Republic, then, was primed for trouble, on that Saturday in April when Reid, as part of his crackdown on suspected trouble-makers in the armed services, ordered his Army Chief of Staff to an Army camp outside Santo Domingo to "cancel the commissions" of four officers thought to be plotting against the government. His suspicions proved sound, but his move merely provoked the suspects, who had apparently been thinking in terms of May or June, to arrest the Army Chief of Staff and launch their rebellion then and there. Had Reid been backed by most members of his military, the whole thing would probably still have collapsed; by nightfall, Radio Santo Domingo, which had been quickly captured by the rebel sympathizers of Juan Bosch and his Popular Democratic Party, was back in government hands. But the military, rallying around General Elías Wessin y Wessin, now saw a splendid opportunity not only to crush the rebels, but to get rid of Reid as well. The latter was quickly done; the former was to prove beyond not only their capacity but their courage. The result, within a few hours, was no government in a position to govern, and, within only a few more hours, civil war and aimless anarchy.

Getting In

Just after the assassination of Trujillo on May 30, 1961, John F. Kennedy "examined the situation realistically," in the words of Arthur M. Schlesinger, Jr. Kennedy said: "There are three possibilities in descending order of preference: a decent democratic regime, a continuation of the Trujillo regime, or a Castro regime. We ought to aim at the first, but we really can't renounce the second until we are sure that we can avoid the third."

By April, 1965, one effort at a "decent democratic regime" had failed. But the Dominican scene had not changed in fundamental ways, and neither, President Johnson would insist, had U.S. policy. "Constitutionalism, *Si;* Communism, No," was his way of putting it, but what he really felt, according to his close associates, was that there could not be another Cuba. So the Johnson policy came down to the same thing as the Kennedy policy —in theory. It was the practice of it that was to cause the argument. And the argument centered on whether the rebellion in Santo Domingo, given timely U.S. encouragement, might not have led to a democratic solution without appreciable risk of producing a "Castro regime." It is a valid argument which will doubtless engage the attention of scholars for years to come. But it has relatively little place in a discussion of Lyndon Johnson's approach to the conduct of foreign policy. If Lyndon Johnson had acted much differently than he did in the early, decisive days of the Dominican crisis, he would have had to invent his own alternatives and ignore the counsel of his principal advisers (only one of whom, Thomas Mann, whose initial influence was marginal, was not a holdover from the Kennedy team). He would have had to discount the overwhelming weight of the intelligence he received from the scene.

And above all, he would have somehow had to find a way around the hard fact that the full weight of the U.S. Government on the scene had been committed to blocking the rebellion before it was 24 hours old—a full four days before the President ordered in the first contingents of Marines.

From that point on, the President was hooked. Only a wholly different reading of the rebel movement—from some source other than official U.S. intelligence—could have halted the natural evolution of the initial "rescue operation" toward an openly acknowledged effort to head off a "band of Communist conspirators." Fewer troops might have been sent. Execution of the U.S. effort could certainly have been improved. A different turn in the tide of the battle might have dictated a different strategy. But the fundamental aim would have remained the same—to hold open the door to a democratic solution, in concert with the OAS if possible, but in any event, to slam the door to outright rebel victory. For the firm conclusion reached at a remarkably early stage by those upon whom Johnson had to rely was that a rebel victory would carry with it an unacceptable risk of a Communist regime.

This is not to say that the President would not have dispatched the Marines to cover the evacuation of stranded American and other foreign nationals at the beleaguered Hotel Embajador in the absence of a Communist threat. Both he and his aides insist he would have. It also seems certain, however, that U.S. troops would have been landed *had there been no Americans to save,* if that had been considered necessary to forestall a rebel victory. Not the least of the lessons of Santo Domingo is that President Johnson was remarkably at the mercy of the advice and activities of his subordinates on the scene. The record strongly indicates that the major preoccupation of the American Embassy in Santo Domingo and the decisive element in its counsel to Washington was the ebb and flow of rebel fortunes rather than the degree of danger to American and other foreign nationals.

The "Cuban syndrome," in short, was exerting a profound and perhaps decisive influence on U.S. policy and strategy from the very start, from the bureaucratic organization up, as well as from the President down.

By Sunday, April 25, for example, there had not been so much as a word in public about a possible Castroite content in the incredibly confusing conflict just then getting under way. But by late afternoon, while Ambassador W. Tapley Bennett was still in Washington, where he had been involved in home-office consultations when the trouble broke out, his Chargé d'Affaires, William Connett, reported that "all members of the country team [the top officers of State, the Agency for International Development, the Peace Corps, the Central Intelligence Agency, and the military attachés] feel Bosch's return and resumption of control of the government is against U.S. interests, in view of the extremists in the coup and Communist advocacy of Bosch return." Connett recommended against a show of U.S. force "at this time," but he said he had already agreed "reluctantly" to a plan adopted by Wessin y Wessin and leaders of the "loyalist" antirebel group to "fight to block return of Bosch . . . even though it could mean more bloodshed." The U.S. military attachés, furthermore, had impressed upon Wessin & Co. "our strong feeling everything possible should be done to prevent a Communist takeover."

In other words, the United States was *promoting* the antirebel fight at this stage, so great was the Embassy's interest in heading off a rebel success, even though no responsible U.S. official was then ready to identify a single key Communist in the rebel movement or to document the degree to which it might be subject to Communist influence. Later, evidence was assembled which indicated the presence of known Communists or Communist sympathizers at rebel gatherings or their participation in distributing arms and ammunition on Sunday. But the bulk of this data, by the State Department's own admission, was not assembled or thoroughly evaluated until at least 48 hours after the fact. Indeed, an official State Department recapitulation detailing Communist activity concedes at the outset that "much of the information concerning the first few days was obtained only after the landing of U.S. forces on [Wednesday] April 28."

On Monday, the Wessin forces began to move. While the rebels were busy handing out captured arms, the Dominican Air Force was bombing rebel installations and other key points in the capital, stirring bitter public resentment and feeding the rebel propaganda mills. By this time, the CIA in Santo Domingo and in Washington was beginning to speak of the Communist threat (privately), though it was still not mentioned by Administration officials as an element in the struggle. Wessin seemed to be winning. In Washington, Bennett was getting ready to return to his post and he received a reminder from the President himself, if any was needed, stating just what sort of outcome Johnson *didn't* want. The President reportedly stressed his desire for a non-*trujillista* solution; but he also is said to have emphasized even more emphatically the unacceptability of "another Cuba in this Hemisphere." Some would argue later that by doing this, the President was fixing limits on the counsel he would get thereafter from his man on the spot. But by that time, the U.S. course had been fixed almost irreversibly. Bennett, from all the evidence, was as determined as any of the principals involved to block a rebel takeover of the government.

By Tuesday, Bennett was back at his desk in Santo Domingo, and the events of that day throw more light on the U.S. frame of mind. Law and order had almost completely broken down. Evacuation of civilians had begun. In the morning, shooting erupted at the Embajador, where evacuees were milling around awaiting transportation to the United States. Though U.S. spokesmen laid the blame on rebel ruffians, the facts were as confused as most things in this tangled revolt. By the word of one American official who witnessed the event, antirebel sympathizers actually opened fire first, as one of their number was being dragged away by the rebel gang. In the melee, shots sprayed the hotel. At that point, American citizens were probably in greater danger than at any other point in the rebellion of encountering the mass slaughter Johnson later pictured as their likely fate, had the Marines not intervened.

Yet on Tuesday, there was no plea for help from the U.S. Embassy. True, the rebels were on the run, or so it seemed to U.S. officials there, and it could have been argued that law and order might soon be restored. But it could as easily have been argued that if the rebels were on the run, the real reason for summoning the Marines—to bolster the antirebel forces—was less compelling.

The first hint of rebel disintegration came at 3:00 p.m. that day, when Colonel Francisco Caamaño Deñó, and Colonel Miguel Angel Hernando Ramírez, two leading figures of the uprising, showed up together with six associates at the U.S. Embassy and were ushered into the office of Embassy First Secretary Benjamin Ruyle. Unanimously, they asked for U.S. help in arranging a cease-fire. When the point was made that the rebel movement had a "President," PRD leader José Rafael Molina Ureña, and that he ought to be in on the discussion, Ruyle suggested they seek him out together at the palace, which had been under heavy bombardment that day. First the rebels suggested it was too dangerous, then they agreed to go, and finally they vanished while Ruyle was checking with Bennett. The First Secretary boldly set out in the company of a police major and found Molina "huddled in a tiny corner deep inside the palace," surrounded by a handful of dejected associates.

Still defiant, Molina resisted the cease-fire proposal, then finally agreed, under strong urging from Ruyle—throwing sharply into question rebel charges that Bennett rudely rebuffed the rebels in a second, better-publicized encounter with their chieftains later in the afternoon. Bennett is a soft-spoken, courtly career man, incapable, as he himself would say, of "bad manners." But he did have the impression at the later session that he was being asked to negotiate a cease-fire largely in order to restore some semblance of balance in a struggle which the rebels seemed on the verge of giving up. Bennett could see no point in rescuing the rebels through the use of American good offices. He had no authority to do so in any case. He did, by his own admission, read them a stern lecture on the evils of allowing Communists to "take advantage of their legitimate movement." As the rebels trooped out, he later cabled Washington, some of them held back "as though trying to avoid going out again into the cruel world."

Both Bennett and Ruyle dared to hope that night, as Molina vanished into asylum, that the rebel cause was lost.

But it was not. "I went to bed that night thinking it was all over," Ruyle recalls. "The next day I woke up and it had started up again." What started it up, most authorities now believe, was the refusal of Wessin to risk his depleted forces, and especially his precious tank units (which come close to representing the real source of power in the Dominican Republic) in the crowded, narrow, rebel-infested streets of downtown Santo Domingo. After one brief foray across the Duarte Bridge into town, he had pulled back. When he was advancing menacingly, the record shows, the rebels were in disarray, with some of their leaders fleeing into asylum and others lying low. When it became apparent that the "loyalists" had no stomach for a mopping-up operation downtown, the rebels popped up again.

Wednesday, April 28, the view from the U.S. Embassy was bleak, and Bennett decided the United States would have to edge into the action a little more decisively. The scattered antirebel units urgently needed communications gear for morale, as well as for military effectiveness. "They go hours without contact," he cabled Washington, in a message which went on to spell out in unmistakable terms the degree of U.S. commitment to quashing the rebel threat at almost any cost. Excerpts from that message to Washington follow:

"While I regret reliance on a military solution for a political crisis engendered by confused, democratic left, all valid elements of which are either in hiding as much from extremists (in their own camp) as from the military forces, the plain fact is that while leftist propaganda may fuzz the issue, *the issue here now is a fight between Castro-type elements and those who oppose* [author's italics]. I do not wish to be overdramatic but we should be clear as to the situation. If we deny communication equipment and the antirebel forces lose for lack of heart, we may well be asking in the near future for landings of Marines to protect U.S. citizens *and possibly for other purposes* [author's italics].

Pointedly he inquired: "Which would Washington prefer?"
Washington's answer was cautious, but also revealing; what it

said, in effect, was that the U.S. was not anxious to intervene to help restore law and order "unless the outcome is in doubt"— a formulation which suggests more than a little multiplicity of purpose in the Washington concept of intervention, too. Still, by mid-day Wednesday, McGeorge Bundy was betting against a landing of Marines and so, reportedly, was the President. Johnson had been watching the Dominican Republic warily since Saturday. U.S. warships, including the carrier "Boxer" with 1,800 Marines aboard, had been standing off the coast since Sunday; the CIA had actually recommended the fleet movement on Saturday. But whatever may have been the private expectation or desire of individual officials, the weekend movement of ships had been precautionary—designed as a contingency measure at the time. The President had meetings scheduled that afternoon to deal with Vietnam and related matters, with Rusk, McNamara, Bundy, Ball, and others, and a later session at the Treasury on balance-of-payments problems.

By 3:00 P.M. Bennett was beginning to get edgy. The head of a "loyalist" junta, Colonel Pedro Bartolomé Benoit, had telephoned a breathless request for U.S. help, including 1,200 U.S. Marines to help restore order. "He was given no encouragement," Bennett reported. "I do not believe the situation justifies it." But the Ambassador's appraisal did not deal with the threat to civilian life and limb. Rather, it was a battle report. "Wessin is not advancing beyond the Duarte Bridge," Bennett's message said. "It is not an impressive showing." The Ambassador added that the outcome was still in doubt. The latest message from the Department was "perhaps unduly optimistic. Logically, junta forces should be able to control the situation. But the situation is not really very logical and a severe test of nerves is in process . . ."

At 4:54, Bennett passed along the text of a formal "loyalist" request for U.S. military assistance (which had also been denied). Its phrasing is interesting. Benoit was arguing that the "present revolt is directed by Communists . . . and [it is] of authentic Communist stamp." The evidence, he said, could be found in "excesses, mass assassinations, sackings of private property." If it prevails, it will be "another Cuba," he concluded, asking for "unlimited and immediate U.S. assistance."

Then, shortly after 5:00 P.M. came the crucial Bennett telegram, recommending the landing of Marines. It suggested this could logically be done for the purpose of protecting the evacuation of American citizens. But, again, what Bennett focused on most was the tide of war. Though noting that the police chief had indicated he could no longer control the rampage in Santo Domingo, it dwelt at greater length on the dispirited state of mind of the "loyalists" out at the San Isidro air base, where they had made their headquarters. The Wessin y Wessin forces, Bennett reported, are "tired and discouraged." The head of the U.S. military-aid program had visited San Isidro, found one leading "loyalist" in a "hysterical mood, urging retreat . . . a number of officers weeping." Benoit had apparently repeated a request for U.S. troops. This time Bennett was prepared to go along.

At the White House, the President and his advisers were caught short. They would have preferred to sound out the OAS. Yet, close advisers to the President frankly admit that this could have been a dangerous course. The Hemisphere organization is notoriously slow, given to endless deliberation and a fascination with legalistic quibbling. "It was," one White House aide said later, "getting close to cocktail time, which is not the best moment for rounding up OAS ambassadors." More important, there was a real danger that the OAS would vote "no," or at least drag out the debate. Yet there was the Bennett recommendation on the record. Loss of American life *was* a possibility. And inaction in the face of the Ambassador's request would have been difficult to justify at home. But intervention in the face of an adverse OAS vote would have been still more damaging in the Hemisphere. Later, comparisons would be made with Kennedy's handling of the missile crisis, but this was scarcely relevant. Kennedy had time to prepare his case and his "consultation" left no question of what the United States intended to do. His terms made it impossible for the Organization to do anything but go along; he had, moreover, photographs of the Soviet missiles. Johnson had no such evidence. So only the briefest consideration was given to a formal appeal to the OAS, which had briefly discussed the Dominican issue that very afternoon without indicating any inclination to get involved.

When Bennett's "critic" cable was brought into the President's office, a call had been made to Tom Mann, who was meeting with his staff at State. Meanwhile at the White House, there was a brisk, brief discussion. One man who was there reported later that nobody felt much need to say anything. "One or two spoke up, and the general conclusion was that there was no real choice. The President asked if there was any other view. By the time Mann called back with his recommendation, the decision had really been made to send in the Marines."

There followed the inevitable rush to call in Congressional leaders, notify Latin ambassadors, and prepare a carefully worded public statement in which no mention was to be made of a Communist threat. Officials insist that in the initial decision-making, the Communist-threat aspect was barely discussed. It wasn't, in fact, necessary to discuss it at all. While no one was unaware of the Communist potential, it was at that point impossible to document. The landing of Marines served the dual purpose of protecting American lives and keeping open the option of U.S. force for whatever Communist threat might materialize. It was a holding operation until the precise situation could be more carefully assessed. For the moment, it would be enough to base everything on the argument for saving lives.

And just to be sure that *was* the argument for the initial intervention, Colonel Benoit's request for U.S. intervention was needed in writing, and in terms considerably less controversial than his earlier frantic appeal for help to head off "another Cuba." If the oas was to be expected to take part in a collective peace-keeping operation, it would be important that there have been an appeal from Dominican authorities for U.S. help on arguable, nonpolitical grounds. So Washington requested, in effect, a toned-down request; that evening, Bennett sent his Air Attaché on a 16-mile helicopter ride to secure from Benoit a brief, one-paragraph appeal in writing, which said simply that "American lives are in danger and conditions of public disorder make it impossible to provide adequate protection. I therefore ask you for temporary intervention and assistance in restoring order in this country." This missive, later to appear as part of the record of a special oas investigative committee, was duly transmitted to Washington early in the morning of April 29.

That evening, the President did not mention Communism in his brief televised announcement of the landings. The State Department was playing down the Communist threat for public consumption, too. In downtown Santo Domingo, said one official, "there are a great many people peddling their separate wares." Mann was perhaps readier than the other leading advisers to the President to stress the "wares" peddled by pro-Communists. He was putting emphasis on reports, however inconclusive, that Communist sympathizers trained in Cuba and some of the Eastern European satellite countries had been filtering back into the Dominican Republic in recent weeks. But on Wednesday, the CIA's Admiral Raborn, who was unjustly blamed for filling the President's head full of Communist scare stories in advance of the landing, could not summon up the names of more than two or three known Communists thought to be playing an influential role in the rebellion. By the time he phoned these names in to the President (insisting on use of a scrambler telephone for maximum security), Johnson had already ordered the Marines to land. Raborn had just assumed his job that day; it was not until the next few days that he bombarded the rest of the government with facts and figures on the degree of Communist penetration of the rebel movement. In Santo Domingo, there was the controversial matter of "the lists." Mistakenly, in the view of almost all concerned (including Johnson), officials on the scene allowed themselves to be badgered into a numbers game; a list was hastily compiled naming 54 "Communists" or "pro-Communists," with predictable results. Duplications were found, partly because two different categories—known party members and persons known to have received Communist-bloc training—were consolidated. There were reports that a few on the list were dead, out of town at the time, or in jail. This became a matter of great controversy. The real damage, again, was to credibility. The point being made in Washington in belated defense of the U.S. action was that a dozen trained Communists, in the right place at the right time, might have captured control, or at least gained a solid foothold, in any rebel government coming to power under such chaotic conditions.

This was the crux of Johnson's thinking, according to those

closest to him. For him, it was never necessary to satisfy himself that the revolution was Communist-controlled, or that it *would* produce another Cuba. The point was that it *might*. That risk he found unacceptable. In this conclusion, he was strongly reinforced by Dean Rusk, who tended to see the Dominican Republic not in isolation, but as part of a global Communist conspiracy and therefore a factor affecting the U.S. position everywhere in the world, and above all, in Vietnam. Rusk, according to intimates, saw it as yet another test of U.S. resolve, whether it was something deliberately planned in Moscow or something which materialized spontaneously, but which the Communists could inevitably be expected to exploit. If the United States failed the test, its hand would, by this reasoning, be weaker in Vietnam.

But Johnson was also reinforced in his view by his own political instincts. For its potential impact on his political position, on Congress, on his legislative program, on funds for the *Alianza*—for all these reasons, almost any detectable risk of "another Cuba" was unacceptable. So there is no neat way to characterize that first landing of Marines—or even the steady, rapid buildup of U.S. forces to a size which many onlookers thought excessive. It was, in a way, Vietnam all over again; as at Pleiku, he did what he thought to be the bare minimum. At the outset in the Dominican Republic, he strove to hold open the option to whatever else might be judged necessary. As in Vietnam, he switched from one purpose to another almost imperceptibly: in Vietnam, from reprisal raids to systematic bombing; in the Dominican Republic, from a mercy mission to a rebellion-blocking mission. Was the ultimate objective always the real one? Probably not even his closest aides know, for Johnson tips his hand as he makes his decisions—one step at a time.

Certainly, by Thursday, April 29, Johnson was aware that his rescue operation might swiftly change character. He confided to visitors that he knew much more about the Communist threat than he was telling, but that to talk about it would have complicated the job of the OAS. He had a low opinion of that organization. "The OAS couldn't pour - - - - out of a boot if the instructions were written on the heel," he said scathingly. Meanwhile, the Hemisphere group quibbled and argued and delayed and resisted after-the-fact U.S. appeals to assume collective responsibility for what the United States had undertaken unilaterally.

But he was aware that the OAS would be even less likely to reach agreement on collective measures if the United States seemed to be taking sides. Criticism was building up at home, as first the 82nd Airborne Division and then still more U.S. troops poured in. The argument that it was all for the sake of saving American lives began to wear thin. By Friday, Johnson was shifting ground. He began to talk not just about the safety of American lives but about the danger to "thousands of Dominican citizens." And for the first time, he referred to "signs that people trained outside the Dominican Republic are seeking to gain control." Then on Sunday, on short notice (not more than two hours, by some accounts), he demanded television time for an address. (The appearance of hasty preparation was increased by a mishap with the Teleprompter which caused him to recite one passage twice.) He said that 3,000 foreign nationals, Americans included, had already been evacuated but that more than 5,000 evacuees including 1,500 U.S. citizens, awaited transportation.

But that was not his real point.

"Communist leaders, many of them trained in Cuba, seeing a chance to increase disorder, to gain a foothold, joined the revolution," he declared. "And what began as a popular democratic revolution, committed to democracy and social justice, very shortly moved and was taken over and really seized and placed into the hands of a band of Communist conspirators."

If this analysis is to be believed, it raises the question of why the U.S. Government opposed that "popular democratic revolution" from its inception. Still more questions were raised in the minds of liberal Democrats—and argued bitterly—by Johnson's assertion that the revolution had been "taken over and really seized and placed into the hands of a band of Communist conspirators." Not even the most zealous Red-hunters could document that statement; indeed, by the time the President got around to making it, the influx of American troops had convinced a good many of the pro-Communist elements in Santo Domingo, according to reliable recapitulations by U.S. authorities, that the game was up. Within a few days, they were drifting away, going underground, or carrying their arms off to the countryside.

The Reason Why

Though it is always tempting to invest desperate acts with logic, there was a logic of sorts in what the United States was doing—though there was less to be said for the way it went about explaining why it was doing it. The reconstruction of events by men closest to Johnson at this time runs like this:

Almost from the outset, there were two threats—the danger to American lives and the menace of a new Castro. Neither one, in the confusion, could be precisely evaluated at any given time. But for Johnson, the man of fundamental caution, both were real. And, as one aide put it quite candidly: "Though we knew there was some Communist threat without being able to prove it, we didn't need that argument for the first landings. If fifty or one hundred or one thousand Americans were slaughtered, what President could stand that?"

Once ashore, however, the United States had a new problem on its hands. The rebels had the momentum. The "loyalists" were not only dispirited but discredited. If the Marines hadn't landed when they did, the rebels would almost certainly have seized the government. "Twenty-four hours later, and we would have had to shoot our way in," said a State Department official at the time. It follows that if the United States had swiftly pulled out after evacuating the last American citizens, the rebels would still have carried the day. So what was needed—as any former Majority Leader could readily appreciate—was a counterweight, a new, antirebel "government." Without one, there was danger that the rebels would begin to solicit and gain diplomatic recognition as the legitimate government, thereby hardening the division and perhaps inducing a "loyalist" collapse. But a new, antirebel government could begin to provide the basic necessities of a compromise. Then there would be two sides of more or less equal strength. In the middle would be the forces of the United States (later to be expanded by token OAS contributions into the Inter-American Peace Force) as the buffer to enforce stalemate and encourage a settlement. Almost certainly, it was not planned so precisely in advance, but that was the general idea behind a move that startled Latin Americans and shocked liberal sentiment. Suddenly the United States seemed to embrace one of the Dominican Republic's most dubious figures, Antonio Imbert Barreras, a one-time manager of a ready-mix cement factory. He was the sole survivor of the assassination team which bushwhacked Rafael Trujillo, and he had received an honorary Brigadier General's commission as reward. A tireless intriguer, he had no political principles and scant popularity for all his heroics. Imbert's hunger for public office was whetted by one of the perquisites of Dominican office-holding—a large armed guard. He was, in the words of one American official, a "hood—but with all the advantages of a hood." He was tough, bold, opportunistic. He had even originally offered his services to the rebel side. When spurned, he waited for signs of "loyalist" disintegration, then rounded up several hundred men and captured the nearly deserted National Palace. He now had a power base—and when John Bartlow Martin, at Johnson's request, came looking for somebody to help assemble an antirebel junta, Imbert, after a few perfunctory disavowals of political ambition, took on the job. Quickly he was tagged as Washington's man. But if this was the hope or the plan of some U.S. officials who saw Imbert as the least of several evils, it was not the original intent of the top policy-makers. One of them said: "Imbert has a Kleenex position—useful, but disposable."

As it turned out, Imbert was not that easy to dispose of. President Johnson's first frenzied efforts to wring a compromise out of the opposing camps were to demonstrate, for all the high-level effort put into it on the spot (McGeorge Bundy, Deputy Defense Secretary Cyrus Vance, Thomas Mann), that compromise, or even reason, comes hard in the Dominican Republic. Ultimately, a makeshift compromise was reached under García Godoy, and the hard and precarious business of preparing the Dominican Republic for elections was handed over to the U.S. Government's prime diplomatic trouble-shooter, Ellsworth Bunker, who had served as Ambassador to Argentina, Italy, and India. A veteran of the West Irian and Yemen disputes, he has a rare talent for tackling seemingly insoluble disputes.

By 1966, almost everybody still involved in the Dominican affair was increasingly hedging bets and still speculating over what course the conflict might have taken had Lyndon Johnson stood aside. But most likely Johnson could not have stood aside, even if he wanted to. His own oft-repeated insistence that "I make the decisions here" is only technically true. For he is, in a certain sense, an organization man. Johnson has expressed scorn for Kennedy's penchant for probing deeply into the bureaucracy to study problems before they become full-fledged crises, to learn the ins and outs of obscure situations, to talk to desk men as well as Cabinet officers. "I talk to Dean Rusk, not to some fifth-desk man down the line," said Johnson on one occasion. "If Rusk doesn't know more than the fifth-desk man, he shouldn't be Secretary of State."

Once the crisis is full-fledged, the number of talks is bound to be huge. Johnson himself has noted that between April 25 and May 2, the crucial days of Dominican decision-making, he had 42 meetings with his top advisers and 225 phone calls with them, including 86 with Bundy, 31 with McNamara, 15 with Rusk, and 10 with Raborn.

Some Kennedy holdovers prefer the Johnson approach, on the grounds that it keeps him from wasting his time and theirs on international situations before the facts are clear, before "they are ripe for serious Presidential attention," as one sub-Cabinet man put it. The crisis in the Dominican Republic, however, was never very clear. And before it became "ripe" for Presidential decision, desk men, or their equivalent, had embarked the United States almost irrevocably on the course that it was to follow, more or less consistently, after Lyndon Johnson took the helm. Later it was argued that the President could not have ignored a plea for help from his "entire country team" on Wednesday, April 28. But if this is so, he was still less able to ignore, as a matter of prudent politics as well as Hemisphere security, the much earlier judgment of his men on the scene that the rebellion carried with it the risk of "another Cuba."

The Other
Johnson

"If we didn't have Vietnam . . ."

By the middle of 1965, this was the preamble to practical discussion of almost everything, and it continued to be, with mounting intensity, in 1966. Vietnam pervaded Lyndon Johnson's
relations with Congress, with his own bureaucracies, with foreign
nations large and small. At home, it menaced the Great Society—
and the President's popularity. The polls showed a majority behind his Vietnam policy; the volume of the voice of the minority
in open opposition was plainly out of proportion to its size. But
there was also latent and dangerous opposition among the majority in support, for Vietnam had crystallized a relatively quiescent hard core of militancy among Americans who also wanted

to end the war but thought the way to do it was by waging it still more furiously.

One result was the image of Lyndon Johnson, the gung-ho, quick-on-the-trigger, war President. But a second result was to produce some revealing insights into another Johnson—perhaps the real Johnson—and to the policies he would follow in a world without Vietnam. For the pressures of Vietnam worked two ways. If they impelled Lyndon Johnson to play to the cold warriors one day, they also impelled the master balancer of the political processes to play to the apostles of peace the next. Vietnam pressures put a premium on the use of carrots as well as sticks.

So it was that at a time of widening warfare in Vietnam, when the American public was being exhorted to stand fast in global confrontation with Communist aggression, when European allies were being asked to stand up and be counted into the U.S. struggle against Asian Communism, and when Vietnam was increasingly a litmus test for fixing U.S. attitudes towards the "non-aligned," President Johnson was simultaneously—

One: Proposing a revolutionary new approach to U.S. foreign assistance abroad, an approach more sweeping in scope than had ever been offered before and—potentially—more generous.

Two: Advocating liberalized East-West trade and other contacts with the Soviet bloc, and pressing for arms control, all on terms more far-reaching than anything that had been attempted since the beginning of the cold war.

Three: Moving toward the rebuilding of NATO on a basis, which, if carried to its logical conclusion, would give the European partners proportionately more weight in decisions involving the common defense and the U.S. proportionately less.

Four: Beginning to sketch, in barely perceptible rough outlines, a modified China policy which would couple continued hostility to Peking so long as Peking remained unremittingly hostile with acceptance of a highly diverse non-Communist Asia whose common denominator would be not so much anti-Communism and still less pro-Westernism, but a reasonable independence from Chinese control; as part of the process, he was launching a "Marshall Plan" for Asia, in which the Russians would be free to participate as partners with the United States, and of which the North Vietnamese could some day be beneficiaries.

The problem was with that initial "if." There *was* an expanding war in Vietnam and it *was* stirring the cold warriors in Congress, endangering the President's control over his legislative program, robbing his more controversial international proposals of their cutting edge, even blunting his ability to extract them from his own bureaucracies without prodigious efforts by the President-protectors on the White House staff.

Vietnam also injected a high tactical content in every move Johnson made towards balancing those processes—a good measure of hard-headedness and a tendency to propose things for the sake of appearance and then to let them drop when opposition showed itself to be too strong. Utility remained the test. Measures for easing East-West tensions or uplifting Asia which had plainly been proposed for their appearance as an offset to napalm and troop-landings, were therefore commonly discounted by the President's critics as nothing more than that.

And, conceivably, rightly so, for as long as the Vietnam miasma beclouded everything, nobody could see clearly enough to be completely sure about the President's intent. What with Vietnam, there was little scope for profitable dealings with Russia, or for a new cast to U.S. Asian policy, or even profound improvement in the U.S. relationships with its European allies. The new Johnson view of foreign aid could be made to sound sweeping. But if the money was still snatched away from those who crossed purposes with Lyndon Johnson on Vietnam at a time when he was particularly sensitive to being crossed on any question touching any aspect of the U.S. conflict with international Communism, the full reach of his foreign-aid revolution could not be proved. Generosity was not the basic ingredient in the Johnson approach to foreign aid, in any case. The key to it would always be a quid pro quo—whether it was some measure of understanding for the U.S. cause in Vietnam, or serious, visible efforts toward self-help, or consideration for U.S. business interests, or a favorable U.N. vote. The emphasis on reciprocity was fundamental. "The President will never believe you can't get more for foreign-aid money than we've been getting," said one visitor to the LBJ Ranch, in the fall of 1965, when Johnson was actively engaged in a reappraisal of American aid policy. Equally fundamental was the instinctive lashing back when Johnson thought he was being pushed around on any issue. That, too, would survive a Vietnam settlement.

But there were, nevertheless, revealing reflections of enduring significance in much of what else Johnson was doing without attracting much public notice. For the essence of this "other Johnson" was the essence of Lyndon Johnson's life.

The roots ran to the modest beginnings, the good-hearted patrons and mentors (FDR and Sam Rayburn); the interplay of Texas businessmen and Texas politics; the *vaqueros* and land-poor farmers of Texas and what the New Deal did for them (and what they did for Johnson); the hard work rewarded by loyalty; the give and take of Congress; the stunning successes that stemmed from all of this and a deeply felt awareness that an equal opportunity ought to be available to others. Finally, it was all rooted in an instinctive feel for the limitations, as well as the potential, in the power he achieved and exercised en route to the Presidency.

When it all came together in Johnson's conduct of the Presidency, the end product could only be confusing. He spoke publicly in terms of a global crusade against Communism and inveighed against appeasement. But he could also hold forth privately in terms with which Senator Fulbright and Walter Lippmann could only concur. He once suggested, in tones of impatience and frustration, that the United States had perhaps been gulled by its own "propaganda about being leader of the free world." He decried the ease with which foreign leaders could say, "Pay me or I'll go Communist," and wondered whether it wasn't time to "let some people sweat a bit—let them go right to the end of that street and see what happens."

Up to a point, his concept of foreign aid was almost synonymous with that of Senator Fulbright, his arch-opponent on Vietnam. And so, in fundamental respects, was his view of foreign policy in the larger scheme of things. It was Fulbright (though it could have been Johnson) who said in early 1965 that "the solution of our domestic problems has a vital bearing on the success of our foreign policies," and added that it was time to turn more U.S. attention and resources to the "problems of slums and crime and poverty and inadequate education in the United States."

The main difference between them was that in speech after speech, on health, education, the problem of food and population and poverty, there ran the grander Johnson theme of a Great Society for export on a scale that could only gratify the most ambitious of the "globalists."

"The President is not conceptual," an associate once said, meaning that Johnson, in his own thinking, does not tend to deal in terms of specific ingredients—an MLF, a new international monetary unit, a regional development bank, a most-favored-nation clause, a nonproliferation pact—that give body to foreign policy. "But he has visions, he has dreams," the same man added, meaning that Johnson knows broadly but profoundly where he would like to head, and what he would like to do, whether in foreign or domestic policy. He knew he wanted to wage war against "the ancient enemies of mankind" as enumerated by Barbara Ward, rather than against the Vietcong. He knew that he wanted to help uplift whole regions while encouraging the nations within the regions to do more individually and collectively to uplift themselves. He knew that something more durable than an unlimited commitment to pour troops into threatened Asian countries was needed to contain the Communist Chinese. He believed in building bridges to Eastern Europe, and in rampant good neighborliness in Latin America. The problem was how to do all this without "scatteration" of U.S. resources, as Walter Lippmann put it, and while engaging in an increasingly costly war.

Operation "Short String"

Lyndon Johnson took one quick look at foreign aid early in his Presidency and wasted almost no time setting to work to change the rules of the game. The end result, in accord with the Johnson pattern, was more impressive than his first move. But the over-all strategy was to be consistent from the start. Foreign aid, he concluded, had become a bad word in Congress, because it was being doled out in too large amounts to too many of the wrong people for too many wrong reasons. It was time for abrupt, perhaps even violent, change. That way everybody could start afresh. Once it was done, both the United States and Lyndon Johnson would be playing with a stronger hand.

The change began the day after Christmas in 1963, when Lyndon Johnson announced formation of a new study group to "approach the problem of foreign aid with fresh minds not bound by precedent or by existing procedure or arrangements." To begin with, it wasn't really a new study group, but an old one that had been quietly set in motion by Kennedy just before his death. Kennedy had charged it with finding ways to insulate the next foreign-aid program sent to Congress from the nearly disastrous drubbing the last program had taken in the 1963 session. (That year, Kennedy had started out asking for nearly $5 billion in appropriations for the 1964 fiscal year, trimmed it himself to about $4.5 billion after receiving the findings of a private study panel headed by retired General Lucius Clay, then trimmed it again while it was before Congress to little more than $4 billion; Congress had then knocked out almost another $1 billion.) Now Johnson dressed the study group up with some new names, including that of Eugene Black, and while some were still puzzling a day or so later about the whole thing, the new President climbed on top of a bale of hay and used that rustic podium to give a large part of the plot away. The Committee would be giving serious consideration to some specific reform proposals from Congressmen, he told a press conference. "But I have some definite views of my own," he added. "I communicated them to the committee. . . . They are considering my views and all other information they can get. They will come up with recommendations. If they are as close to my views as I hope they will be, we will probably adopt them."

So much for "fresh minds not bound by . . ."

The study group considered the views of Congressional leaders before it even made its report, and found the House Foreign Affairs Committee and its Chairman, Thomas Morgan, firmly opposed to at least one of the President's "definite views," which would have involved splitting apart economic and military aid. At a late-evening White House meeting with Morgan and other interested lawmakers, the President decided, in effect, to abandon his other reforms (including special treatment for the Alliance for Progress and a further splintering of the program by placing long-term development in a category of its own) as well. Instead of this effort to make foreign aid look less bulky, Johnson settled in 1964 for a program which started out smaller than any that had been submitted to the Congress in a decade or more; he repeated that tactic in 1965. This was the first major Johnson change in the rules; where once it had been part of the game to give Congress an outsized program and to give the lawmakers the credit for slashing it, the Johnson Administration adopted the "bare-bones" approach and, by skillful legislative maneuvering, made it work. Johnson was to be able to claim in 1964 and 1965 that his programs had suffered less damage at the hands of Congress than those of any of his predecessors, which was true. But it was true only because they were sent to Congress preshrunk by the President.

It was hard to tell how much of the reshaping of foreign aid which culminated in a markedly new foreign approach in 1966 was done at the instigation of Johnson and how much was done by the able, reform-minded head of the Agency for International Development, David Bell. What is clear is that the thinking of the leading AID men paralleled that of the President in certain key respects. There was a determined effort to cut the number of beneficiaries and concentrate the bulk of the effort in key countries: India, Pakistan, Turkey, Nigeria, Korea, Chile, Colombia, and (after the removal of the Goulart Government) Brazil. There was a growing emphasis on self-help, initiated by the Kennedy Administration and carried forward by the Johnson Administration. Tax reform, land reform, sound fiscal policies, social-welfare efforts, and the like were increasingly made a precondition to U.S. help. Greater emphasis was placed, where possible, on multilateral institutions, such as the World Bank's lenient-lending offshoot, the International Development Association, and the Inter-American Development Bank in the Western Hemisphere. Countries such as Greece, Nationalist China, and Israel, which were reaching self-sufficiency, were removed from the rolls of beneficiaries. Long-term aid arrangements, particularly those involving shipments of surplus American food, were allowed to lapse as they expired; they were subject to renewal only under tighter rules enforcing self-help.

Those were the trends. But there is also no doubt that the President gave them considerable added impetus. The big change, in fact, can be dated from one controversial incident—Johnson's abrupt postponement of a state visit by Pakistan's President Ayub Khan in the spring of 1965, which in turn led him to postpone a visit by the late Prime Minister Shastri of India, scheduled for later in the year. There were loud cries of anguish and rage in Pakistan and India. From New Delhi, Ambassador Chester Bowles cabled that 15 years of patient efforts to build a working relationship between the United States and India had been undone. The White House was quick with explanations that no snub had been intended and that certainly no hard feelings were involved. The President, it was said, had simply felt that the visits of both leaders would be more fruitful all around if they were delayed until after Congress had finished work on the pending foreign-aid appropriations.

That was the explanation offered officially to India and Pakistan, and there was some basis for it. Pakistan had fallen from grace in the eyes of Congress, as well as of the President, for multiple offenses—closer ties with Communist China, opposition to the U.S. policy in Vietnam, support for Indonesia's "confrontation" with Malaysia, and a marked slackening of interest in its membership in the SEATO and CENTO pacts, a large part of the basis for a friendly and exceedingly generous U.S. attitude towards Pakistan in the past. So Ayub's presence in town probably wouldn't have helped the prospects for the foreign-aid bill. It was reasoned, after that, that to bar him and receive Shastri (with whom he was violently at odds over Kashmir) would have been open U.S. favoritism and too much of an affront to Pakistan.

But few officials in a position to read the President's mood at the time believed the "disinvitation" of Ayub was as simple as that. "The President simply lost his temper," said one man who was intimately involved in the matter at the time. "He thought he was being used." Johnson reacted furiously in private to any suggestion that he had acted impetuously or for any reason other than the one the White House gave. But his own explanations, in private, hardly reinforced the argument that it was a considered, thoughtful act. "Suppose your mother-in-law dropped in on you five minutes before you were going to go out to a ball game," was one analogy he employed. But a better clue to his reasoning appeared when he was asked why he did not have time to receive the leaders of India and Pakistan when he did have time to welcome to Washington, at about the same time, the head of the staunchly pro-Western government in South Korea? His answer, in paraphrase, was that it was the difference between spending time with Senator Majority Leader Mansfield, or Minority Leader Dirksen, on the one hand, and a member of the Texas legislature on the other. In other words, it was the difference between spending time with somebody with whom he could do business and with somebody with whom he could not.

Criticism lingered on, despite the President's protestations, and flared up again when Pakistan provoked a small war with India over the disputed Kashmir in the fall. Some authorities were even prepared to argue cause and effect—that Ayub was moved to save face and salvage honor by instigating the Kashmir "war."

But the real significance of the Ayub-Shastri affair lay elsewhere. As things turned out, the war was brought under control, (in large part by Lyndon Johnson's decision to throw the full weight and influence of the United States behind U.N. efforts to work out a cease-fire in tacit concert with the Soviets). Late in 1965 and early in 1966, the "other Johnson" was to be seen at work. By then, elements of the U.S. aid packages to India and Pakistan had been either wholly suspended or reduced to a month-by-month basis, pending a cessation of hostilities in Kashmir. Ayub's postponed visit was back on the calendar for December, 1965, and it became the occasion for a candid statement of U.S. foreign-aid policy. The statement came in the form of a ranch-house backgrounder given by Bill Moyers for a handful of newsmen then in attendance on the convalescing President. It amounted to a blueprint of Johnson thinking, rendered from notes of a conversation with the President himself, in which Pakistan and India were made, in effect, an object lesson for any nation receiving or expecting U.S. aid.

The President, it was said, was prepared to resume large-scale foreign aid to Pakistan and to India—at a price. He was acutely aware that the United States had provided a total of nearly $10 billion to the two countries in their 18 years of independence, as part of a wider effort to shore up not only the Asian subcontinent but all of Asia against Communist encroachment. Yet India, while directly menaced by China, could not seem to see the Communist threat in South Vietnam, nor see fit to support the U.S. effort there. Pakistan, which had been heavily armed by the United States, seemed more interested in fighting India than in joining in a common effort for the subcontinent's defense. And the Indians hadn't done enough to patch up their quarrel with Pakistan. So, to start with, there must be no more shooting, and there must be a reasonable effort towards a lasting settlement.

Moreover, both the President and Congress had been increasingly disturbed by Pakistan's steady drift towards alignment with Communist China and open opposition to "U.S. imperialism" in Vietnam. That, too, would have to stop, if Pakistan was to expect a resumption of U.S. aid. Nor could the United States be expected to be generous with its aid in Pakistan if the Pakistanis continued to accuse the U.S. of "betrayal" on the grounds of American aid to India; the U.S.–Pakistan alliance, Mr. Ayub was to be reminded, was against the Communists.

As for India, (which, in contrast with Pakistan, had an exceptional record of making sound use of U.S. economic help), more effort must be made in New Delhi to come to grips with the Indian food problem by building fertilizer factories instead of steel mills, and by promoting food output in other ways. The United States, the President felt strongly, could not be expected to go on feeding an increasingly populous India—or an increasingly populous world, for that matter—indefinitely.

This was not the first instance of a tougher Johnson line—but the care that was taken to promulgate it was the most convincing evidence thus far that there was nothing hit-or-miss about the evolving Johnson foreign-aid philosophy. "More and more, we are putting these so-and-sos on a short string," said one AID official at the time. Already President Nasser had gotten the "short-string" treatment. When he persisted in undermining U.S. efforts to damp down the Belgian Congo crisis, continued trouble-making in Yemen in ways which threatened a U.S. ally, Saudi

Arabia, and agitated for the ouster of the U.S. from its airbase in Libya; his long-term aid agreement was allowed to run out. Peru, Colombia, and Ghana were others whose aid programs were cut back or halted at one time or another under toughened aid policies.

This was one side of the Johnson aid strategy—the process referred to by some as "wiping the slate." But there was a second side, once the slate was relatively clean and everybody understood each other all around. For as soon as Johnson became convinced that he and the United States were not being used—or as one White House aide put it, that he "had found the right levers for bringing U.S. influence to bear"—it was his habit to respond with reasonable generosity. At that point, aid was usually restored—but on a shorter "string." Despite a proposal by the U.S. Embassy in Cairo, for example, for another three-year surplus-food deal with Nasser, only a six-month agreement was authorized. After the December encounter with Ayub, the money began flowing again; and while officials were reluctant to discuss just what assurances of better behavior the President had obtained in his talk with Ayub, there was general agreement that the atmosphere between the two countries improved measurably afterwards. "If we said how, it wouldn't last," one official contended at the time. One implication was that the President, by taking a hard line, had given Ayub the leverage *he* needed against extremist elements in *his* government.

As one White House adviser summed it up: "The President knows by instinct that he is dealing with a man at the other end of the line who has political problems—and he wants the other fellow to know that we have political problems too. The test for foreigners is not really what they say. It's what they do to cause Johnson political problems at home. That's why the personal contact is so important to him. But it doesn't work, of course, unless the stage has been properly set."

Whether it works at all, some would argue, would remain to be seen. Theorists of foreign aid argue, with logic, that U.S. political gain has no place in long-range economic development. They contend that aid recipients cannot be expected to make hard-headed social and economic reforms at home unless a continued flow of money is assured. Such self-help is a proper precondition for American aid, the theorists agree. Their point is, however, that long-term economic uplift of the world's poor is more important to the United States, both politically and morally, than short-term considerations, such as reaction to a USIA–library burning. But here, too, Johnson was moving foreign aid away from traditional concepts, away from the economists and the trend lines and the technicalities of growth rates, per capita income, and "take-off points." In January, 1966, he sent Congress a foreign-aid program which could be termed a genuinely new departure —but a program whose make-up also lent itself to adjustment when the U.S. did not think the performance of the recipient or its leader justified continuing the aid flow. The emphasis was away from long-term, "impact" projects, which, once started, cannot lightly be abandoned out of political pique. Instead, the Johnson approach concentrated on the basics—education and health and nutrition and population control—as the prerequisites to effective use of the long-term development loans and outright cash grants that had dominated the aid program in earlier days. Included in his outline of the essentials was some unprecedented tough talk:

"The U.S. is unwilling to subsidize those who do not assume responsibility for their own fate. Those who do not fulfill their commitments to help themselves cannot expect help from us. Neither can we nor they afford waste, and we will not continue any partnership in which only we recognize that fact."

For those who "are determined to help themselves" and "are not hostile to us," Johnson promised the benevolence of the rich to the poor in an attack on "the root causes of misery and unrest." Some of the rhetoric was familiar from past foreign-aid messages. The difference was in emphasis and in application, and it was in the latter that the most fault was found by those critics who remained nostalgic for the Kennedy approach to what had been termed the Third World. The Kennedy Administration wooed it with an intellectual approach and, in the popular idiom, identified with its revolutionary zeal: professors were dispatched as ambassadors—an Arabist to Cairo, economists to Rio and New Delhi. They tended to approach the Third World in ideological terms. The difference is perhaps best measured by the fact that in the Johnson White House, the Third World was more often referred to as "countries that want something from us."

But it wasn't all a case of the back of the U.S. hand to "hostile" nations, or a blatant play for Congressional support by an unmitigated hard line. Asian experts cited, with approval, Johnson's handling of Indonesia, although an angry rupture of all relations might well have drawn applause on Capitol Hill. (Indeed, a legal case would have been constructed that the United States was obliged to remove the last remnants of its aid program in Indonesia under the terms of a restrictive amendment to the foreign-aid bill.) But the State Department and other agencies argued that a small foot in the door might prove fortuitous, should Sukarno lose his grip and forces less bent on tight alignment to Communist China come to the fore. Johnson was "quite able to see the advantages of even a little something being better than nothing in a place like Indonesia," said one interested diplomat, adding that "the President went so far as to take it up quietly with the right people on the Hill; there was a conspiracy of silence and the point was never raised." As a result, there was at least a modest U.S. "presence" in Djakarta when Sukarno, for all practical purposes, was removed from power. The army, with which the United States had close connections because of a long-standing military aid program, seemed to have turned decisively against the Communists in March, 1966.

The handling of Indonesia was a minor illustration of the other Lyndon Johnson. A major one could be found much closer to home—in his handling of Panama. Here the issue was not as overbearing as Vietnam, but a similar problem was involved: to achieve an international objective without unsettling the atmosphere in Congress.

Once the election was safely passed, Lyndon Johnson surprised many of his most critics on the left by taking what was probably the single most significant U.S. initiative in relations with Panama since Theodore Roosevelt's original adventure into its politics:

"This Government has completed an intensive review of policy toward the present and future of the Panama Canal. On the basis of this review I have reached two decisions.

"First, I have decided that the United States should press forward, with Panama and other interested governments, in plans and preparations for a sea-level canal in this area.

"Second, I have decided to propose to the Government of Panama the negotiation of an entirely new treaty on the existing Panama Canal."

The stage had been carefully set for these words from President Johnson. Not only had the United States held its election the month before, but Panama had elected a new President the preceding May; domestic political pressures on both sides had been considerably eased. Meantime, the United States had edged back into giving Alliance for Progress aid for Panama. As in all of Lyndon Johnson's foreign-aid programs, the emphasis for almost all aid beneficiaries was on shorter-term programs dealing with such basic social necessities as education and housing, rather than on big, splashy "impact" projects. More important, the critical question, the future of the Panama Canal, had been skillfully placed in a wholly new perspective. For the first time, the United States and Panama had gotten down to serious talk about things that mattered, such as how quickly the ditch might become obsolete or incapable of carrying the load of expanding world shipping, whether a new canal might be built, and where and how would it be run.

Although the U.S. Government had been thinking and planning about these problems for a good many years, almost nothing had been done to bring Panama into the process of studying the whole question. The existing canal was vulnerable to terrorism, just as the whole U.S.–Panama relationship was vulnerable to leftist agitation. There was little question that the U.S. could defend the Canal by brute force, but the problem was to remove this extreme alternative and replace it with something more constructive. There was a variety of alternate canal routes under consideration, some in Panama, some in neighboring Central American nations. All had to be considered, together with the question of whether nuclear explosives could be used to blast out a new canal; if they could, the cost would drop dramatically. There were more than enough alternatives and unanswered questions to pose the possibility that another route might be found outside Panama. Through a series of studies initiated in the spring and summer, the President managed to hold open for the sober consideration of the Panamanians the possibility that the United States might ultimately settle on a route in Colombia, or possibly prospective routes through Nicaragua or Costa Rica. But it was emphasized that if proper treaty terms could be arranged, the best site might very likely be an alternate route through Panama. The success of this balancing act has yet to be fully tested.

But on September 24, 1965, the long preliminary negotiations finally brought an agreement in principle between President Johnson and President Robles of Panama, and the agreement had an illuminating history. Robles had political troubles at home. His parliament was about to reconvene and the Canal question was certain to provoke debate. When Johnson heard of this, he decided to give his Panamanian counterpart a helping hand. "Johnson lived up to his quid pro quos," a White House aide said at the time. "But if you want a favor from Johnson, you have to do a favor for him."

Robles had been accomodating, so Johnson agreed to a public progress report on the canal negotiations, stating that the two nations had reached "general areas of agreement." This included the understanding that the 1903 Treaty would be scrapped, that the new treaty would effectively "recognize Panama's sovereignty over the area of the present Canal Zone"; that the new treaty covering the existing canal would expire after a certain number of years, or on the date of the opening of a second Panama Canal; that the Canal Zone and the rest of the Republic of Panama would be integrated much more closely, politically, economically, and socially; and that employees of both nations working for the canal would be entitled to more equitable treatment. Finally, the two nations agreed that the United States should maintain military bases in Panama to safeguard its security interests in the canal.

By almost any measurement, both the December, 1964, and September, 1965, breakthroughs were historic. They were also a tribute, as President Johnson said in making public the September agreements, to his own faith in "reasoning together."

Whatever the awkwardness of the initial phase of Lyndon

Johnson's Panama policy, the second phase had all the earmarks of a political work of art. Johnson had delayed, but he could hardly be said to have dallied. Consensus had been achieved, not just with Panama, but within the Administration and across the great political middle ground in the United States, and this last gain may have been even more important for future U.S.–Panama relations. Getting the Department of the Army to agree with almost anybody else in the U.S. Government is feat enough; getting the Army and the Defense Department and the State Department in line is that much harder. But by the time Lyndon Johnson was ready to announce his really critical decision, at the end of 1964, to propose the negotiation of an entirely new canal treaty, he was able to say that this move reflected the unanimous judgment of "the Secretary of State, the Secretary of Defense, and the Joint Chiefs of Staff" and was "based on the recommendations of Ambassador Robert Anderson, Secretary [of the Army] Stephen Ailes, Secretary Thomas Mann, and Ambassador [to Panama] Jack Vaughn" and has "the full support of Mr. Truman and General Eisenhower." For good measure, he noted that the idea of a new treaty, together with the plans for a sea-level canal in Central America, had also "been reported to—and sympathetically received by—the leadership of the Congress." The result was that what Lyndon Johnson believed he could not possibly do in January, 1964, he did in December, 1964—and with barely a ripple of public dissent. By September, 1965, the American public seemed bored by the whole subject. There was none of the outcry that might have been expected and probably too little praise as well.

Alianza, Johnson-Style

Toward the end of 1965, the "other Johnson" was also in evidence in Latin American affairs, in other ways. He had engineered an effective administrative overhaul of the *Alianza* workings in Washington; improved the aid operations themselves; and, more important, given impetus in December, 1965, at an inter-American conference in Rio de Janeiro, to the most significant alteration in *Alianza* concepts since its founding. For the first time, the United States had unequivocally pledged to support the *Alianza* indefinitely, beyond the 10-year life span agreed upon in 1961 at its founding. Regionalism, a fundamental Johnson concept in foreign aid, had also been written into the inter-American system; what had been seen largely as a bilateral U.S. aid program to the southern half of the Hemisphere was to become much more of a mutual-aid operation, under which the members pledged to help not only themselves but each other to knit tighter economic connections and to share the responsibility for the common effort.

"People in Latin America measure Johnson against the Kennedy charisma, and he fails completely, through no fault of his own," said one veteran State Department hand after the Rio meeting. "But the President's personal pledge to maintain U.S. support for the *Alianza* after 1971 had a tremendous impact. The big thing that emerged in that meeting was the general impression that we are really serious."

Rio was a bright spot for Johnson, but the turning point in his efforts to project his own approach to Hemispheric uplift almost certainly dates back to a speech he made on August 17, 1965, the fourth anniversary of the Alliance. It was an address that went far to erase the poor impression made when he appeared at an earlier commemorative occasion in the thick of the Panama crisis in March, 1964.

Now, in the August, 1965, speech, he pledged U.S. support for a new fund to promote multinational road-, river-, and communications-improvement projects. He offered U.S. help for another multilateral scheme to create a Latin American equivalent of the European Coal and Steel Community—but dedicated to communal production, on a continent-wide basis, of fertilizer, pesticides, and other products to spur farm output. He spoke movingly of his Great Society at home and of its aim in common with that of the Alliance for Progress— to "enlarge the dignity of man everywhere." He spoke of his own country's shortcomings and those of the Hemisphere as a common problem to be tackled in concert. "In my nation, like yours," he declared, "we are still struggling to find justice for all of our people. And because we are fortunate in abundance, we feel that morality requires that we must also try to help others who seek it for their own people, too."

In the opinion of close associates, those ideas are at the heart of the Johnson vision for the world—the vision of a "global populist" with a genuine yearning to bring to backward areas everywhere what had been brought to the backward areas of Texas three decades earlier.

And yet, one long-time observer of the Latin scene returned from a Hemisphere tour that fall to report that "Lyndon Johnson could not visit any Latin country without creating a police problem." Most American diplomats on the scene would have agreed that Lyndon Johnson remained a controversial figure with most Latin Americans. The Dominican intervention was probably part of it, though its impact on anti-Americanism was always overrated. It was a convenient rallying cry for leftist agitators—but one they did not really need.

The largest liability for the "other Johnson," a good many experts felt, and the issue likeliest to fuel a hostile demonstration were he to voyage to Latin America or anywhere else was deepseated, widespread, popular antipathy to the U.S. war effort on behalf of South Vietnam.

Birth of a Bank

A primary example of the "other Johnson" may be read between the lines of a statement made by Vice President Humphrey in March, 1966, making clear that the Administration wanted to present a face other than one of unremitting hostility toward Peking. Humphrey suggested that U.S. policy toward China should be one of "containment without necessarily isolation," and that the United States should attempt to approach China much as it approached the Soviet Union in the late 1950's—both with military firmness and with active efforts to explore better relations. Humphrey's words followed an Administration decision to move cautiously to encourage qualified persons—scholars, doctors, and journalists—to pursue their contacts to arrange visits to China.

To some extent, this strategy placed the onus on China for U.S.–Chinese antagonisms, much as Roger Hilsman's December, 1963, statement sought to do. It also drew attention to the steps the United States had taken, and it suggested not a change of policy, but the idea that a reappraisal was being considered in hopes of more peaceful coexistence.

This was one indication of the kind of world Lyndon Johnson would like. An earlier and more substantial one came in 1965, when the germ of a Johnson policy for Asia first publicly appeared. It came together with the glimmering of a chance for parallel action with the Soviet Union, perhaps even collaboration with it, in the containment of China.

By the spring of that year, Lyndon Johnson was beginning to feel the need for a more appealing mix in the U.S. approach to Asia—something more constructive than shot and shell and scattered bilateral foreign-aid programs. The concept of an Asian Development Bank to finance regional economic-development projects in the vast area stretching from Teheran to Tokyo had been kicking around for more than two years. It was an idea that found favor largely in Japan; to the free-trading Japanese, dependent on industrial exports to finance food imports, a regional bank with Japan as a major member could be a commercial open-sesame to her Asian neighbors, and a useful instrument in the new Japanese economic coprosperity sphere. But the trouble was that only Japan had much money to put into it; other Asian nations were cool to lukewarm about contributing the needed capital. The United States, already busy bankrolling a clutch of international lending institutions, was smiling distantly on the project, but without offering capital or encouragement. But the idea kept recurring, and it was due to be discussed in Wellington, New Zealand, on March 17, 1965, at a meeting of the Economic Commission for Asia and the Far East, a regional economic body of the United Nations. It was necessary for the United States once more to take a stand.

In the State Department, there was at least some support for an Asian bank. Some foreign-aid theorists liked the idea because they liked any multilateral instrumentality for dispensing American aid without incurring all the political problems inherent in bilateral beneficence. Some "grand strategists" liked it because it would bring the Asians into a common effort to cope with their staggering economic problems. It would also open up a channel for aid to Asia from the United States, from European nations, and, most important of all, to many, from the Communist bloc; for Russia, as well as other non-Asian nations, was to be invited to join.

This was the feature that appealed most strongly to some of President Johnson's closest White House advisers. The bank itself would be modest and have little impact economically for some time; but as one adherent put it, "The shadow it would cast is the kind of shadow we must increasingly try to cast in that part of the world." His point was that the day was past when the United States could stand alone in Asia, as the sole guardian of non-Communist Asia against Chinese expansion. The white man, with his military bases, his anti-Communist treaties and pacts, and all his fire-power, no longer had the whole answer. Sooner or later, the Asians would have to come to recognize their communal responsibility, and the United States, for its part, would have to recognize that the containment of Chinese expansion could only be done in the context of diversity, by accepting a broad spectrum of nonaligned countries, even Communist nations of the Titoist stripe, as the wave of the future. Practically speaking, it would never be easy in the near future to engage in bilateral aid programs in Cambodia or in Indonesia, where American aid was being spurned. But the violent anti-Americanism, the outright hostility toward the Western "imperialists" that was daily being aggravated by the war in Vietnam, was an argument for creating machinery which would enable the West to offer, through multilateral channels, some alternative to those who did not wish to fall wholly under Communist Chinese sway. There was, then, a lot of ideology wrapped around what otherwise was merely a proposal for another regional bank.

But to the Treasury Department, it still looked like a bank. Worse, it looked like a trouble-making bank, and the Treasury had enough trouble with Congress as it was. That was enough for Treasury Secretary C. Douglas Dillon. He did not wish to make the case on Capitol Hill for another regional bank, especially since the Treasury had a low estimate of the utility or efficiency of the Latin American precedent, the Inter-American Development Bank. Dillon did not like the idea of an ineffective

Asian bank draining money away from more efficient institutions, such as the World Bank or the International Development Association. He didn't like the effect that any American contribution would have on the U.S. balance of payments. The thought of trying to explain to Congress the virtue of belonging to the same bank with Russia—at a time when the Vietnamese war was stirring cold war fervor—was a chilling one.

All these arguments were contained in a March memorandum from Dillon to the State Department. There they reached the receptive ear of Tom Mann, who thought that the State Department, for its part, had enough trouble with Congress and no need of another controversial project to place before it. Mann's heart was with the Inter-American Development Bank, and he was not interested in setting up a rival institution which might compete with the IDB for U.S. money.

David Bell, AID's Director, was more favorable to the project, and he and Mann had reached an agreement to maintain an open-minded U.S. position. But Dillon's memorandum was just what Tom Mann needed; and at the crucial moment, while instructions were being given to the U.S. mission to the ECAFE meeting in Wellington, David Bell was out of town. The result was that the instructions were not open-minded at all. It was Tom Mann's intention to tell the delegation to make clear that the United States had no plans to contribute capital to the bank, even though it was prepared to concede that such an institution might serve a useful purpose if the Asians themselves set it up on a sound basis and ran it that way. Mann believed that they would not, and, indeed, that there was little momentum behind the idea at all. At the eleventh hour, word reached the White House that the instructions to the U.S. delegation were to be essentially negative.

Most likely, Lyndon Johnson knew nothing about any of this and was scarcely aware of the existence of the idea of an Asian bank. But he had been thinking and talking about the U.S. position in Asia. He had a general vision of a different position, and an anxiety about the impression created by the martial American stance in Vietnam, and, for that matter, in all of Asia. What followed was a classic example of the machinations of Big

Government under Lyndon Johnson. It is also an example of how a policy of sorts can evolve from a Johnson concept or state of mind. The state of mind would have to be translated by staff advisers into a program and a policy, all the time working against the innate inertia of bureaucracy. It was a clear example, too, of option-keeping: a door was about to be slammed at just the moment when, in the judgment of White House staff members, Lyndon Johnson might find it in his interests to walk through it. There was urgent telephoning, and the thin edge of a wedge was inserted to keep that door open. It was a very thin edge, to begin with; the instructions for the Wellington delegation were modified only a little: U.S. officials were to state U.S. disinterest in joining an Asian bank, but were to add the phrase "at this time." The United States was to express at least a qualified readiness to render technical assistance to the bank and to engage in joint ventures, with both U.S. and bank capital, for projects too large for the bank to handle alone.

The U.S. position was still essentially negative, but it made a curious positive effect simply by generating Asian dismay. This proved decisive, for the mission was able to report back that Asian yearning for an Asian bank was a lot stronger than it had seemed when there had been no prospect of U.S. participation. The White House and the State Department—which is to say, for all practical purposes, Tom Mann—had reached a tacit compromise that a real show of Asian interest would be the test. Obviously, Johnson would not want to ask Congress to finance an Asian bank that the Asians were not interested in. As this test was met, during the course of the Wellington meetings, the White House staff acquired the leverage to revise the mission's instructions still more liberally. By the end of the meeting, the American delegation was taking a far more open-minded position than it had started with. The United States was saying, in effect, that it would consider membership in an Asian bank, always depending on the kind of bank that was set up and the terms under which the United States might be asked to join.

With that door wedged open, plans went forward for the President's April 7 speech at Johns Hopkins. Here Johnson made his first major effort to recast the U.S. approach to Asia, enlarging the carrot to offset the adverse impact of the stick. Politically, the major concession was the "unconditional discussions" which Johnson said the United States was prepared to take part in; until that point, the United States had seemed unwilling to do any talking until the North Vietnamese stopped their "aggression" against the South. But the President plainly wanted to go further in the economic field. While the door was open to the offer of U.S. participation in an Asian bank and in joint efforts to develop the Mekong Basin as part of a special Southeast Asian Development Program, the President characteristically did not wish to take the initiative; again he resorted to a form of judo. Congress, he and his staff felt certain, would be more impressed by an Asian initiative. Instead of proposing U.S. membership in an Asian bank, or talking in specific terms about U.S. aid to development in Southeast Asia, the President asked for suggestions from the Asians themselves. Just to make sure that everybody was following the same script, he took pains to suggest, discreetly, of course, what sort of Asian suggestions would be most welcome.

Adlai Stevenson called on U Thant and asked him how he might reply, if the President were to ask Asian leaders what they wanted. Thant said that an Asian Bank and a specific hydro-electric power project in Laos, known as the Nam Ngum Dam, would be his idea of ways to start. And these were the suggestions that U Thant presented, in a public statement responding to the President's Johns Hopkins speech.

By then, the Asian Bank was beginning to find a secure niche as a permanent piece of U.S. policy. The President enlisted the services of Eugene Black, who has a high rating with Congress as a judge of what is safe and sensible in international financial matters. Black went to see U Thant and other Asian figures at the United Nations and confirmed the estimates of White House and the State Department supporters that there was enthusiasm for the idea. The process spun itself out, with Lyndon Johnson by that time an active ringmaster; the fate of the whole exercise no longer hung on the option-guarding efforts of his staff. He called a high-level meeting of principal advisers in the Cabinet room. There, Black delivered his report, which amounted to a solid endorsement of a serious U.S. effort to help establish an Asian bank and of U.S. participation in it as an active member and major subscriber.

On June 1, 1965, the President asked Congress for $89 million to expand programs of economic aid and social development in Southeast Asia. The first draft of his request had made no mention of an invitation to the Soviet Union to participate, but Lyndon Johnson scribbled into it, in his own hand, a reference to it in the line, "Our role will be vital, but we hope that all other industrialized nations, including the Soviet Union, will participate."

At the time, few American authorities had much hope that the Russians were ready to join the United States in aid programs designed to bolster Asian nations against Chinese blandishments. But the fact remains that the proposal was put to the U.S. Congress; it was implicit in the U.S. approach to the make-up and functioning of the proposed Asian development bank. It was clear that President Johnson was looking forward to the possibility that the United States and Russia might some day have a broader common interest in containing Red China.

The Soviet Union showed some interest in the idea by sending a team of observers to one of the planning sessions, held at Bangkok, prior to the formal establishment of the bank. By so doing, they kept alive the idea that they might join at some future date.

Eugene Black went to Manila on November 27, 1965, for the founding meeting of the Asian Development Bank. When he had met with Johnson a day earlier, the President again repeated the idea of Russian participation in these words: "It is my hope that the industrialized nations of both Western and Eastern Europe that have not yet signified their support [of the Bank] will do so."

The Treasury still had its reservations about the Bank and so did Mann. But essentially, bureaucratic inertia had stemmed from anxiety over Congressional reaction, not just against the Executive Branch, but against the Treasury and the State departments. Neither has political capital of its own to spend on the Hill in large amounts, and the instinct is to resist promoting projects liable to be controversial. But now the processes had carried the project to the White House, and made it a piece of Presidential business. The President, of course, does have capital to spend in the pursuit of his objectives in Congress; a large part of the bureaucratic anxiety had been assuaged.

In this fashion, the processes had lifted a project out of the bureaucracies by a curious sort of interaction between the Presidential vision, a White House staff concept, and a lower-level bureaucratic impulse which had blended in as the project rose to the top. Of all these ingredients, the essential one was the option-guarding efforts of the White House staff. It had the ability to foresee—at a time when the Johns Hopkins approach was barely an idea in the back of the President's mind (and perhaps somewhat further forward in the mind of McGeorge Bundy)—that the way must be kept open for its practical application, and that no potentially useful door could be allowed to slam shut.

Bridge-Building

If it required a complicated reaction between a Presidential vision and a clear-headed concept in the minds of a Presidential staff to give birth to an Asian Development Bank, it required even more powerful chemistry to launch the United States, in 1966, on the most progressive program to promote East-West trade since the beginnings of the cold war. Once again, the instrument involved was scarcely one to quicken the pulse. It was a mundane matter of seeking authority from Congress for the President to grant what is called most-favored-nation treatment to countries of the European Communist bloc on the same basis that it is granted to all other U.S. trading partners whenever the President felt that this would advance U.S. interests. It was, in other words, an opening toward ending trade discrimination against the Eastern European satellite nations—and perhaps Russia as well. Up until 1966, only Poland and Yugoslavia had been granted most-favored-nation (MFN) treatment—another way of saying that only those two nations have been granted the trade concessions, in the form of tariff cuts, which had been negotiated with all other U.S. trading partners over the years. The rest of the Communist countries were still obliged to trade with the United States at tariff levels far higher than those granted other countries on the principle of equal treatment for all who will grant equal treatment in return.

Rumania, for example, is charged 30 per cent more duty on its caviar than is Iran; the tariff on its glassware is 60 per cent of the value, while the rate for competitive items from non-Communist countries ranges from 15 per cent to no more than 50 per cent.

It is important to set aside, however, the thought that an important commercial issue was involved; the satellites and Russia would probably continue to have only a limited opportunity of selling their products in the United States, even on level terms with "most-favored" competitors; they lacked the sales outlets, the merchandising know-how, the simple understanding of a free-enterprise system; indeed, they lacked the goods themselves. But they did want to buy in the U.S. market and they could unquestionably increase their sales there through MFN treatment and thus increase their dollar earnings and their capacity to buy a bit more than they had.

But trade was really never the point. The point was bridge-building, a concept Lyndon Johnson had embraced, in principle and with intensity, almost from the beginning of his Presidency. In a speech in Lexington, Kentucky, at a dedication of the George C. Marshall Research Library, Johnson evoked the memory of the Marshall Plan and its original purpose of bringing "every European nation closer to its neighbors in the relationships of peace." The United States, he said, "will continue to build bridges across the gulf which has divided us from Eastern Europe. They will be bridges of increased trade, of ideas, of visitors, and of humanitarian aid."

Indeed, the man who had always accepted as a simple necessity the keeping open of lines of communication had been a bridge-builder before he reached the White House. "That Iowa farm that Khrushchev saw damned near upset the whole Communist system," he once said, in recalling Khrushchev's 1959 visit to the United States. "That's why I want them [the new Soviet leadership] to come over and see our electronics industry."

But he was also, of course, aware that East-West trade was a red flag to the cold warriors of Congress, to conservative opinion everywhere, and to organized labor, which publicly saw it as a moral question involving the exploitation of Communist slave labor, and privately saw it as a competitive threat that would encourage an influx of cheap goods whose cost could be controlled by the Communist governments concerned. Yet another stronghold of opposition to "trading with the enemy" was in the Commerce Department, whose responsibility for administering export and import controls in general, and restrictions on trade with Communist nations in particular, had given rise to an entrenched bureaucracy dedicated to the principle that Communism could be strangled to death by economic strictures.

So Lyndon Johnson only talked about East-West trade in 1964. When he reverted to this vision in 1965, he was still not ready for a frontal assault on Congress. A State Department suggestion that East-West trade promotion be a feature of the foreign-policy section of his State of the Union Message in January, 1965, was considered, but it was ultimately discarded, apparently on the grounds that the stage had not yet been properly set. In particular, the stage had not been set with AFL-CIO President George Meany, a rigid opponent of the whole idea. But the President did start setting the stage. He appointed a blue-ribbon panel of distinguished private citizens to study the issue and come up with proposals. The committee, under Chairman J. Irwin Miller, chairman of the board of Cummins Engine Co., Inc., was selected with care by White House staffers who knew what the President wanted. In the spring of 1965, he got it, in the form of recommendations from the Miller group which were unequivocal in their espousal of a concerted U.S. effort to establish stronger trade ties with countries behind the Iron Curtain. The report was realistic; it did not project a bright commercial opportunity. Rather, it centered hardheadedly on the aspects of East-West trade that interested Lyndon Johnson: the opportunity to open channels to Communist nations in order to encourage a somewhat larger measure of economic independence from Moscow for the satellites; the necessity for the United States to get in step with the reality of a burgeoning East-West trade between Eastern Europe and Western Europe; the ultimate, long-term advantages of any measures that pulled divided Eastern and Western Europe closer together, that increased mutual trust, that provided contacts, openings, connections, if only for the purpose of resisting the present-day tendency, under the order of things, for the halves of Europe to drift further apart. The nub of the argument against all this was that East-West trade would strengthen the economies of the satellites, and their Communist governments as well, and prolong Communism as their way of life. The counterargument was that the course of natural evolution was bound to weaken Communism's authority and control, especially if the evolution worked toward economic improvement at home rather than toward increasing the number of people under Communist sway.

Originally, the hope in the White House and in some circles in the State Department had been to send East-West trade legislation to Congress in 1965, embellished with the findings of the Miller Committee. But in July, when a draft bill was ready, the President had already promised the Congressional leadership that nothing new would be thrown into the hopper at that late date. The problem then became one of maintaining the bureaucratic momentum. Secretary of Commerce Connor was cool to the Miller findings, reflecting the traditional Commerce Department view, which in turn reflected the thinking of a considerable segment of the business community; the Commerce Department's most vociferous "clients" tend, by and large, to be at the conservative end of the business spectrum. At State, the Under Secretary for Economic Affairs, Tom Mann, was also skeptical, not so much on philosophic or ideological or even international political grounds as on practical domestic considerations. His "clients" also tended to be in the business world, and they were numbered among its more conservative elements. His Capitol Hill connections were of the same ideological stripe and for the same reason; Mann had become the Administration's apostle of conservatism and pragmatism in a liberal parish, though it was almost impossible to tell whether this was out of his profound beliefs or whether because those were the outside connections he had and those were the sort of people he could be most helpful with in the Johnson cause. In any event, he was now, to a large degree, Johnson's favorite go-between with the more conservative segment of business thinking—a segment which Lyndon Johnson had always believed, from his earliest days as a Texas politician, to be well worth cultivating.

The danger became that the Miller Committee report would simply be pigeonholed, for lack of any particular positive effort to keep it alive until its recommendations could be translated into a legislative proposal for 1966. Again, McGeorge Bundy was to play a decisive role. It had been his inspiration to create the Miller Committee in the first place, as a powerful assemblage of outside wise men to render a constructive and favorable verdict on East-West trade. Now it was his inspiration that the conclusions of the Miller Committee be written as indelibly as possible into formal Johnson Administration policy. A task force, he concluded, would do the trick, but only if an intragovernmental task force could be assembled which could be counted on to accept the Miller Committee finding. This would depend largely on who the chairman was. Because it was to be at the Under Secretary level, a logical candidate was Mann. But it was clear, from all that was known about Mann's views, that a study committee chaired by him would not come up with a very positive conclusion. An alternative to Mann was Bundy himself. The decision was put to bridge-builder Johnson, with predictable results. So it was that McGeorge Bundy chaired the intragovernmental committee whose findings, neatly parallelling those of the Miller group, became, in effect, a declaration of U.S. policy, durable enough to last until the time came around to begin drafting the legislation for submission to Congress in 1966.

Yet, even in the face of what would have seemed to be a plain Presidential predilection for promoting East-West trade, when the natural forces of budget-making and program-planning and Congressional message-writing began to bring East-West trade back into focus in December, the opponents were apparently as ready as ever to resist. And once again, resistance grew out of concern on the part of the bureaucracies for their own particular position in Congress.

The process began with the proponents in the bureaucracy. John Leddy, Assistant Secretary of State for European Affairs (embracing Eastern as well as Western Europe) and Anthony Solomon, Assistant Secretary for Economic Affairs, together came up with a proposal which seemed in all logic to fit Johnson doctrine. They recommended that East-West trade liberalization be a high-priority item in the President's package of legislative proposals for the 1966 session, and that it get a suitable send-off in his State of the Union Message. The next way station in the process, under the table of organization, was, however, the office of the Under Secretary for Economic Affairs, and it was Mann's view, according to associates, that Vietnam made 1966 a poor year for bridge-building. East-West trade, Mann apparently believed, could not fit the Congressional mood; even Fulbright and Mansfield were thought to be lukewarm about a fight on that issue in the cold war atmosphere afflicting Congress. It seems likely that Mann did not put a high priority on bridge-building, in any case, and saw it as something that could be put off for a year or so without great loss. Even George Ball, usually a proponent, was said to be worried about the Congressional reaction, and about the effects of a nasty fight and, at best, a narrow victory on the larger purposes of the East-West trade proposal. So the recommendation that finally reached Dean Rusk's desk was ambivalent. Besides, Rusk had other things on his mind. The State of the Union Message was in the process of the usual frantic preparation, and late-blooming candidates for inclusion in it were not likely to qualify. The option-keepers, however, were on the job. They had made it their business to keep an eye on the East-West trade problem as it made its precarious way up to the seventh floor of the State Department and into the Secretary's office. They knew where it stood, but they did not know Dean Rusk's position. To find out, they had to engage Lyndon Johnson's active concern. A staff memorandum bearing obliquely on the East-West trade issue found its way into the President's night-reading file—the preferred technique for attracting the President's considered attention. It was enough to elicit a request for a status report, which was enough to justify an inquiry at State. Even this, however, did not extract from Secretary Rusk a resounding judgment. This was the time of the big peace offensive, with the bombing pause in Vietnam, and it apparently was Rusk's view that a U.S. proffer of more liberal terms on East-West trade should await the outcome of the effort to find a breakthrough in the war. Whatever the outcome of that effort, the Congressional receptivity to an East-West trade bill would be easier to measure when it was clear what course the struggle in South Vietnam was going to take. To the extent that Rusk came down on one side of the issue, he was inclined toward caution and delay, but he was, according to one associate, prepared to take a stronger line if the President wanted him to. This was enough, barely enough, to justify the inclusion of the East-West trade proposal in a draft of the State of the Union Message.

Once more, the custodians of Presidential options had kept open the option that he might finally wish to throw East-West trade into the balance. In the eyes of the world and at home, Johnson was looking more and more like a war President. Vietnam was carrying him off in a direction in which he obviously did not want to be carried. He had every reason to wish to demonstrate his concern and, more specifically, to dramatize, as best he could, the direction in which he would prefer to go. He was asking Congress for huge new sums to wage war and he had equally good reason to wish to signal to the Communist countries of Europe, at least, that he had other aims and other hopes. Those dealing most closely with him—those staff members whose interests were the President's interests and who did not have to concern themselves with the built-in interests of the great bureaucracies—had no doubt that Johnson would wish to have the option of including East-West trade in his program.

But in the first few days of January, when a decision could not be delayed much longer, those who were in favor of the East-West trade legislation believed that the President would decide against it, if only because the government over which he presided seemed incapable of deciding one way or the other.

But they were proven wrong. In his State of the Union Message, the President proclaimed that the "most important principle of our foreign policy is support of national independence." One of the ways "we follow this principle," he declared, is "by building bridges to Eastern Europe. I will ask the Congress for authority to remove the special tariff restrictions which are a barrier to increasing trade between East and West."

Even when this language had been written into the final draft of the State of the Union Message, those who cherished it were not certain it would survive. One of them, while going over the draft with the President, felt obliged to call his attention to the passage on East-West trade. He had read by it, without comment, and might have missed its implications. But it turned out that he had not. Indeed, his reaction suggested that he had expected it would be there all along.

TWELVE

The Confines
of Consensus

In his State of the Union Message to Congress, January 12, 1966, President Johnson placed Vietnam at "the center of our concerns."

But he insisted: "We will not permit those who fire on us in Vietnam to win a victory over the desires and the intentions of the American people. This nation is mighty enough, its society is healthy enough, its people are strong enough to pursue our goals in the rest of the world while still building a Great Society here at home."

That had been the intent—from Pleiku on. The crucial decisions in July, 1965, had artfully balanced another major escalation of the U.S. war effort with business as usual at home. At the end of January, Johnson would break the 37-day pause in the bombing of North Vietnam—but he would break it gently, if that is the word, by beginning at a lower level of intensity and only creeping slowly closer to targets that could bring about risk of war with the Chinese Communists.

But guns-plus-butter was still not much more than a hope in spring, 1966—whatever Lyndon Johnson's intents. For no one could read the will or intentions of Hanoi or Peking, however much some military men and civilian warhawks might claim such omniscience in the course of their argument that given a free rein, American power could crush the Vietnamese insurgency. Still less could anyone correctly gauge the interaction of the Communists and the U.S. President, or, in the last analysis, the President's continuing capacity to balance the domestic political processes bearing upon him.

What was all too evident, however, was that the rapidly increased U.S. war effort in Vietnam had brought the nation perilously close to the ceiling on *its* capacity to wage a war in Asia while pursuing Johnson's goals in the rest of the world and building a Great Society. This, in turn, was creating serious contradictions in the President's fundamental Vietnam strategy.

The crux of the strategy, as summed up in early 1965 by a man in a good position to know, had always been a "larger effort for a lesser reward." The theory accepted by Johnson—if not by all of his advisers—was that a steady intensification of the U.S. effort at best could be counted on only to shift the balance of forces and encourage the Communists either to negotiate or at least stabilize the level of conflict as a first step toward some sort of *de facto* de-escalation of the war. But even this strategy required a poker player's reflexes, a readiness not just to meet an opponent's raise, but to raise back. By early 1966, however, there was little room left for safe raising by Lyndon Johnson unless he dipped into chips earmarked for the pursuit of a Great Society at home and overseas.

And if Lyndon Johnson devoutly hoped to avoid this ever larger effort, the American public seemed unprepared to settle for a "lesser" reward. "A larger effort for a lesser reward" is not a purpose calculated to stir the blood of a people conditioned to think that the object of any contest is victory. It was not in Lyndon Johnson's nature, either, to lead by publicly propounding unappealing propositions. He was a master balancer of the processes, but he had shown scant ability over two and a half years to inspire. For reasons that still had sociologists and political scientists puzzled, he suffered from what the White House inner circle thought of as an "inspiration gap." His consensus for Vietnam had been constructed by enormously skillful manipulation of the processes. But it was also an amalgam of mixed motives and conflicting hopes. The advocates of total victory still had some small hope that this was also Johnson's goal, or that if it wasn't events would make it so. Those who wanted to get the United States out of Vietnam had been given to believe that escalation was the quickest way. Nobody had been encouraged to think that the new Johnson approach to the Vietnam struggle which had opened in the spring of 1965 could well drag on for many springs, though the President warned, for the first time, in that January message to Congress that "we may have to face long, hard combat or a long, hard conference, or even both at once."

Johnson-style consensus, however, rested a good deal less on candor than on the capacity to convince, by whatever means. An old associate said frankly, "You have to ignore the President's own account of why he does things, or even what he has done." Yet people persisted in asking where the war *was* headed and what the President *did* want out of it. The questions would not go away. "I'm still confused," said Senator Fulbright after a four-hour, closed-door meeting of the Senate Foreign Relations Committee with McNamara. Puzzlement over the purpose of it all ran through the public sessions of the Fulbright Committee hearings in February as well. When Vice President Humphrey appeared on "Meet the Press" in mid-March to face a panel of editors and publishers, the first question, from John S. Knight, began with the preamble: "Despite all of the millions of words about Vietnam, the editorial opinion, background, interpretation, and even the Fulbright hearings, the American public is still divided and confused as to our ultimate aims and objectives . . ."

A member of the Senate "peace bloc" came away from a session with the President at about that time convinced that Johnson was a "hard-liner; he talks as if he thinks we can win it militarily." The hard-liners, for their part, complained that the President talked too much about the awful danger that more escalation would bring intolerable risk of a clash with the Communist Chinese. The Johnson art of persuasion, which had served him so well in rallying the nation for a bigger war effort a year earlier, was beginning to fail him, as the size of the effort and its prospective growth rate began to menace all those other "desires and intentions of the American people" at home and abroad, without offering conclusive evidence of commensurate reward.

The stage, in short, was set in the early spring for what modern geopoliticians call the "Crunch"—the moment when something, somewhere would have to give. Or so it seemed when one examined what had gone before.

The Center of Concern

In the spring of 1965, and on into that summer, the South Vietnamese and their American allies were losing the war. McNamara was speaking publicly of a "deterioration" in Vietnam. On the scene, U.S. military men spoke freely of the need for many more U.S. troops and a more active U.S. combat role. Though the number of U.S. troops was climbing rapidly toward 75,000 at the time, their weight was just beginning to be applied. The Vietcong "monsoon" offensive was overrunning district towns, closing in on provincial capitals. The President had dropped the other diplomatic shoe in April, with his offer of "unconditional discussions." In May, he had gestured toward the peace bloc at home and abroad by a perfunctory five-day pause in the bombing of the North. Some argued that at this point, Hanoi could have been lured into negotiations by a longer pause and a more out-going U.S. attitude. But to a large degree, it was an academic argument, because the Johnson high command was convinced it did not have adequate military strength to furnish a sound basis for an acceptable settlement.

"We have to be for negotiations," said a Presidential aide, at about that time. "But under the circumstances, we would also have to go in with pretty tough terms." Johnson told visitors in June that he was "going to cut down on offers to negotiate"; he gave the reason that past offers had been so rudely rebuffed that new ones would be taken as a sign of weakness. But a more basic reason almost certainly was his assessment of the tide of battle at the time. It was going to get worse before it got better, he declared. There would be more casualties. It could be a long war, he was privately conceding. In early June, he let it be known that U.S. troop needs might soar as high as 400,000, and McNamara was speculating aloud that it might be necessary to declare an emergency and call up the reserves. There was talk of a special message to Congress, asking for a new, updated vote of confidence to replace the post-Tonkin resolution with something more relevant to the waging of a far wider war.

It sounded serious, and of course it was. But there is evidence, necessarily circumstantial, that it was also made to sound more serious than it had to be. When the President, on July 28, announced his second major escalation of the U.S. war effort, it fell reassuringly short of the dire measures the public had been conditioned for by the advance build-up—a preconditioning which had stirred new outcries of opposition to the war. Draft calls were increased, but there was no call-up of reserves, no declaration of a state of emergency. A new build-up of U.S. forces to the 125,000-level was announced, and the way was left wide open for further increases. But Johnson carefully avoided mention of ultimate totals nearly as large as some that had been officially bandied about. To some, it was the budget shell game all over again—the careful preparation of the public for measures more extreme than those actually contemplated in order for the actuality to seem mild by comparison.

But close students of the President's methods argued it was a more complex process than that. They saw it as another example of skillful maneuver and artful balancing. General Westmoreland was given all the forces he had been seeking so the military would have no solid basis for complaint. But a backfire of public and Congressional opposition to an even larger effort had been generated in the process by advance hints of the more drastic accompanying measures which the military were also demanding. Having polarized opinion, the President neatly positioned himself inbetween. Everybody got something, even if nobody was quite satisfied. Johnson, for his part, had avoided a degree of mobilization that a diplomatic breakthrough might just conceivably make unnecessary. The enemy had been given less grounds for a bigger raise in return. In the meantime, guns-plus-butter could still be a plausible program for America.

The President insisted in private that there had been nothing stage-managed about it, that his final decision in favor of more moderate measures had been made the morning of the announcement. He had been about to adopt the more stringent measures bruited about in advance, he said, when suddenly a "weak feeling in his stomach" about such drastic moves impelled him to second thoughts. And his primary consideration, he contended had been a balancing not of domestic pressures, but of his position vis-à-vis the Soviet Union. A U.S. move toward semimobilization, he said, would have raised tensions between Washington and Moscow just when he had particular reason not to stir up the atmosphere excessively. U.S. air strikes had just been ordered against North Vietnamese SAM (missile) sites; because these weapons were Russian-supplied, there was at least some possibility that Russians might be killed by U.S. air attacks.

If this was an element in the President's thinking, however, few of his close advisers believe it was the only element, or even the dominant one. Rather, it was another example, reminiscent of the MLF affair, of Johnson injecting his own instincts for his own position, in its totality, at home and abroad, into the counsel he received and coming to a conclusion essentially his own. "It wasn't a matter of the President going against all his advisers, although he would probably argue that it was," said one aide just afterwards. "But it was uniquely his decision, his shaping of a major policy."

As it turned out, 125,000 U.S. troops did not begin to reflect the full reach of this policy. Implicit in acceptance of Westmoreland's requests of the moment was acceptance of a strategy which would require far larger numbers if that was the way the other side chose to play *its* hand.

Hanoi, as it turned out, did raise back. It stepped up its escalation, and toward the end of the year, as U.S. forces plunged deeper into successful if inconclusive combat operations, the center of gravity in the President's war councils underwent a significant shift. McNamara became less confident about the end result of steadily intensified applications of U.S. military power and more concerned about the possibility that this would lead inevitably to a clash with the Communist Chinese. The logic was all too clear. Intelligence studies indicated that the bombing of the North did not materially inhibit Hanoi's capacity to infiltrate the South with ample numbers of men and adequate supplies; projections indicated it never really could, however more difficult it might make the provisioning of the insurgents. But lack of results would logically bring demands for more effective, punishing air strikes at industrial targets. Eventually North Vietnam would want the Communist Chinese to furnish stronger air defenses, probably with Chinese fighter planes. U.S. plane losses would grow. There would be pressure to plaster the airfields more heavily. The Chinese would be asked for more help and be hard put to resist supplying it from airfields in China. The rallying cries of the hawks—"hot pursuit" and "privileged sanctuary"— would grow. It would be awkward for Johnson not to heed them —and so the war would spill over into Communist China. McNamara was not necessarily predicting this; still less was he moving into opposition to basic strategy. But he threw his weight increasingly in favor of a greater effort to find a basis for negotiated or *de facto* settlement. The McNamara-Rusk partnership in Vietnam never had fit the obvious stereotype of a defense chief bent on a military solution and a diplomatic chief placing his faith in bargaining, and it came to fit it less and less. Rusk was not *against* a new diplomatic initiative; indeed, he also supported the idea. But as the President once told a visitor: "Rusk and Bundy are always a litle bit readier to hit than McNamara." By the end of 1965, it was McNamara who was taking the lead in advocating a major new U.S. effort to find a diplomatic breakthrough. In early December, according to reliable accounts, he visited Johnson at the ranch and in the course of a long conversation, argued for a break in the bombing and a fresh effort to promote

a settlement. The initiative was significant, for the modification
it reflected in the thinking of the Secretary of Defense introduced
an added element on the side of caution and restraint in Johnson's high councils at a time when the White House was professing
growing concern over public pressures for a greater show of
militancy. "McNamara has changed from a mechanical optimist
to a mechanical pessimist," said one member of the policy-making
team.

For Johnson, a peace offensive offered multiple opportunities.
There was the off-chance, not rated very high, that a major effort
might actually bring if not negotiations, then perhaps what had
come to be called a "reciprocal reduction of hostilities," requiring
neither side to acknowledge anything but giving both a chance
to edge back from endless, ever widening conflict. In time, if
reciprocity should set in and become tacitly acknowledged by
both sides, the mutual confidence this might engender could
pave the way for bargaining. And at the least, the United States
would have tried; it would thereby be in a stronger position
politically and diplomatically to pursue the struggle if rebuffed
by Hanoi.

Plans for the bombing pause were started accordingly in December—again propelled by mixed motives. The peace bloc
could hope that once it began, it would stick because of the un-
popularity of starting up the bombing again. The hard-liners
could take comfort in the thought that if nothing came of it, the
argument for pummeling the Communists would become inescapable. The initial idea was to let a hiatus in the bombing
grow out of the annual cease-fire which normally is observed
over the four days of Tet, the lunar new year, in the last week
of January. Subsequently, when an exchange of truce proposals
led to a rather loosely observed cease-fire over Christmas, Johnson
seized on that occasion instead. In principle, his air-borne peace
offensive was decided upon in advance—however helter-skelter it
may have appeared at take-off time, when Harriman, Goldberg,
Humphrey, and Bundy were suddenly fired, like acrobats from a
cannon, to the far corners of the world. The seeming spontaneity
sprang largely from Lyndon Johnson's delight in taking people
by surprise.

The result was an undoubted net gain politically, even if some scoffed at Johnson's "rodeo diplomacy." On balance, however, the Johnson Administration improved its position abroad as well as at home. But a month passed, and still there was nothing from Hanoi that the Administration could take as a gesture of conciliation. In the last week of January, Johnson was faced with one of the most difficult decisions of his Presidency.

The pause had carried through to Tet. The question now was whether the fighting would revert to its former ferocity, or whether, just possibly, the pause might elicit a gesture from Hanoi—on the ground, in the battle, if not through diplomacy. As Tet ended, however, the Administration was in an awkward spot; a diplomatic note is one thing to read, but an easing of hostility on the battlefield is something else again. Intelligence-gathering in Vietnam is a murky, imprecise, often necessarily misleading business, and from myriad intelligence sources, the White House received early in that last week of January two quite conflicting assessments. One, the more hopeful, indicated a possible slackening in the number of Vietcong "incidents." But even this, while statistical in nature, could not be a conclusive token of intentions unless it was known precisely what sort or size of incidents were involved. In theory, "incidents" means any assault launched by the Vietcong. As a matter of political practice, however, whether an incident is big or little depends on whether it is successful or unsuccessful. A mortar attack on a U.S. airbase, for instance, could miss most of its targets and make few headlines, though what it said of the intentions of Hanoi might be fully as revealing as an attack that connected. Thus, Johnson had not only to consider what the reports said, but what impression they would have on U.S. public opinion and in Congress.

A second report, also submitted early that week, was less hopeful, because it was prepared in a different way. It took similar raw data, projected it over a longer period, and concluded that the war was really being waged by the other side at approximately the same level of intensity as it had been before Tet. It took three days before the White House finally concluded that the second report was right; a day after the conclusion was reached, bombing was resumed.

Meantime, however, Congress and the public were leaping to conclusions at a time when the Administration itself could find nothing solid on which to base a policy. Pressures were building up on both sides. Fulbright demanded that his Senate Foreign Relations Committee be consulted before a decision was made. Fifteen Senators dashed off a letter to the President urging restraint and got a curt reply. The President met with Congressional leaders, the overwhelming majority of whom were in favor of a resumption of the bombing; he seemed to them to be talking their language. His position in private was that it was becoming increasingly difficult to justify *not* bombing "when American boys are fighting." Yet the President's performance was curious; apart from the intelligence delay, he seemed, once again, to be positioning the opposition, giving more rein to the peace bloc than he normally gave to opposition—or, at least, to unwelcome opposition. He seemed, in his dealing with both hawks and doves, to welcome some expression of their respective sentiments—though, on balance, he would probably have preferred no kibitzing from anyone, and least of all from those who, by his reasoning, risked misleading the enemy by implying a lack of U.S. resolve. But since there *was* opposition from the peace bloc, it had its purposes. Johnson did not wish to take the more extreme counsel he was getting from the "bomb boys." So he split the opposition, once again, by resuming the bombing, though at a limited rate below that of the period before the pause. Before he was through, he had managed again, in his process-balancing, to come up with something for everybody—even for Wayne Morse. Responding to a convenient plea from Pope Paul suggesting that Vietnam be referred to the United Nations for arbitration, Johnson dispatched Goldberg to New York to ask the world body to do what it could—which almost everybody agreed could not be much. Still, Senator Morse was moved to applaud the appeal to the United Nations, which he had been recommending for months on end, even while deploring the ending of the pause.

But the consensus was wearing thinner all the time. More and more the war in Vietnam was shaping up as a test not of firepower but of staying power, and a test of staying power seemed far more of a threat to a thin consensus than a test of strength, which might reasonably be expected to produce a solution, of some sort, soon.

The Joint Chiefs, by March, were already chafing under the bombing restraints imposed after the ending of the pause. The antiwar elements, while numerically small, were less disposed to leave the critical question of negotiations and prospective peace terms to quiet diplomacy, even though efforts to draw the Administration into public discussion of the subject often prompted Johnson to balance things off by a restatement of U.S. objectives in stiffer terms. Meantime, the President and aides kept insisting that their main concern lay with the pressures they saw building up for more war. "That's where the specific gravity of the nation lies," said a White House man in March. And to counter it, there were the first faint signs, largely in private, of a campaign to counter advocates of militancy by sketching in somewhat greater detail a reasonable solution short of total victory.

There were even public suggestions of this. Administration spokesmen were quick to crack down in concert on Senator Robert Kennedy's suggestion that the United States contemplate at least the possibility of an eventual settlement in which the Vietcong would have a place in society, politics, and in the government. But when the cross-fire of controversy finally died away, it became apparent that Kennedy's position wasn't all that far removed from the private thinking of the Administration.

The real problem, officials kept insisting, was that saying so publicly would be to propound final settlement terms before any bargaining had begun.

But how else to prepare U.S. public opinion for what would, if achieved, almost certainly be a rather soggy settlement? Could a consensus behind generous—perhaps even risky—settlement terms be developed at all without spelling out the final U.S. position in advance to the other side? And if no effort to do so were made, was it not reasonable to expect that as casualties mounted, the public attitude would be more than likely to echo that of Maxwell Taylor at the Fulbright hearings—"Having embarked on this course, I hope we strike them hip and thigh."

Indeed, does consensus work for Vietnam, or in any major matter involving foreign policy?

It was no time for flat and final answers and no time for prophecy. For the answer to Vietnam in the spring of 1966 was the answer to almost everything. If the answer to Vietnam could not be read in Hanoi, still less could it be read in the complicated maneuverings of an essentially inscrutable President.

But there is a Johnson record, in Vietnam, and in the rest of the world, and with Lyndon Johnson, more than with most men, past performance is always more meaningful than efforts to interpret current maneuvering.

—The Rest of the World

In the final months of 1965, while convalescing at his Texas ranch house from a gall bladder operation, the President did some reflecting on the world situation apart from South Vietnam, and on what that world might be like if there were no Vietnam war at all. His thinking, conveyed at great length for attribution to "informed sources" or other authoritative mirrors of the Presidential mind, was characteristically hopeful—and hyperbolic— but no less revealing on that account.

Vietnam, the President was said to believe, had distracted attention from significant and encouraging trends. He saw a growing sense in much of the world that the domination of one nation by others in the pursuit of extreme nationalist or ideological ambitions was less and less a winning game. The year 1965, he believed, had been a pretty good year for the moderates and a bad year for extremists—in Indonesia, in a number of African nations, in the subcontinent of Asia, even in the Dominican Republic and some other Latin American lands. Everywhere he turned, indeed (except for Vietnam, of course), the President was heartened. He looked for constructive progress in strengthening the NATO Alliance. He had had successful talks with the leaders of Britain, Germany, and Italy. While progress toward *rapprochement* and *détente* with the Russians had been discouraging, opportunities for knitting closer ties with Eastern Europe through a relaxation of the rules on U.S. trade behind the Iron Curtain were promising. Discussions were under way leading toward improvements in the free world's international monetary arrangements. Rhodesia to the contrary, extremism was on the wane in Africa, and the United States was pitching in to punish Rhodesia's white-supremacy government. Things looked brighter in Yemen. U.S.

relations with the United Arab Republic and Algeria were look-ing up a little, and in our own Hemisphere, the Alliance for Progress was showing some progress at last. By and large, again leaving Vietnam aside, the President saw growing awareness of the need for peaceful collaboration among nations in the solution of common problems. The great need, the President said, was for people to approach the world's problems with a more realistic understanding of the world as it is.

It was a rosier view of things than many observers would have rendered, but it was also remarkably in consonance with the ap-praisal offered three years earlier by John F. Kennedy, with hardly much more time in office (and with, to an astonishing degree, substantially the same men helping shape his view of the world, for Johnson, in foreign affairs, held on tenaciously to most of the top foreign-affairs men of the Kennedy team).

Kennedy had seen large tides running against the "monolithic toward the pluralist idea—away from Communism and toward national independence and freedom." Kennedy had concluded that "beyond the drum-fire of daily crisis . . . there is arising the outline of a robust and vital community, founded on nations secure in their own independence and united by allegiance to world peace."

Plainly, Johnson was moving toward that conclusion, wherever he may have started out. And the world was continuing to con-firm, in early 1966, his estimate of it. Indonesia took one more firm step away from Communist influence. Castro was railing against the Communist Chinese. The Communists were the losers, who-ever might be the ultimate winners, in upheavals in Ghana and Nigeria. The odds on a Dominican Republic election, if not a stable Dominican Republic, had picked up perceptibly.

De Gaulle looked troublesome. But a case could be made that he was playing into Johnson's hand. Johnson had plans all ready for rebuilding an Alliance without France, and De Gaulle's back-of-the-hand to NATO in March was turning the rest of Europe increasingly in search of an alternative—a NATO without France—which Johnson might just possibly help to construct on lines the United States had been favoring all along.

Communist China was in deep trouble, reappraising policy, recalling her ambassadors systematically for consultation, plainly concerned by repeated setbacks around the world. And the United States was prepared, under Johnson, to help shape the reappraisal if it could. That was at least part of the purpose of a new note of flexibility in the Administration's talk of Chinese "containment without necessarily isolation." It was not all talk; Johnson had moved to promote contacts by clearing the way for some Americans to visit mainland China if Peking would permit it. U.S. China policy was loosening up, moving back up to and a bit beyond the "open door" approach proclaimed by Hilsman about the time that Johnson came to power.

Lyndon Johnson, despite the constraints of Vietnam, was moving with the world. If in the first two years, there were no glittering accomplishments, little conclusive to crow about, there were advances—in foreign aid, monetary reform, in the U.S. acceptance of the validity of parallelism with the Soviet Union (and in practical application of that thesis in the Kashmir crisis), and—very faintly—in Asia, even in Vietnam. Those who might quarrel with the course could not fault the lack of innovation.

Above all, the seemingly impulsive can-do man had slammed no doors; nothing had been irrevocably foreclosed.

Yet foreign policy remained, if not a blot on Johnson's escutcheon, at least the main point of attack and the chief source of anxiety about his performance at home and overseas. Criticism centered on the President's conduct of the war in Vietnam, on whether opportunities for negotiated settlement had been missed, on whether U.S. involvement was not unnecessarily deep. Some found the President's performance in the Dominican Republic even more disquieting; and while the public argument against U.S. policy in Santo Domingo was that the Johnson Administration did not properly sympathize with leftist revolutionary movements in Latin America or elsewhere, the private concern was more personal and had to do with the performance of the President himself. The word used by one of the most respected elder statesmen was "scary," though he admitted he couldn't quite define what he meant. It was simply something in the President's conduct and manner that raised doubts about his ability to deal with foreign policy, even though nobody was questioning his capacity to handle domestic affairs.

At home he had a slogan—the Great Society—and specific,

identifiable programs whose public acceptance was beyond serious dispute. And while he was rapidly beginning to apply the Great Society concept to the world at large, the twin specters of Vietnam and the Dominican Republic all but obscured whatever else the President might be attempting to do abroad, even when he was attempting to do quite a lot and in ways that were unmistakably his own.

Why then was it still difficult to discern and define a distinctive Johnson foreign policy?

Part of the fault may lie with the term "foreign policy." It smacks of something worked out painstakingly by policy-planners, chewed over by their superiors, thrashed out by the top men, decided by the President, and resoundingly propounded to the world. But the term has been overworked to the point that it is now applied not only to the most vapid generalities but to every tactical twist and turn.

And part of the fault may lie with the man. For Lyndon B. Johnson, foreign policy could only be politics on an international scale—but it was still politics, and therefore an essentially pragmatic, preferably impenetrable, sometimes inchoate, and often unpredictable way of life. He had listened and learned, spoken and acted, erred and admitted it by changing course. Panama and Cuba, Saigon and Santo Domingo, Cyprus and the Congo, Harold Wilson and Ho Chi Minh, Ayub Khan and Charles de Gaulle— all these and more had received some measure of the Johnson Treatment in the first turbulent years, and all had left their imprint in one way or another on the U.S. President.

He still defied precise definition—as evidenced, perhaps, by the fact that some would still call him a hawk, while others complained that he was too much a dove. In practice, he merely confirmed by his conduct of the foreign policy of the United States that this particular formula for categorizing American policy and policy-makers was one of the least fortunate ever submitted to a complex world. Even its inventors gave up in despair as they watched the Cuban missile crisis turn all the participants into "hoves" and "dawks."

Lyndon Johnson had started out in a hurry. He would probably always be hurrying, although there was evidence that he had come to a fundamental realization—that the world would *not* work to his, or anybody's, clock. "We must deal with the world as it is," he said recently, "if it is ever to be as we wish." He had discovered that one phone call would not settle a crisis in Panama, that even months of patient, skillful diplomacy brought no promise of a lasting settlement. He had discovered that a measured taste of American air power would not chasten Hanoi. By January, 1966, he felt obliged to tell the nation that "we just cannot know what the future holds" in Vietnam.

He remained as he always had been in his political life: cautious by instinct, wary of commitment, tireless in pursuit of that "reasonable majority" behind his every move. And it is here, perhaps, that something will have to change if the Johnson visions are ever to be transformed into reality.

Vietnam in 1966 was more than ever the key to all of Johnson's aims. But Vietnam was becoming less and less susceptible to cure by consensus. People and politicians were questioning more, and liking the answers less. Credibility, the keystone of consensus-building, was visibly crumbling. And consensus itself, as applied by Johnson, had lost its true definition; it had come to mean endless machination and maneuver and compromise and delay in quest of jerry-built majorities. It had come to mean balancing existing forces rather than bending them into new shapes. It had come to mean posturing and dissembling to produce public approval; it had come to mean barely disguised efforts to stifle public dissent.

The test of a great President, it has been written, is morality. It is not necessary to pass judgment on whether Johnson has it to argue that he does not radiate it, that he does not exert moral leadership, that he does not inspire. Another test is courage. "The trouble with Johnson's style," said an admirer of Johnson who knows the raw, earthy force of the man, "is that he doesn't have the courage of it."

If the ability to inspire and the courage of one's strength are, indeed, what make a President the master of events, by mid-1966 Johnson had yet to prove himself. For Lyndon Johnson and the world, the test would almost surely be Vietnam. And the question kept coming back hauntingly: could consensus be counted on to fix a safe course in so dangerous and deep a sea?

Index